The promise of AI as an active agent in modern society has been with us for more than half a century, and has had its boosters and its skeptics. Recent developments, especially in GAN technology, have made it clear that the bud is flowering, with implications in every field of human endeavor. Architects, planners, designers, and all citizens seriously contemplating "smart cities", "autonomous vehicles", and "intelligent bots" – among many other cyber-artifacts appearing on the world stage – need good information and critical thinking to guide them. This book fills a real need in that regard.

**Stephen M. Ervin**, *MLA, PhD,*
*Assistant Dean for Information Technology,*
*Harvard University Graduate School of Design*

*A History of Artificially Intelligent Architecture* is a much-needed book that provides both practitioners and academics with a comprehensive account of the origins, development and possible future(s) of AI and design practice. A must-have text to everyone interested in AI and its inevitable impact on the AEC industry.

**Silvio Carta**, *Associate Professor, University of Hertfordshire, UK*

# A History of Artificially Intelligent Architecture

*A History of Artificially Intelligent Architecture: Case Studies from the USA, UK, Europe and Japan, 1949–1987* provides a comprehensive survey of architectural projects exhibiting intelligence since the Late First Century right up to the present day.

Tracing the social, scientific and technological developments, this book analyses case studies from both conceived and executed architectural projects by architects and cyberneticians from the United States, United Kingdom, Europe and Japan from 1949–87. From the Late First Century through to the Seventeenth Century, the scientific endeavors of the Hero of Alexandria, Ramon Llull, Paracelsus, René Descartes, Jacques de Vaucanson, Pierre Jacquet-Droz and Charles Babbage have been presented in which they attempted to review, analyse and conclude the notion of artificial intelligence. Coming to the twenty-first century and witnessing a period, particularly from 1949–87, where nothing had been constant, architects and cyberneticians whose architectural projects attempted to simulate intelligence include Cedric Price, Richard Saul Wurman, Nicholas Negroponte, Kenzo Tange, Arata Isozaki, Charles Eames, Ezra D. Ehrenkrantz, Richard Rogers, Renzo Piano and Gordon Pask respectively. This book asks: How have polymaths, architects and cyberneticians simulated artificial intelligence in their scientific/architectural projects? Is it possible to define intelligence purely based on the history of architecture? Or, on a more extensive level, is it possible to view artificial intelligence originating from the history of architecture instead of computational paradigm?

The transdisciplinarity of the book makes it of interest to researchers and students of technologically advanced architecture's history, theory and criticism, artificial intelligence, cybernetics, information and communications, urban and sustainable design, ergonomics, computer applications and digital design and fabrication.

**Danyal Ahmed** is a Licensed Architect holding a PhD in Architecture and Building Science from Tohoku University, Japan, and ETH Zürich, Switzerland. He specialises in the history, theory and criticism of technologically advanced architecture with a focus on the role the emerging technologies, particularly, artificial intelligence, internet of things and big data had, is and will play with reference to architecture. He has presented his research at the platforms of the Architectural Institute of Japan, Architectural Society of China, Architectural Institute of Korea, Association of Pacific Rim Universities, European Association for Japanese Studies, University of Manchester (UK) and University of New South Wales (Australia). Being an AI researcher within the continents of Asia, Australia and Europe, he has been a recipient of grants and scholarships from prestigious governmental and higher education institutions such as the Ministry of Education, Culture, Sports, Science and Technology (MEXT) – Government of Japan, Tohoku University (Japan) and University of Manchester (UK) – and holds internationally appreciated architectural designs, research papers and conference proceedings to his credits. Among his invited talks, *Architecture in the Age of Artificial Intelligence* (TEDx Tohoku University) and *CIBSE IBG: What is Artificial Intelligence when it comes to Architecture?* (Chartered Institute of Building Services Engineers, London) can be accessed online.

# Routledge Research in Architecture

The *Routledge Research in Architecture* series provides the reader with the latest scholarship in the field of architecture. The series publishes research from across the globe and covers areas as diverse as architectural history and theory, technology, digital architecture, structures, materials, details, design, monographs of architects, interior design and much more. By making these studies available to the worldwide academic community, the series aims to promote quality architectural research.

**The Spatialities of Radio Astronomy**
*Guy Trangoš*

**The Ambiguous Legacy of Socialist Modernist Architecture in Central and Eastern Europe**
*Mariusz E. Sokołowicz, Aleksandra Nowakowska, Błażej Ciarkowski*

**Architecture, Ritual and Cosmology in China**
The Buildings of the Order of the Dong
*Xuemei Li*

**Art and Architecture of Migration and Discrimination**
Turkey, Pakistan, and their European Diasporas
*Edited by Esra Akcan and Iftikhar Dadi*

**Rem Koolhaas as Scriptwriter**
OMA Architecture Script for West Berlin
*Helena Huber-Doudová*

**A History of Artificially Intelligent Architecture**
Case Studies from the USA, UK, Europe and Japan, 1949–1987
*Danyal Ahmed*

For more information about this series, please visit: www.routledge.com/Routledge-Research-in-Architecture/book-series/RRARCH

# A History of Artificially Intelligent Architecture

Case Studies from the
USA, UK, Europe and Japan
1949–1987

**Danyal Ahmed**

LONDON AND NEW YORK

Designed cover image: © Getty Images

First published 2024
by Routledge
4 Park Square, Milton Park, Abingdon, Oxon OX14 4RN

and by Routledge
605 Third Avenue, New York, NY 10158

*Routledge is an imprint of the Taylor & Francis Group, an informa business*

*British Library Cataloguing-in-Publication Data*
A catalogue record for this book is available from the British Library

ISBN: 978-1-032-50404-9
ISBN: 978-1-032-51360-7
ISBN: 978-1-003-40185-8

DOI: 10.4324/9781003401858

Typeset in Times New Roman
by Apex CoVantage, LLC

To Saria, Saandal, Jasrat
and my parents Liaqat Ali, Nayyar Nazir

# Contents

| | | |
|---|---|---|
| *List of Figures* | | *x* |
| *List of Tables* | | *xiii* |
| *Acknowledgements* | | *xiv* |
| 1 | The Hero of Alexandria to Charles Babbage: Tinkering with artificial intelligence | 1 |
| 2 | Cedric Price, Richard Saul Wurman and Nicholas Negroponte: Information-dissemination machines | 22 |
| 3 | Kenzo Tange and Arata Isozaki: Cybernetic environments | 57 |
| 4 | Richard Rogers and Renzo Piano: Change as the only constant | 108 |
| 5 | Gordon Pask: Information, communication and feedback | 152 |
| 6 | Artificially Intelligent Architecture: Futuristic prospects | 201 |
| | *Index* | *207* |

# Figures

1.1    Experimentations of the Hero of Alexandria exhibiting controlled architectural settings.    6

1.2    Llull's rotating discs – as in Prima, Secvnda, Tertia and Qvarta Figvra.    8

1.3    Vaucanson's venture towards artificial life – The Mechanical Duck.    11

1.4    The Writer, Draughtsman and Musician by Jaquet-Droz.    13

1.5    A woodcut print showing a portion of Babbage's Difference Engine No. 1.    14

2.1    Fun Palace Brochure that presented it as a short-term plaything for realising the possibilities and delights of the twentieth century.    24

2.2    Site and Ground Floor Plans and a Section showing details of the Eidophor projection system in combination with the hydraulic movable floors in a proposal for the regeneration of the Oxford Corner House by Price. These movable floors facilitated the triple projection system for the large Eidophor screens, and viewers were seated as in theater-like arrangements.    31

2.3    John and Julia Frazer presented this model to Price.    37

2.4    In an email message with the author on January 30, 2023, John Frazer captioned this photograph as "Working electronic model showing the electronic components proposed to be embedded in every part of the building fabric[,] 1979–80."    38

2.5    In an email message with the author on January 30, 2023, John Frazer captioned this photograph as "Computer program by John and Julia Frazer for organizing the site on a day by day basis. Pen plot during development of the software[,] 1978."    39

2.6    The Urban Observatory's City Comparison App enables its users to compare and contrast cities against a number of themes.    43

2.7    Spectators observing the Seek (1969–70).    46

2.8    Gerbils were introduced into this computerised environment in order to challenge the strictly rectilinear programming of the machine.    47

2.9    Negroponte (left) with Interdata Model 3 Computer that was responsible for managing the intelligent behaviour of the roaming electromagnet hung overhead in the Seek.    48

2.10    Seek's intelligent response to the unpredictable actions of
        gerbils proved it as capable of exhibiting responsible behaviour.    49
3.1     According to Tange, when the functions of a city with 10
        million people are distributed along a line, the communication
        linking them can be carried-out in a minimum of time.    60
3.2     A perspective of the central civic communications axis from A
        Plan for Tokyo (1960–61) showing the communal axis and the
        community facilities (left) and the residential area (right).    61
3.3     Floor plan and axonometric of the exhibit Electric Labyrinth
        (1968).    75
3.4     The Arai or Responsive House (1968–69) was a cybernetic
        house that responded to the behaviour of its occupants.    76
3.5     The Computer Aided City deployed supercomputers acting
        as brain of the city as they exchanged, processed and stored
        information (1970–72).    78
3.6     Terminologies such as satellite brain, town brain, centre, corner
        and street terminals, mobile terminals, home terminals and
        information, traffic and energy terminals were used in order
        to indicate the processing of information and communications
        within this brain of the city.    79
3.7     The two rows of buildings in the city centre consisted of layers
        performing multiple functions, such as a hospital, laboratory,
        office and shopping complexes, local community centre,
        convention hall, etc.    80
3.8     The master plan of the Osaka Expo '70 (1966–69).    84
3.9     Robot cranes were designed by Isozaki for the Festival Plaza for
        lifting and re-arranging of movable seating stands, stages and
        trolleys. These robot cranes were capable of moving across the
        railways and performed multiple functions.    89
3.10    The Festival Plaza's mobile apparatuses, including seating
        stands, stages and trolleys, made numerous festival
        arrangements possible with the help of robot cranes.    92
3.11    Isozaki was influenced by science fictions while designing the
        cybernetic environment of the Festival Plaza.    95
3.12    The main control room of the Osaka Expo '70. As the system of
        the Expo was controlled from this room, Isozaki believed that
        the whole city could be controlled with such city brains.    98
4.1     The Eames House (1949).    111
4.2     The caption of the photograph reads, "This section of the east
        elevation is characteristic of the buildings. Of the three stucco
        panels shown here, one is pure white, one is brilliant blue,
        and one is black behind white crossed tension rods. The small
        rectangular panels and the sash are the natural warm grey of the
        Cemesto board; the two panels above the door are covered with
        gold leaf. The drapes are a natural coloured rayon and linen fabric."    112

4.3     Truscon open webbed joists and Ferro-board decking formed
        the exposed ceiling throughout the house and the studio except
        for the bathrooms.                                                    113
4.4     Technologically advanced self-decision-making kitchen
        appliances were used in the Eames House, including
        automatic kitchen appliances manufactured by Sunbeam, for
        example, Wafflemaster, Coffeemaster, Mixmaster, Ironmaster,
        Shavemaster, Toaster, etc.                                            115
4.5     Some of the technologically advanced products that were merit
        specified by Soriano to be used in the Case Study House 1950.         117
4.6     Automatic built-in gas cooking unit by Western-Holly
        Appliance Company.                                                    119
4.7     Kierulff Sound Corporation's HI-FI Home Music System
        advertisement.                                                        120
4.8     Prefabricated wall panels of the Case Study House #18.
        Details regarding their standardised components, connection
        simplification and ease of installation.                             122
4.9     Open plans or free space achieved with the light and modular
        structures in the Italian Industry Pavilion for the Japan World
        Exposition Osaka (1970) and the office spaces for B&B Italia,
        Novedrate (1971).                                                     134
4.10    The Center Pompidou, Paris: An information-disseminating
        machine acknowledged as a convergence of the plastic arts,
        architecture, music, cinema, industrial creation, etc.               137
4.11    Facades facing Rue Saint-Martin and Rue du Renard.                    142
4.12    Flexible and free spaces of the Center Pompidou, Paris.               144
5.1     The Musicolor System, its power boxes and reflector display.          168
5.2     Electrochemical system attached with the Musicolor System.            172
5.3     The Colloquy of Mobiles.                                              173
5.4     The interaction of mobiles in the dark.                              175
5.5     Toruses, or doughnuts, as suggestive of information and
        communication processes going-on within the Intelligent Plaza
        or Architecture of Knowledge.                                         184
5.6     Droege's proposal *Technology For People: A Campus City Guide*.        190

# Tables

| | | |
|---|---|---|
| 1.1 | A list of architectural projects case studied in this book. | 4 |
| 2.1 | "A List of 70 Projects for a Fun Palace" by Dr. John Clark. | 29 |
| 3.1 | The architects, designers and their responsibilities for Expo '70 under Tange's leadership. | 83 |
| 5.1 | Panel for the jury of the competition. | 156 |
| 5.2 | Advisors appointed for the competition jury. | 157 |
| 5.3 | Details of the winning entries. | 188 |
| 5.4 | Details of Droege team. | 191 |
| 5.5 | Components of the Intelligent Places. | 193 |

# Acknowledgements

This book is a map of those wonderful senses, experiences, emotions and memories that I enjoyed and collected during the course of my doctoral studies at Tohoku University, Sendai, Japan, and Swiss Federal Institute of Technology (ETH), Zürich, Switzerland, and during my research visits in greater Europe, East Asia and Australia from 2017–21. This book is an expression of gratitude to those who allowed me an easy access to primary sources, became available for interviews, permitted their exciting and intricate works to be reproduced, offered their valuable time and suggestions, helped me when I was lost on an unknown airport, railway, tram or subway station heading to visit archives in that new city, translated foreign languages for me and in doing so, to be concise, unintentionally made those vibrant and colourful cultures and those exciting, unforeseen journeys more enjoyable with their sublime presences. You all are going to stay with me forever, from every corner of the world where we first met, as if we are knitted in an everlasting bond of respectable friendship.

This book is an extensively revised version of my doctoral dissertation that I researched while availing the prestigious *Monbukagakusho* (MEXT) Scholarship for doctoral program by the Ministry of Education, Culture, Sports, Science and Technology, Government of Japan. First, this book would have not been possible without the knowledgeable, thought-provoking and creative suggestions by my advisors at Tohoku University (Junichiro Higaya) and at ETH Zürich (Ludger Hovestadt). The patience, tolerance and stamina with which they pushed me towards broadening my experiences whether in Japan, Switzerland or abroad and a passionate thrust towards experimentation led me towards writing this book on a pioneering field of study. I will always be an ardent admirer of the depth of knowledge they possess on historically significant as well as contemporary architectural discourses, and I am extremely grateful to them for the guidance and knowledge that will always be an inseparable part of myself.

This book would not have been comprehensive and thorough without the influence of professors with whom I had detailed discussions, Yasuaki Onoda and Taro Igarashi, for their guidance regarding minute details and technicalities of this book. I am also grateful to Masashige Motoe, who, during our late-night, after-lecture walks, clarified my concepts regarding the significance and consideration of technology in Japanese culture and lifestyle. He was the one who suggested that Japanese do not consider any segregation between technological artefacts and nature, and for them, these are two sides of the same coin. This concept led me to write some of the most wonderful research papers during the course of my PhD. I enjoyed attending his special and intensive courses and the after-discussions we had. The discussions I had with him not only let me find my way out of a cluster of ideas but also clarified my approach towards technologically advanced architectural systems. There are a number of people who took time to share their reminiscences and expertise with me (in alphabetical order): Alison Browne, Andrew D. Gordon, Antoine Picon, Barbara Wilcox, Ben Sweeting, Caroline A. Jones, Daniele Lauro, Daniele Santucci, Deljana Iossifova, Derek Clements-Croome, Ewan Branda, Hikaru Kobayashi, Jasia Reichardt, Jean-Louis Cohen, John Frazer, Joshua D. Lee, Kevin Liar, Koji Shidara, Kosuke Sakai, Manabu Nakagawa, Marincic Nikola, Miro Roman, Mohsen Mohammadzadeh, Mohsen Mostafavi, Molly Wright Steenson, Nobuyoshi Yabuki, Orit Halpern, Paul Pangaro, Peter Droege, Phillip G Bernstein, Richard Staley, Robert Iliffe, Ryan Burns, Sacha Menz, Silvio Carta, Simon Sadler, Stephen M. Ervin, Theodora Vardoulli, Thomas Daniell, Tong Yang, Viktor Mayer-Schoenberger, Wenyi Zhu, Yangang Xing, Yoshio Tsukio, Yukio Lippit and Yuriko Furuhata. I have tried my best to be comprehensive, but I apologize if I cannot recall any of you at this moment, for you all will always be a refreshing memory in my mind.

As this book is based on primary sources, it has benefitted from the use of several archives for which I'm extremely grateful to: Adam Crothers from St John's College Library, Cedric Price Collection, Cambridge; Brigitte Bouvier from Fondation Le Corbusier, Corwyn Travers Braschi – trustee and on behalf of *Arts and Architecture* magazine; Hisako Kato from Kawasumi-Kobayashi Kenji Photograph Office; Jean-Philippe Bonilli from Archives Department of the Center Pompidou, Paris; Marcus J. Carney from Heinz von Foerster; Gordon Pask & Cybernetics Archives, Department of Contemporary History, University of Vienna; Mary O'Connell from Wiley; Maya Gervits from Architecture Library, Littman Library, New Jersey Institute of Technology; Melanie Lenz from Digital Art, V&A Museum, London; Miki Irie from Tange Associates; Naoko Hatta from Misa Shin & Co. on behalf of Arata Isozaki and Associates; Nicoletta Durante from Fondazione Renzo Piano; personal archives of John Frazer, Peter Droege and Richard Saul Wurman; Philippe Lüscher from Musée d'art et d'histoire de Neuchâtel, Suisse; Rebecca Merriman from Jewish Museum, New York; Sayaka Ueki from Josai University Press; Tim Klähn from Cedric Price Fonds, Canadian Centre for Architecture, Montréal; and Yuma Ota from Toyo Ito and Associates, Architects. I'm deeply grateful to Miyoko Okazaki at Tohoku University, Sendai, Japan, and Guala Mario at ETH Zürich, Switzerland, for their support regarding administrative matters.

I wish to express my gratitude to the publication house – Routledge – for making this work accessible to millions of readers around the globe, whose suggestions and comments I'll be welcoming wholeheartedly. I especially commend the commissioning editor for this book – Caroline Church – for her appraisal, suggestions and patience for this work. A gratitude to all the production team, editorial assistant – Meghna Rodborne; project manager – Spandana PB; and cover designer – Jo Griffin; whose untiring efforts turned this draft from a cluster of ideas to a well-organised, captivating book. Many thanks to Gita Devi Manaktala, who, early in this project, extended support regarding book publication procedures from the Massachusetts Institute of Technology (MIT) Press.

I owe my greatest debt to my father, Liaqat Ali, who, being a passionate book reader, a successful book publisher and an ardent photographer of the historically significant architecture, taught me since gaining consciousness how to love and read books and how to feel their true essence. It is only due to his encouragement that I gained interest in reading the history of the world and started digging its other aspects, such as synchronisations of the wonderful cultures of the world and their appreciations. My mother, Nayyar Nazir, being a retired secondary school principal, always had been an inspiration to me regarding her passion for academics. This book would not have been possible without the support of my wife, Saria Chaudhry, who, by taking the charge of my parental responsibilities, allowed plenty of time for the completion of this book. Our sons, Saandal Vance and Jasrat Vance, are the ones, who, in the difficult most times, just instilled fighting power in me through their innocent and energising smiles. This project would not have been completed without you all. Being blessed, I surely want all of you to be with me all of my life!

# 1 The Hero of Alexandria to Charles Babbage

Tinkering with artificial intelligence

## What is artificial intelligence when it comes to architecture?

Architecture in the age of artificial intelligence? What is artificial intelligence when it comes to architecture? Is there any relationship between artificial intelligence and architecture? These are some of the titles of my talks that I delivered in 2019 and recently in 2022 through the platforms of TEDx Tohoku University, Japan, and the Chartered Institution of Building Services Engineers, United Kingdom. There is no one answer to these complex questions. It depends on the context in which these questions are placed and allowed to form interactive friendly relationships, thus generating transdisciplinary formulations. Architecture itself is a transdisciplinary field. While getting trained as an architect, I had to go through a whole breadth of courses, including but not limited to the history, theory, criticism, visual communication, materials and construction systems, structures, environmental control systems, surveying and levelling, landscape design, interior design, environmental psychology, urban design, business management, architectural conservation, research methodology, building economics, sustainable design, computer applications, including digital design and fabrication, etc. It has been due to this inherent quality of transdisciplinarity in architectural studies that many of my class fellows pursued specialisations in as diverse fields as textile designing or culinary arts. Viewed in this context, artificial intelligence seems no alien to the discipline of architecture, but both seem to complement each other. This interaction between the two can said to be suggestive of an experimental discipline that can be titled as *Artificially Intelligent Architecture*.

Artificially intelligent architecture is a vast discipline that adopts technologies from the fields of artificial intelligence, information and communications, cybernetics, heuristics, set and graph theory, machine learning (a subset of artificial intelligence) and computer science, etc. It is difficult to segregate and define these technologies independently, as they are highly interdependent and work in collaboration. Gordon Pask's (whom we'll meet again in Chapter 5) collaborator, Paul Pangaro, Professor of Practice at Carnegie Mellon University, suggests that artificial intelligence has been originated from the field of cybernetics, and both of these disciplines are inherently intermeshed and contribute each other. The pioneer of cybernetics, Norbert Wiener, also presented the same line of thought in his book

DOI: 10.4324/9781003401858-1

*Cybernetics: Or Control and Communication in the Animal and the Machine* published in 1948. Kenzo Tange and Arata Isozaki (awaiting us in Chapter 3), while designing cybernetic environments, utilised technologies of information and communications, cybernetics and computer sciences, etc. In order to have a definition of artificially intelligent architecture, are these facts able to support our argument, or do we have to look somewhere else?

## Artificially intelligent architecture, by definition(s)

In an attempt to define artificially intelligent architecture, almost every architect, cybernetician or technologist, whose project has been case studied in this book, tried to introduce some notion of intelligence in their architecture. This book thus, by limiting the scope of its study, attempts to define artificially intelligent architecture on the basis of the word *intelligence*. Understanding and summarising intelligence is not a new concept, and numerous scholars from different walks of life have attempted to define it since before the Common Era.[1] Twentieth-century architects, cyberneticians and technologists explored innovative ways of incorporating intelligence in their projects. This notion has sometimes taken the direct form of expression, and sometimes it had to be understood in veil as it took a backstage. *Baukasten* (Construction Kit) concept was introduced by Walter Gropius and Adolf Meyer in 1925. In 1933, Robert W. McLaughlin designed a prefabricated modular international-style house called the Winslow Ames House, and in 1945, Buckminster Fuller presented the Dymaxion House. Meanwhile, the first artificial intelligence technology boom starts, spanning a period of 1950–69. In 1956, a summer workshop called the *Dartmouth Summer Research Project on Artificial Intelligence* was conducted by a group of mathematicians and scientists at the Dartmouth College in New Hampshire. This workshop is considered as the founding event of the discipline of contemporary artificial intelligence. In 1957, Patrick J. Hanratty develops Pronto that further leads to the development of computer-aided design (CAD) and computer-aided manufacturing (CAM) softwares. Further in 1960, Luigi Moretti presents Stadium N project at the Parametric Architecture exhibition, at 12th Milan Triennial. Christopher Alexander presents *Notes on the Synthesis of Form* published in 1964, and Moshe Safdie designs Habitat 67 for Montréal Exposition 1967. Another important benchmark in the evolution of artificially intelligent architecture is the formation of the Architecture Machine Group at the Massachusetts Institute of Technology by Nicholas Negroponte in 1968 that led to significant developments. Meanwhile, the second artificial intelligence boom arrives from 1975–89. In 1982, Koichi Furukawa initiates the Fifth Generation Computer Project in Japan that runs till 1992 and culminates in despair. Autodesk releases its first commercial AutoCAD also in 1982, and in 1997, a collaboration between Frank Gehry, Jim Lymph and computer-aided three-dimensional interactive application (CATIA) software produces the Guggenheim Bilbao. In 2008, Patrick Schumacher coins the term Parametricism, and in 2015, the third artificial intelligence technology boom starts that is still progressing. One of the prominent names from pioneers of contemporary artificial intelligence, Marvin Minsky

(1927–2016), defines intelligence in his paper titled *Steps Toward Artificial Intelligence*:

> Should we ask what intelligence "really is"? My own view is that this is more of an esthetic [sic] question, or one of sense of dignity, than a technical matter! To me "intelligence" seems to denote little more than the complex of performances which we happen to respect, but do not understand. So it is, usually, with the question of "depth" in mathematics. Once the proof of a theorem is really understood its content seems to become trivial. . . . But we should not let our inability to discern a locus of intelligence lead us to conclude that programmed computers therefore cannot think. For it may be so with man, as with machine, that, when we understand finally the structure and program, the feeling of mystery (and self-approbation) will weaken[2] [emphasis in original].

Minsky defines intelligence as a phenomenon that encourages engagement and excitement through stimulating activities and computer programs. He suggests that once the participant discovers the underlying factor of engagement, he loses the feeling of mystery and self-approbation. This is the reason why this quality of engaging the participants and not letting them become bored is present in the architectural projects by Cedric Price, Nicholas Negroponte, Richard Saul Wurman, Kenzo Tange, Arata Isozaki, Richard Rogers, Renzo Piano and Gordon Pask that have been case studied in this book. None of them wanted users of their artificially intelligent architectural systems to get bored while going through these processes and so they utilised whatever advanced technologies that may had come across in order to keep presenting participants with new perspectives on the world around them.

## Artificial intelligence technology booms

This chapter approaches the narrative of artificially intelligent architecture by dividing it into two sections. Section I presents the history of artificially intelligent architecture from the Late First till Seventeenth Century. Polymaths whose work has been discussed include the Hero of Alexandria, Ramon Llull, Paracelsus, René Descartes, Jacques de Vaucanson, Pierre Jacquet-Droz and Charles Babbage. In their experiments, they attempted to review, analyse and conclude the notion of artificial intelligence. Section II refers to the history of contemporary artificially intelligent architecture starting from the twentieth century. Tracing the origins of artificial intelligence in the war-born technologies carried over from World War I and II, this section presents the contribution of artificial intelligence to architecture concluding as in technologically advanced architectural systems of today. The contemporary history of artificial intelligence presents a scattered and discontinuous narrative due to the lack of impactful technological breakthroughs and insufficient fundings from the government and other organisations, thus resulting in three post–World War technological booms of 1950–69, 1975–89 and consequently,

2015–present. The case studies selected for this book belong to the first and second artificial intelligence technological booms, as major advancements have been observed in these periods. Similarly, countries or continents with major advancements in artificial intelligence during the first and second artificial intelligence technological booms tend to be the United States, United Kingdom, Europe and Japan. Thus, architectural projects selected on the basis of these selection criteria are from 1949–87 and include both built and unbuilt projects. A list of architectural projects case studied in this book has been presented in Table 1.1.

This book explores the relationship between artificial intelligence and architecture through the projects of architects, cyberneticians and technologists. Whether these projects were executed or not has not been taken into consideration. A characteristic common to all of these projects is their ability to exhibit some notion of

*Table 1.1* A list of architectural projects case studied in this book.

| First AI boom: 1950–69 | | Second AI boom: 1975–89 | |
|---|---|---|---|
| Eames House | 1949 | Center Pompidou | 1971–77 |
| Case Study House | 1950 | UOP Factory | 1973–74 |
| New Case Study House | 1953 | PA Technology Lab | 1975–85 |
| Case Study House #17 | 1956 | Generator | 1976–80 |
| Case Study House #18 | 1958 | Japnet, Kawasaki | 1986–87 |
| WHO Headquarters | 1959 | | |
| MIT Boston Harbor | 1959 | | |
| A Plan for Tokyo | 1960–61 | | |
| School Construction Systems Development | 1961–67 | | |
| Fun Palace | 1961–85 | | |
| Tsukiji Project in Tokyo | 1963 | | |
| Yamanashi Communications Center | 1964–67 | | |
| Plan for Skopje | 1965 | | |
| Oxford Corner House | 1965–67 | | |
| Festival Plaza - Osaka Expo '70 | 1965–70 | | |
| Urban Observatory | 1967–71 | | |
| Reliance Controls Electronics Factory | 1967 | | |
| Electric Labyrinth | 1968 | | |
| Responsive House | 1968–69 | | |
| Rogers House | 1968–69 | | |
| Zip-Up Enclosures | 1968–71 | | |
| Italian Pavilion - Osaka Expo '70 | 1969 | | |
| Seek | 1969–70 | | |
| Extension to Design Research Unit | 1969–71 | | |
| Computer Aided City | 1970–72 | | |
| Association for Rural Aid Medicine Module | 1971 | | |

intelligence. One of the most interesting facts that this book relies on is the practice of simulating intelligence by polymaths not only in their innovations but also in their everyday lives. In other words, it can also be said that they were inspired by their surroundings to produce such intelligent systems. Whether it was produced just for the elites or was intended for the social good is a debate that has been left to the intellectualities of the reader!

The purpose and significance of this book lies in the fact that first, it is a historical comprehension of the subject. Through the analysis of history and case studies of artificially intelligent architecture, the aim has been to unearth the intentions of designers involved in these projects that have been case studied and, most importantly, the contributions their systems made to the discipline. To be concise, a wider historical perspective has been intended. Second, on the basis of this historical comprehension, this book further aims to figure-out the characteristics and futuristic prospects of artificially intelligent architecture.

## The Hero of Alexandria to Charles Babbage: tinkering with artificial intelligence

The concept of artificially intelligent architecture is not new. A whole breadth of research exists since the Late First Century indicative of scientific and architectural projects somehow simulating intelligence. As the concept of artificial intelligence has always intrigued innovators and particularly, their audiences, this section of the chapter presents a longer history of artificial intelligence and documents those projects that can said to be the predecessors of contemporary artificial intelligences. Transdisciplinarity tends to be a characteristic shared by all of the scientific and architectural projects.

Hero of Alexandria, an ancient Greek mathematician and engineer from the Late First Century, appears to be the earliest transdisciplinary writer experimenting within the fields of mathematics, mechanics, physics and pneumatics. Probably through very first accounts of formal research into the discipline of cybernetics, he designed programable architecture that performed tasks on its own. Through controlled experimental set-ups, he tested architectural elements against air, steam and water or a combination of these in order to present them as fully automated. For example, in one such controlled set-up, sounds were produced whenever a door of a temple was opened (Figure 1.1a). The mechanism comprised of a door attached to a container having an inverted vessel in it. Whenever the door was opened, it stretched the attached rod that descended the inverted vessel in the container filled half with water. Consequently, the sound of a trumpet was produced through the expulsion of air contained in the vessel. Similarly, he proposed an automaton in which the doors of a temple were opened whenever an altar was set to fire (Figure 1.1b). In this controlled experiment, a micro-sized temple was proposed on a pedestal such that its altar was connected to its main door and a globe and bucket placed underneath. When the fire grew hot, the air in the altar expanded. This air then passed into the globe, driving out its liquid, either water or quicksilver, through a siphon into the suspended bucket.

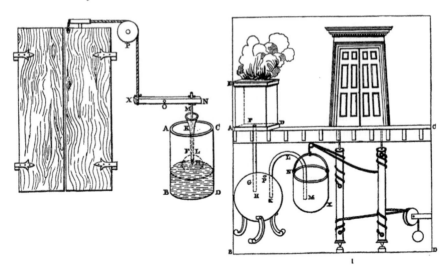

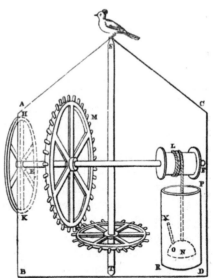

*Figure 1.1* Experimentations of the Hero of Alexandria exhibiting controlled architectural settings. Clockwise from top left:

a.  A controlled set-up that produced sounds whenever the door of a temple was opened.
b.  A set-up exhibiting opening of temple doors when an altar was set to fire.
c.  A shrine on which a bird sang and turned around by worshippers turning a wheel while entering it.

*Source*: Bennet Woodcroft, ed., *The Pneumatics of Hero of Alexandria: From The Original Greek*, trans. J. G. Greenwood (London: Taylor Walton and Maberly, 1851), 33, 57, 93.

This bucket then descended due to its weight consequently tightening the chains and opening the doors. In another example, whenever worshippers entered the shrine, they turned a wheel so that a bird made to sit at the top of the shrine made a note and turned around as well (Figure 1.1c). The mechanism consisted of three interconnected wheels and a weight suspended in a vessel filled with water. Whenever a wheel was turned, the weight submerged into the water and produced the note of a black-cap by the expulsion of air. The revolutions of wheels were responsible for the turning around of the black-cap.[3]

Ramon Llull (1232–1316?) – a Catalan philosopher and theologian from the late Middle Ages – acquired knowledge in the fields of medicine and astronomy and was aware of the ideas of medieval physicians. His transdisciplinary concepts have been influential in infusing computational thinking into the arts, culture and technology of today. One of his major contributions have been the overlapping rotating discs with linguistic symbols, terms and alphabets on them (Figure 1.2). Through combinations of these, he intended to invent a universal language, a method of assigning logic and stability to the uncertain world. These overlapping paper discs are said to be inspirations from astrolabe and medieval volvelle and in turn inspired a cryptographic device known as a cipher wheel. Although this mechanical device was not able to provide the intended solutions it was meant for at that time, it did inspire Gottfried W. Leibniz (1646–1716) – a German mathematician, philosopher and theologian, who broke down arguments into their constitutional parts and then recombined them through automatic processes in order to reach philosophical truths. In this way, Leibniz was able to formulate a binary system of numerals that has significant connections with modern computer science and theory of information. Consequently, the fundamental principles of these universal machines tend to be ones defined by Leibniz as of dividing a task into basic operational steps, reducing the complexity of a language to a few symbolic elements and the transformation of intangible symbols, terms and alphabets and their possible combinatory properties to hardware.[4]

Paracelsus (1494?–1541), born Philippus Aureolus Theophrastus Bombastus von Hohenheim, was a Swiss physician, alchemist, lay theologian and philosopher. He is credited for presenting a recipe for the artificial generation of men. He believed that some truth exists in this fact, and it has already been concealed for a very long time. Doubts and questions were raised in great details by the ancient philosophers, he said, and whether it was possible for nature or art to beget a man out of the body of a woman was full of concerns. To this, he answered that this problem would find its solution in the art of alchemy and nature, and it is absolutely possible to generate an artificial man, or *homunculus*, by following the recipe as follows:

> Let the Sperm of a man by itself be putrefied in a gourd glass, sealed up, with the highest degree of putrefaction in Horse dung, for the space of forty days, or so long until it begin to be alive, move, and stir, which may easily be seen. After this time it will be something like a Man, yet transparent, and without a body. Now after this, if it be every day warily, and prudently nourished and

*Figure 1.2* Llull's rotating discs – as in Prima, Secvnda, Tertia and Qvarta Figvra (First, Second, Third and Fourth Figures, clockwise from top left) – having linguistic symbols, terms and alphabets, providing its reader with infinite combinatorial opportunities in order to discern philosophical truths.

*Source*: Ramón Llull, *Ars brevis (S. XVIII)*, S. XVIII [18th Century], copia de la edición hecha en Barcelona en 1565 [copy of the edition made in Barcelona in 1565], Ars brevis (h. 1–38v.), Notas de teología y filosofía lulianas (h. 39–88) [Notes on Llullian Theology and Philosophy (pp. 39–88)], 88 pages (15 × 11 cm), 10–15, Biblioteca Virtual del Patrimonio Bibliográfico, Ministerio de Cultura, Subdirección General de Coordinación Bibliotecaria, Madrid [Virtual Library of Bibliographic Heritage, Ministry of Culture, Subdivision General of Library Coordination, Madrid], accessed December 29, 2022, https://bvpb.mcu.es/ca/consulta/resultados_ocr.do?id=134288&tipoResultados=BIB&posicion=4&forma=ficha. Use permitted under Creative Commons Attribution 4.0 International.

fed with the Arcanum of Mans blood, and be for the space of forty weeks kept in a constant, equal heat of Horse-dung, it will become a true, and living infant, having all the members of an infant, which is born of a woman, but it will be far less. This we call *Homunculus*, or Artificial[5] [emphasis in original].

René Descartes (1596–1650) was a French philosopher, scientist and mathematician credited as a prominent figure in the emergence of modern philosophy and science. He presents a number of philosophical issues regarding our existence and resulting relationships with our surroundings in his book *Meditations on First Philosophy* published in 1641. In *Meditation II: On the Nature of the Human Mind, which is Better Known than the Body*, and *Meditation VI: On the Existence of Material Objects and the Real Distinction of Mind from Body*, he prioritises thorough understanding of physical objects in our surroundings thus enhancing the judging power of our minds. Physical characteristics of objects that we comprehend through our senses, such as qualities of being tangible or visible and respective preconceived mental images are of lesser significance.[6] Existence is not dependent on a physical substance, as he said that "'I am, I exist' must be true whenever I state it or mentally consider it"[7] [emphasis in original]. Contrary to this, he stated that there must be an understanding substance in which his abilities would reside. While considering himself as a *thinking thing*, he stresses that it is with the judgement in his mind and not with the deceiving senses that he comprehends surrounding objects. If he stops thinking, then this thinking thing would cease to exist. He defined this thinking thing as "a mind, soul, understanding, or reason . . . [s]omething that doubts, understands, affirms, denies, wills, refuses, and also senses and has mental images."[8] As a thinking thing, he distinguishes between his mind and body and stresses that body by its nature is divisible while mind is indivisible because "[t]he abilities to will, sense, understand, and so on can't be called parts, since it's one and the same mind that wills, senses, and understands."[9]

In *Treatise on Man – Part I: On the machine of the body*, Descartes alternates the human body and its parts with that of a machine by saying that "I suppose the body to be just a statue or a machine made of earth, which God forms with the explicit intention of making it as much as possible like us."[10] He defines veins as tubes and stomach and intestines as a much larger tube that is perforated with little holes. He describes brain as "the seat of the common sense, of the imagination, and of the memory."[11] He states that this machine has been gifted all the colours and shapes of our body, and the interior has also been composed of all the parts required for walking, eating, breathing and imitating all of those functions that we carry. He stated that position of a rational soul in this machine is in its brain. He further strengthens his argument by stating:

the nerves of the machine that I am describing can indeed be compared to the pipes in the mechanical parts of these fountains, its muscles and tendons to various other engines and springs which serve to work these mechanical parts, its animal spirits to the water that drives them, the heart with the source of the water, and the brain's cavities with the apertures. Moreover, respiration and similar actions which are normal and natural to this machine, and which depend on the flow of spirits, are like the movements of a clock or mill, which the normal flow of water can make continuous.[12]

Although Descartes alternates the human body with a machine, in doing so, he carefully assigns all the bodily and sensory functions to machines, giving us the impression that machines are very well capable of conducting such operations with and within their systems. The functions he assigned included the following:

digestion of food, the beating of the heart and the arteries, the nourishment and growth of the bodily parts, respiration, waking and sleeping, the reception of light, sounds, odours, smells, heat, and other such qualities by the external sense organs; the impression of the ideas of them in the organ of common sense and the imagination, the retention or imprint of these ideas in the memory; the internal movements of the appetites and the passions; and finally the external movements of all the bodily parts that so aptly follow both the actions of objects presented to the senses, and the passions and impressions that are encountered in memory.[13]

He intended all of these functions to be followed by this machine just as "the movements of a clock or other automaton follow from the disposition of its counterweights and wheels."[14]

Jacques de Vaucanson (1709–82) was a French inventor of innovative automata. He is particularly known for his first all-metal lathe known as the mother of machine tools that played a significant part in the Industrial Revolution by leading to the invention of other machine tools. In a letter to Abbe De Fontaine, Vaucanson elaborates regarding an automaton – a Duck that performed the operations of eating by stretching out its neck to take corn out of a hand, drinking, digesting and, consequently, discharging it with the help of mechanical intestines (Figure 1.3). All the functions of a natural digestive system were imitated through circumvolutions of flexible pipes: "First, to swallow the Corn; secondly, to macerate or dissolve it; thirdly, to make it come out sensibly changed from what it was."[15] The duck was able to play in the water with his beak and also made a gurgling noise, imitating a real living duck. Vaucanson wanted his audience to view this mechanical duck being more than a mere machine operating on some autonomous principles, as he said:

To shew that the Contrivances for moving these Wings are nothing like what is made use of in those wonderful Pieces of Art of the Cock mov'd by the Clock at Lyons, and that at Strasburgh, the whole Mechanism of our artificial Duck is exposed to View; my Design being rather to demonstrate the Manner of the Actions, than to shew a Machine. . . . In a Word, they [persons of skill and attention] will be sensible of a prodigious Number of Mechanical Combinations. This Machine, when once wound up, performs all its different Operations without being touch'd any more.[16]

*Figure 1.3* Vaucanson's venture towards artificial life – The Mechanical Duck.

*Source*: Jacques de Vaucanson, "Le mécanisme du fluteur automate, presenté a Messieurs de l'académie royale des sciences [The mechanism of the automaton flutor, presented to the Gentlemen of the Royal Academy of Sciences]" ca. M. DCC. XXXVIII (1738), 11 [i.e. 23] p.: front., 26 × 20 cm, Paris: Chez Jacques Guerin, Library of Congress, Washington, DC, accessed December 30, 2022, www.loc.gov/resource/muspre1800.100207/?sp=1&st=image&r=-0.255,-0.026,1.53,0.764,0. Use permitted under Public Domain Content from Library of Congress, Music Division.

Pierre Jaquet-Droz (1721–90) was a Swiss philosopher, mathematician and watchmaker. He is famous for his three doll automata – The Writer, Draughtsman and Musician – constructed between 1768–74 (Figure 1.4). The Writer's set-up comprises of a child of about three years sitting on a stool and holding a goose quill in his right hand and sliding the mahogany writing pad underneath with his left hand (Figure 1.4a-b). His head and eyes follow the letters being traced, and his attitude is attentive, but the gestures seem a little bit jerky. Jaquet-Droz accommodated the complete mechanism within the body of the child. The movements of the wrist have been controlled with the help of the elbow and arm. There are two sets of gears that function alternately and are responsible for the movement of the wrist that is holding a pen. The pen is designed to move in both horizontal and vertical directions, thus tracing the letters with thick and thin strokes. This mechanism is adjustable and can be made to write any text to a maximum of forty letters or signs. The automaton writes a number of sentences, for example, "Les automates Jaquet Droz a neuchatel" that can roughly be translated to English as "Jaquet Droz vending automaton in Neuchâtel" or "Es lebe die Stadt Albrecht Duerers" translated from German as "long live the city of Albrecht Duerer." The Draughtsman, another automaton constructed by Jaquet-Droz's son, Henri Jaquet-Droz (1752–91), with the assistance of Jean-Frédéric Leschot (1746–1824), is said to be constructed between 1772–74 (Figure 1.4c-d). Looking very similar to the Writer, the Draughtsman was not designed with a moving writing pad. It is able to draw a profile or a subject with extraordinary attention to detail. The working mechanism of it is much similar to the previous automaton but is said to be much less complicated. The system is capable of generating four drawings – the portrait of Louis XV, Marie-Antoinette, the drawing of *Toutou* (a dog) and Cupid driving a chariot drawn by a butterfly. The Draughtsman also blows on his drawing with the help of a bellows placed in its head in order to clean all the dust that accumulates during the drawing process. The trio also collaborated in order to construct the Musician (Figure 1.4e-f). The automaton comprises of a lady playing a musical organ, but in fact, the music comes from the automaton itself. It plays five different musical themes. The mechanism of the system rests on a cylinder transcribed with melodies. Whenever a melody transcribed on the rotating cylinder is read by a mechanical component, the Musician plays notes or chords under her hands.[17]

Charles Babbage (1791–1871) was an English polymath – a mathematician, philosopher, inventor and mechanical engineer. He commenced his Difference Engine No. 1 in 1823, and its construction was abandoned in 1842 (Figure 1.5). He defines his difference engine in a letter to the Astronomical Society of London as a piece of machinery, or an engine, that with the application of a moving force computes any of the tables required for astronomical and mathematical purposes.[18] The engine was capable of computing the numbers as fast as any assistant or calculator could write them down. The engine was comprised of a small number of different parts that were repeated frequently. It is interesting to note that Babbage presented this machine as to perform one of the lowest operations of human intellect of "intolerable labour and fatiguing monotony of a continued repetition of similar arithmetical calculations."[19] He argued that a

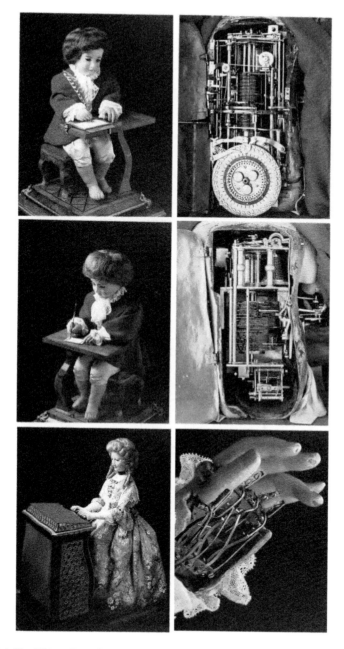

*Figure 1.4* The Writer, Draughtsman and Musician by Jaquet-Droz.
    a–b. The Writer and his internal mechanism.
    c–d. The Draughtsman and his body mechanism.
    e–f. The Musician and her hand's internal workings.

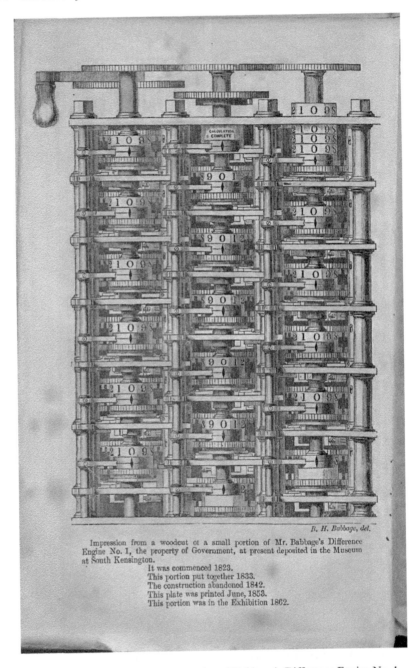

*R. H. Babbage, del.*

Impression from a woodcut of a small portion of Mr. Babbage's Difference Engine No. 1, the property of Government, at present deposited in the Museum at South Kensington.

It was commenced 1823.
This portion put together 1833.
The construction abandoned 1842.
This plate was printed June, 1853.
This portion was in the Exhibition 1862.

*Figure 1.5* A woodcut print showing a portion of Babbage's Difference Engine No. 1.

*Source*: Charles Babbage, *Passages from the Life of a Philosopher* (London: Longman, Green, Longman, Roberts, and Green, 1864), frontispiece, accessed January 5, 2023, https://archive.org/details/TO00961792_TO0324_62184_000000/page/n7/mode/2up?view=theater.

gentleman employed by the publishers of a valuable collection of mathematical tables for correcting the press was being paid the amount of just three guineas a sheet, "a sum by no means too large for the faithful execution of such a laborious duty."[20] Although Babbage was utmost confident regarding his contrivance, he sought the support of the president of the concerned society and scientific friends who examined it, as he said:

> I am aware that the statements contained in this Letter may perhaps be viewed as something more than Utopian, and that the philosophers of Laputa may be called up to dispute my claim to originality. Should such be the case, I hope the resemblance will be found to adhere to the nature of the subject rather than to the manner in which it has been treated.[21]

One of the interesting aspects of difference engine was the usage of signs for expressing its actions, a process Babbage later called as *mechanical notation* of machinery. He stated that it was very difficult and inconvenient for him to find out the state of motion or rest of any individual part at any given instant of time from the drawings of the engine. He wanted to contrive a method by which he, at a glance of the eye, could trace its relation with other parts of the machine and, if needed, track the sources of its movement through all the successive stages to the original moving power. Thus, the purpose of the notation was intended "to be at once simple and expressive, easily understood at the commencement, and capable of being readily retained in the memory from the proper adaptation of the signs to the circumstances they were intended to represent."[22] Regarding the advantages of this labelling, he said:

> The advantages which appear to result from the employment of this *mechanical notation*, are to render the description of machinery considerably shorter than it can be when expressed in words. The signs, if they have been properly chosen, and if they should be generally adopted, will form as it were an universal language; and to those who become skillful in their use, they will supply the means of writing down at sight even the most complicated machine, and of understanding the order and succession of the movements of any engine of which they possess the drawings and the mechanical notation[23] [emphasis in original].

Babbage was keen in promoting this mechanical notation as a universal language. In a paper titled *Laws of Mechanical Notation*, circulated in July 1851, a note under the title states that "[t]his short paper, upon the principles of lettering mechanical drawings, was printed and given away by Mr. Babbage in considerable numbers, to foreigners as well as to his countrymen, during and after the Great Exhibition of 1851."[24] Another note that appears at the end of this paper states that "Mr. BABBAGE *will feel obliged by any criticisms, or additions to these Rules of Drawing, and to the Mechanical Alphabet, and requests they may be addressed to him by post, at No. 1, Dorset Street, Manchester Square.* July, 1851"[25] [emphasis in original].

### On your mark, get set, go

This book case studies architectural projects that simulated intelligence in a number of ways from the United States, United Kingdom, Europe and Japan. Architects, cyberneticians and technologists, whose projects have been case studied, include Cedric Price, Nicholas Negroponte, Richard Saul Wurman, Kenzo Tange, Arata Isozaki, Richard Rogers, Renzo Piano and Gordon Pask respectively. The work of Price, Negroponte and Wurman has been presented in Chapter 2 that case studies the architectural projects of Fun Palace (1961–85), Oxford Corner House (1965–67) and Generator (1976–80) by Price. Negroponte's project that has been case studied is the Seek (1969–70). Wurman's project that has been included is the Urban Observatory (1967–71). Chapter 3 aims to discuss the interchanging characteristics of cybernetic environments and suggestive artificially intelligent architecture by case studying the projects of Kenzo Tange and Arata Isozaki. Projects designed by Tange that have been case studied include World Health Organization Headquarters (1959), Massachusetts Institute of Technology Boston Harbor (1959), A Plan for Tokyo (1960–61), Tsukiji Project in Tokyo (1963), Yamanashi Communications Center (1964–67) and Plan for Skopje (1965). Projects designed by Isozaki that have been case studied include Electric Labyrinth (1968), Responsive House (1968–69) and Computer Aided City (1970–72). The last section of the chapter case studies Tange and Isozaki's collaborative project called the Festival Plaza (1965–70) of the Japan World Exposition Osaka 1970. Chapter 4 aims to find out the interchanging characteristics of kit-of-parts discourse and suggestive artificially intelligent architecture by case studying the Center Pompidou, Paris (1971–77). This chapter consists of three sections. The first section discusses the pre-history of the Center Pompidou, Paris, by case studying the Case Study House Program (1945–62) and the School Construction Systems Development (SCSD) (1961–67) projects. In the Case Study House Program (1945–62), projects that have been case studied include the Eames House (1949) designed by Charles Eames, Case Study House (1950) by Raphael S. Soriano and New Case Study House (1953), Case Study House #17 (1956) and Case Study House #18 (1958) designed by Craig Ellwood. For the SCSD Project (1961–67), Ezra D. Ehrenkrantz acted as the project architect among other team members. The second section of this chapter case studies projects designed by Rogers and Piano during 1971–77. Projects by Rogers that have been case studied include Reliance Controls Electronics Factory (1967), Rogers House (1968–69), Zip-Up Enclosures No 1 and 2 (1968–71), Extension to Design Research Unit (1969–71), Association for Rural Aid in Medicine Module (1971), Universal Oil Products Factory (1973–74) and PA Technology Laboratory (1975–85). A project by Piano that has been case studied is the Italian Industry Pavilion Osaka Expo '70 (1969). The third and last section of this chapter case studies the Center Pompidou, Paris (1971–77). Chapter 5 aims to figure-out the characteristics of an artificially intelligent architectural environment by case studying the reactive and adaptive cybernetic environment proposed by Gordon Pask in his competition entry called the *Japnet, Kawasaki* (1986–87). This competition entry was submitted in response to an international concept design competition that was launched by the city of Kawasaki in 1986. The aim of the competition was to transform Kawasaki into an information-intensive city experimenting with new scientific methods and technologies. Intelligent Plazas, Kawasaki Institute of Technology, Campus City Festival and Intelligent Network were the four competition themes that the administrators requested participants to consider in their proposals. Finally, Chapter 6 presents prospects of artificially intelligent architecture from 1988 till present and discusses some futuristic issues regarding the subject.

In the chapters to come, we will see how architects, cyberneticians and technologists attempted to simulate intelligence in their architectural projects, particularly in the decades of 1960s' and 1970s'. While merging the information and communication technologies with their architectures, they tried to portray the image of architecture as an information-dissemination machine. It was to perform as an antenna, a symbolic avatar disseminating all sorts of routine essentials for its users. This is the subject of the next chapter in which Price, Negroponte and Wurman propagated intelligent architecture as generative, having a life and intelligence of its own. They promoted it as exhibiting responsiveness, individuality and excitement as its significant components consequently yielding fully automatic, self-organising architecture. It was a procedure for processing of information through visual data centres. To return to questions that opened this chapter, let us answer "What is architecture in the age of artificial intelligence? What is artificial intelligence when it comes to architecture? And is there any relationship between artificial intelligence and architecture?" through the case studies in the next chapter.

## Notes

1 For details regarding the evolution of intelligence since before the Common Era till the twenty-first century, a chapter called *Time Line: The Evolution of Intelligence* in McCorduck's book *Machines Who Think* can be consulted. Pamela McCorduck, "Timeline: The Evolution of Intelligence," in *Machines Who Think: A Personal Inquiry into the History and Prospects of Artificial Intelligence*, 2nd ed. (Natick, MA: A K Peters, Ltd., 2004), 523–533, accessed June 27, 2021, https://monoskop.org/images/1/1e/McCorduck_Pamela_Machines_Who_Think_2nd_ed.pdf.

2 Marvin Minsky, "Steps Toward Artificial Intelligence," in *Proceedings of the IRE* 49, no. 1 (January 1961): 27, accessed June 26, 2021, http://www-public.imtbs-tsp.eu/~gibson/Teaching/Teaching-ReadingMaterial/Minsky61.pdf.

3 Hero of Alexandria frequently mentions elementary parts of machinery, particularly steam engines, in his work and stresses that he must not be considered as the inventor of these machines, as these have been handed down to him from his predecessors and his contributions are limited only to necessary additions. For further details regarding his pneumatic experiments, consult the following:

Bennet Woodcroft, ed., *The Pneumatics of Hero of Alexandria: From the Original Greek*, trans. J. G. Greenwood (London: Taylor Walton and Maberly, 1851), 33, 57–58, 93–94.

4　*Selected Works of Ramon Llull (1232–1316)*, ed. and trans. Anthony Bonner, 2 vols. (Princeton: Princeton University Press, 1985), accessed July 2, 2022, https://archive. org/details/selectedworksofr00v1llul/page/n11/mode/2up?view=theater.

5　Paracelsus, "Of the Nature of Things: The First Book, Of the Generations of Natural Things," in *Nine Books of the Nature of Things*, trans. J. F. M. D. (London: Richard Cotes, for Thomas Williams, at the Bible in Little-Britain, 1650), 8–9, accessed October 23, 2022, https://archive.org/details/newlightofalchym00sedz/page/8/mode/ 2up?view=theater.

6　Rubin clarifies regarding the usage of term *mental image* as "While it's usual to translate the Latin verb '*imaginari*' with 'to imagine,' I've often translated it with a phrase like 'to have a mental image.' In English, the verb 'to imagine' can simply mean 'to suppose.' But, when Descartes uses the verb '*imaginari*,' he's talking about *picturing* a thing as if looking at it, not just about pretending or supposing that something is the case" [emphasis in original]. Ronald Rubin, "Translator's Preface," in *Meditations on First Philosophy*, trans. Ronald Rubin, 2nd ed. (Claremont: Areté Press, 1986), vii, accessed August 19, 2022, https://archive.org/details/meditationsonfir0000desc_v7t3/ mode/2up?view=theater.

7　René Descartes, "Meditation II: On the Nature of the Human Mind, Which is Better Known than the Body," in *Meditations on First Philosophy*, trans. Ronald Rubin, 2nd ed. (Claremont: Areté Press, 1986), 7, 9, accessed August 17, 2022, https://archive.org/ details/meditationsonfir0000desc_v7t3/mode/2up?view=theater.

8　Ibid., 8–9.

9　René Descartes, "Meditation VI: On the Existence of Material Objects and the Real Distinction of Mind from Body," in *Meditations on First Philosophy*, trans. Ronald Rubin, 2nd ed. (Claremont: Areté Press, 1986), 50, accessed August 19, 2022, https:// archive.org/details/meditationsonfir0000desc_v7t3/mode/2up?view=theater.

10　René Descartes, "Treatise on Man," in *The World and Other Writings*, trans. and ed. Stephen Gaukroger (Cambridge: Cambridge University Press, 2004), 99, accessed December 25, 2022, https://archive.org/details/worldotherwritin0000desc/page/98/ mode/2up?view=theater.

11　René Descartes, "The Description of the Human Body and All Its Functions, Those that Do Not Depend on the Soul as Well as Those that Do. And also the Principal Cause of the Formation of its Parts," in *The World and Other Writings*, trans. and ed. Stephen Gaukroger (Cambridge: Cambridge University Press, 2004), 172, accessed December 25, 2022, https://archive.org/details/worldotherwritin0000desc/page/98/ mode/2up?view=theater.

12　Descartes, "Treatise on Man," 107.

13　Ibid., 169.

14　Ibid.

15　M. Vaucanson, "A Description of an Artificial DUCK, Eating, Drinking, Macerating the Food, and Voiding Excrements; Pluming her Wings, Picking her Feathers, and Performing Several Operations in Imitation of a Living Duck: Contrived by the Same Person," in *An Account of the Mechanism of an Automaton, or Image Playing on the German-Flute: As it Was Presented in a Memoire, to the Gentlemen of the Royal-Academy of Sciences at Paris*, trans. J. T. Desaguliers (London: Printed by T. Parker, and Sold by Mr. Stephen Varillon, 1742), 22, accessed July 22, 2022, https://archive.org/ details/b30358711/page/n1/mode/2up?view=theater.

16　Ibid., 22–23.

17　Laura Casalis, ed., *Androids: The Jaquet-Droz automatons* (Milan: Scriptar and Franco Maria Ricci, 1979), 28–37, 40–49, 52–79, accessed August 2, 2022, https://archive.org/ details/androidsjacquetd00carr/page/n7/mode/2up?view=theater.

18  Charles Babbage, "Note on the Application of Machinery to the Computation of Astronomical and Mathematical Tables: From the Memoirs of the Astronomical Society of London, Read 14th of June, 1822," in *Babbage's Calculating Engines: Being a Collection of Papers Relating to Them; Their History, and Construction*, ed. Henry P. Babbage (Cambridge: Cambridge University Press, 2010), 211, accessed December 25, 2022, https://archive.org/details/babbagescalculat00babb/page/n5/mode/2up?view=theater.

19  Charles Babbage, "A Letter to Sir Humphry Davy, Bart., President of the Royal Society, &c. &c., on the Application of Machinery to the Purpose of Calculating and Printing Mathematical Tables," in *Babbage's Calculating Engines: Being a Collection of Papers Relating to Them; Their History, and Construction*, ed. Henry P. Babbage (Cambridge: Cambridge University Press, 2010), 212, accessed December 25, 2022, https://archive.org/details/babbagescalculat00babb/page/n5/mode/2up?view=theater.

20  Ibid., 215.

21  Ibid.

22  Charles Babbage, "On a Method of Expressing by Signs the Action of Machinery: From the Philosophical Transactions. 1826. Vol. 2, page 250," in *Babbage's Calculating Engines: Being a Collection of Papers Relating to Them; Their History, and Construction*, ed. Henry P. Babbage (Cambridge: Cambridge University Press, 2010), 236, accessed December 25, 2022, https://archive.org/details/babbagescalculat00babb/page/n5/mode/2up?view=theater.

23  Ibid., 240.

24  Charles Babbage, "Laws of Mechanical Notation (For Consideration.) July, 1851," in *Babbage's Calculating Engines: Being a Collection of Papers Relating to Them; Their History, and Construction*, ed. Henry P. Babbage (Cambridge: Cambridge University Press, 2010), 242, accessed December 25, 2022, https://archive.org/details/babbagescalculat00babb/page/n5/mode/2up?view=theater.

25  Ibid.

## Bibliography

This chapter has benefitted from the archives of Bibliographic Heritage, Ministry of Culture, Subdivision General of Library Coordination, Madrid. This bibliography only lists the name of the collection that has been consulted instead of the specific items. It is in accordance with the guidelines of *The Chicago Manual of Style*, 17th ed. (Chicago: University of Chicago Press, 2017) and for more details, section 14.222 can be consulted. The details of specific items have been listed in the notes. Unless otherwise noted, all translations are by the author.

Babbage, Charles. "Laws of Mechanical Notation (For Consideration.) July, 1851." In *Babbage's Calculating Engines: Being a Collection of Papers Relating to Them; Their History, and Construction*, edited by Henry P. Babbage, 242–245. Cambridge: Cambridge University Press, 2010. Accessed December 25, 2022. https://archive.org/details/babbagescalculat00babb/page/n5/mode/2up?view=theater.

Babbage, Charles. "A Letter to Sir Humphry Davy, Bart., President of the Royal Society, &c. &c., on the Application of Machinery to the Purpose of Calculating and Printing Mathematical Tables." In *Babbage's Calculating Engines: Being a Collection of Papers Relating to Them; Their History, and Construction*, edited by Henry P. Babbage, 212–215. Cambridge: Cambridge University Press, 2010. Accessed December 25, 2022. https://archive.org/details/babbagescalculat00babb/page/n5/mode/2up?view=theater.

Babbage, Charles. "Note on the Application of Machinery to the Computation of Astronomical and Mathematical Tables: From the Memoirs of the Astronomical Society of London, Read 14th of June, 1822." In *Babbage's Calculating Engines: Being a Collection of Papers Relating to Them; Their History, and Construction*, edited by Henry P. Babbage, 211. Cambridge: Cambridge University Press, 2010. Accessed December 25, 2022. https://archive.org/details/babbagescalculat00babb/page/n5/mode/2up?view=theater.

Babbage, Charles. "On a Method of Expressing by Signs the Action of Machinery: From the Philosophical Transactions. 1826. Vol. 2, Page 250." In *Babbage's Calculating Engines: Being a Collection of Papers Relating to Them; Their History, and Construction*, edited by Henry P. Babbage, 236–241. Cambridge: Cambridge University Press, 2010. Accessed December 25, 2022. https://archive.org/details/babbagescalculat00babb/page/n5/mode/2up?view=theater.

Babbage, Charles. *Passages from the Life of a Philosopher*. London: Longman, Green, Longman, Roberts, and Green, 1864. Accessed January 5, 2023. https://archive.org/details/TO00961792_TO0324_62184_000000/page/n7/mode/2up?view=theater.

Casalis, Laura, ed. *Androids: The Jaquet-Droz Automatons*. Milan: Scriptar and Franco Maria Ricci, 1979. Accessed August 2, 2022. https://archive.org/details/androidsjacquetd00carr/page/n7/mode/2up?view=theater.

Descartes, René. "The Description of the Human Body and All Its Functions, Those That Do Not Depend on the Soul as Well as Those that Do. And also the Principal Cause of the Formation of its Parts." In *The World and Other Writings*, translated and edited by Stephen Gaukroger, 170–205. Cambridge: Cambridge University Press, 2004. Accessed December 25, 2022. https://archive.org/details/worldotherwritin0000desc/page/98/mode/2up?view=theater.

Descartes, René. "Meditation II: On the Nature of the Human Mind, Which is Better Known than the Body." In *Meditations on First Philosophy*, translated by Ronald Rubin. 2nd ed., 6–13. Claremont: Areté Press, 1986. Accessed August 17, 2022. https://archive.org/details/meditationsonfir0000desc_v7t3/mode/2up?view=theater.

Descartes, René. "Meditation VI: On the Existence of Material Objects and the Real Distinction of Mind from Body." In *Meditations on First Philosophy*, translated by Ronald Rubin. 2nd ed., 40–53. Claremont: Areté Press, 1986. Accessed August 19, 2022. https://archive.org/details/meditationsonfir0000desc_v7t3/mode/2up?view=theater.

Descartes, René. "Treatise on Man." In *The World and Other Writings*, translated and edited by Stephen Gaukroger, 99–169. Cambridge: Cambridge University Press, 2004. Accessed December 25, 2022. https://archive.org/details/worldotherwritin0000desc/page/98/mode/2up?view=theater.

Llull, Ramón. *Ars brevis (S. XVIII). Biblioteca Virtual del Patrimonio Bibliográfico, Ministerio de Cultura, Subdirección General de Coordinación Bibliotecaria, Madrid* [*Virtual Library of Bibliographic Heritage, Ministry of Culture, Subdivision General of Library Coordination, Madrid*].

Llull, Ramon. *Selected Works of Ramon Llull (1232–1316)*. Edited and translated by Anthony Bonner. 2 vols. Princeton: Princeton University Press, 1985. Accessed July 2, 2022. https://archive.org/details/selectedworksofr00v1llul/page/n11/mode/2up?view=theater.

McCorduck, Pamela. "Timeline: The Evolution of Intelligence." In *Machines Who Think: A Personal Inquiry into the History and Prospects of Artificial Intelligence*. 2nd ed., 523–533. Natick, MA: A K Peters, Ltd., 2004. Accessed June 27, 2021. https://monoskop.org/images/1/1e/McCorduck_Pamela_Machines_Who_Think_2nd_ed.pdf.

Minsky, Marvin. "Steps Toward Artificial Intelligence." *Proceedings of the IRE* 49, no. 1 (January 1961): 8–30. Accessed June 26, 2021. http://www-public.imtbs-tsp.eu/~gibson/Teaching/Teaching-ReadingMaterial/Minsky61.pdf.

Paracelsus. "Of the Nature of Things: The First Book, Of the Generations of Natural Things." In *Nine Books of the Nature of Things*, translated by J. F. M. D., 1–13.

London: Richard Cotes, for Thomas Williams, at the Bible in Little-Britain, 1650. Accessed October 23, 2022. https://archive.org/details/newlightofalchym00sedz/page/8/mode/2up?view=theater.

Rubin, Ronald. "Translator's Preface." In *Meditations on First Philosophy*, translated by Ronald Rubin. 2nd ed., v–viii. Claremont: Areté Press, 1986. Accessed August 19, 2022. https://archive.org/details/meditationsonfir0000desc_v7t3/mode/2up?view=theater.

Vaucanson, Jacques de. *Le mécanisme du fluteur automate, presenté a Messieurs de l'académie royale des sciences* [*The Mechanism of the Automaton Flutor, Presented to the Gentlemen of the Royal Academy of Sciences*]. Washington, DC: Library of Congress.

Vaucanson, M. "A Description of an Artificial DUCK, Eating, Drinking, Macerating the Food, and Voiding Excrements; Pluming Her Wings, Picking Her Feathers, and Performing Several Operations in Imitation of a Living Duck: Contrived by the Same Person." In *An Account of the Mechanism of an Automaton, or Image Playing on the German-Flute: As it Was Presented in a Memoire, to the Gentlemen of the Royal-Academy of Sciences at Paris*, translated by J. T. Desaguliers, 21–24. London: Printed by T. Parker, and sold by Mr. Stephen Varillon, 1742. Accessed July 22, 2022. https://archive.org/details/b30358711/page/n1/mode/2up?view=theater.

Woodcroft, Bennet, ed. *The Pneumatics of Hero of Alexandria: From the Original Greek*. Translated by J. G. Greenwood. London: Taylor Walton and Maberly, 1851.

# 2 Cedric Price, Richard Saul Wurman and Nicholas Negroponte
## Information-dissemination machines

### Cedric Price: generative architecture having a life and intelligence of its own

Cedric Price (1934–2003) – an English architect who presented extensive pro-posals on the artificially intelligent, interactive, self-generative and responsive architecture – proposed a scheme for a framework that can be adjusted accord-ing to the activities being carried-out in it which was named as the Fun Palace (studies carried out from 1961–85, predominantly from 1961–74) (Figure 2.1). The Fun Palace started as a collaboration between Price and the radical English theater director Joan Littlewood (1914–2002) with the aim of designing an artificially intelligent architecture that eliminates the division between work and leisure. The sociopolitical talk of the time classified work as imposed and leisure as voluntary activity and debated less hours for work and more for leisure. It was assumed that working environments were mentally and hygienically unbearable, suppressing the productivity of the workers, while "a new mentality" was assumed to be awakened during periods of self-willed leisure activities. While pointing towards the increase in wealth, personal mobility, flexibility of labor and decreased social interdepend-ence as constituents of the change in the patterns of imposed activity (i.e. work over the past twenty five years), Price was a strong proponent of the belief that a division between work and leisure must not exist, as he stressed:

> The increasingly obvious reduction of the permanence of many institutions
> . . . allied with the mass availability of all means of communication, has
> demanded . . . experiences open to all at all times[.] . . . A short-life toy of
> dimensions and organisation not limited by or to a particular site is one good
> way of trying, in physical terms, to catch up with the mental dexterity and
> mobility exercised by all today.[1]

As a result, the Fun Palace was conceived as a short-life toy spanning for ten to fifteen years of dimensions and organisation as a visiting mobile structure. It comprised of a huge steel frame that integrated movable, modular components of portable stairways, pivoting escalators, moving walkways, projection units, mobile gantry cranes for placing ceiling and floor modules and other pneumatic

DOI: 10.4324/9781003401858-2

structures, etc., as and when needed. This mobility and flexibility on the one hand being accounted for its innovative and transformatory characteristics resulted in great difficulties for both Price and Littlewood. Not only were they not able to persuade changing governmental authorities for budget and site allocation and construction of this project but also, the project itself switched a number of sites during its paper lifetime and consequently remained unconstructed. From 1961–63, the project was designed and programmed, and from 1962–64, its feasibility studies were undertaken, considering various large metropolitan sites. In 1964, Fun Palace was included in the Civic Trust's Lea Valley Development Plan (East London), and in 1966, the Fun Palace Foundation was registered as a charitable trust. The board of trustees was comprised of Yehudi Menuhin, R. Buckminster Fuller, Joan Littlewood, Lord Ritchie Calder and George Henry Hubert Lascelles, Earl of Harewood. In 1966, Fun Palace was withdrawn from the Lea Valley site due to strongly contested variation in the extent of particular site, and till 1968, there was no scheduled construction site and date.[2]

Unspecific, indefinite and unplanned activities of the participants were the most significant aspect of the Fun Palace. The public was supposed to enter it as *Input of Unmodified People*, and after passing through these unplanned activities, they were supposed to exit as *Output of Modified People*. The form of the structure was a resultant of the activities generated within it. Price collected the details of these activities through punch card questionnaires over the years. In total, 6,000 questionnaires were sent out to persons of any age group, and around 3,000 responses were received. People were requested to elaborate the things they would like to do, and responses such as "Lying on my back with a glass of wine observing giant spiders" were taken seriously in order to be processed in architectural design.[3] The fund-raising brochure for Fun Palace summarised its layout in greater detail and stated that passers-by would be able to view what's happening inside it through the information screens installed. There would be no entrance – no doors, foyers, queues or commissionaires. A visitor can enter the structure from anywhere. Lifts, ramps and escalators would facilitate a visitor to explore whatever seems interesting to him. Whether a participant wanted to learn the handling of tools, paint, babies and machinery or just wanted to listen to his favourite music and dance or to tune in to see what's happening in other parts of the city would be an enjoyable event. 24/7 activities were planned, and participants were encouraged to relax even in the thunderstorms, as *artificial clouds* were able to keep oneself cool or make rainbows! In answer to why all this stuff was being arranged and this level of freedom was being granted to its users, Price and Littlewood quoted Robert Vaughan from 1843 as "If any nation is to be lost or saved by the character of its great cities, our own is that nation." They intended the Fun Palace as a short-term plaything, where anyone was able to realise the possibilities and delights of a twentieth-century city environment.[4]

On the basis of the documentation of activities of its participants, this temporary frame of activities could be called a cybernetic system. It incorporated the processing of and feedback from the information gathered regarding the activities of its participants that resulted in its self-organising, artificially intelligent architecture.

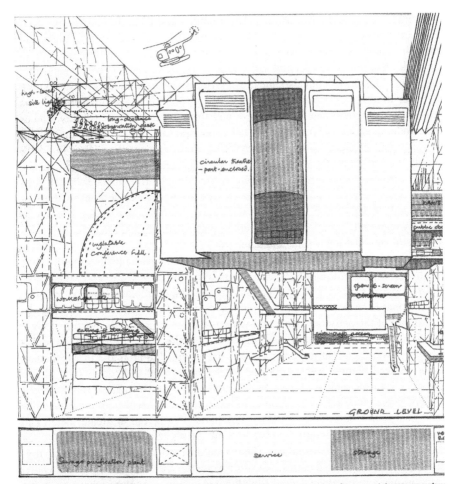

ARRIVE AND LEAVE by train, bus, monorail, hovercraft, car, tube or foot at any time YOU want to - or just have a look at it as you pass. The information screens will show you what's happening. No need to look for an entrance - just walk in anywhere. No doors, foyers, queues or commissionaires: it's up to you how you use it. Look around - take a lift, a ramp, an escalator to wherever or whatever looks interesting. CHOOSE what you want to do - or watch someone else doing it. Learn how to handle tools, paint, babies, machinery, or just listen to your favourite tune. Dance, talk or be lifted up to where you can see how other people make things work. Sit out over space with a drink and tune in to what's happening elsewhere in the city. Try starting a riot or beginning a painting - or just lie back and stare at the sky.

*Figure 2.1* Fun Palace Brochure that presented it as a short-term plaything for realising the possibilities and delights of the twentieth century.

*Source*: Cedric Price, Fun Palace Promotional Brochure, ca. 1964, poster: illustration, 60 × 36 cm folded to 21 × 30 cm. Price/1/6/16/2, St John's College Library, Cedric Price Collection. By permission of the Master and Fellows of St John's College, Cambridge.

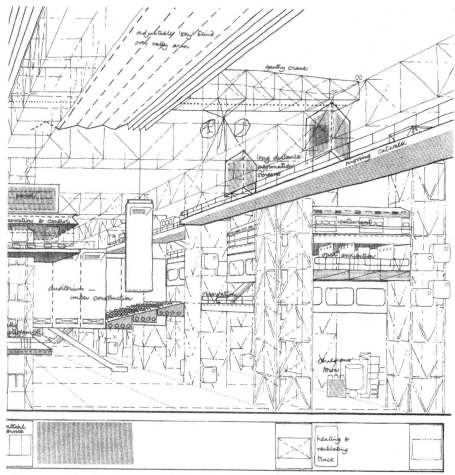

WHAT TIME IS IT? Any time of day or night, winter or summer — It really doesn't matter. If it's too wet that roof will stop the rain but not the light. The artificial cloud will keep you cool or make rainbows for you. Your feet will be warm as you watch the stars — the atmosphere clear as you join in the chorus. Why not have your favourite meal high up where you can watch the thunderstorm?

WHY ALL THIS LOT? "If any nation is to be lost or saved by the character of its great cities, our own is that nation". — Robert Vaughan 1843

We are building a short-term plaything in which all of us can realise the possibilities and delights that a 20th Century city environment owes us. It must last no longer than we need it.

*Figure 2.1* (Continued)

Littlewood proposed that for the successful functioning of the Palace, it was extremely important that the information it generated was equally available not only to its immediate neighbors but also to people from the national and regional levels. She also stressed that Fun Palace must also allow random time usage. These varied communication routes must be of a metropolitan or regional network passing through the site, she said, so that the *occasion* and *event* could also synchronise themselves with the changing scale and intensity of the metropolitan region.[5] Classifying the Palace as a cybernetic system, Littlewood stressed that the aim was of gathering information through a wide range of activities of the participants and then this information was intended to be

> handed over to the cyberneticians with specific requests for threshold conditioning, visiting patterns etc., to be investigated at an early stage. Once satisfactory feedback was achieved then previous hunches on, say, the desirable periods of transformation from one total configuration to another could be tested.[6]

Gordon Pask (1928–96) – an English cybernetician who elaborated the relationship between the field of cybernetics and the discipline of architectural design – presented the scheme of a Cybernetic Theater in his *Proposals for a Cybernetic Theatre* research that he conducted for Price's Fun Palace project.[7] A Cybernetic Theater, according to Pask, is such a theater in which the audience is able to control the performance of the actors during the play through feedback. This cybernetic play is only successful when both the stakeholders – the audience and the actors – contribute each other. The statement of the audience controlling the actors during a play in a Cybernetic Theater seems imaginary, but Pask detailed the rules and principles for this set-up. According to him, the plot and dialogues of the actors are fixed, and the actor is allowed to vary only the details of emphasis or interpretation in response to the feedback that he receives from the audience during the play. Also, if any member of the audience wishes to participate and is interested in sending his feedback, he should select an actor initially to whom he will be sending his feedback, and when he gets experienced enough, he may feedback as many actors as he wants to.[8] In this way, after some experience, both the Cybernetic Theater and the play contribute each other and also advance towards changing each other's nature, such as writing a play becomes similar to writing a computer program for the Cybernetic Theater.

Pask proposed detailed technical specifications and certain ergonomic factors for the realisation of this Cybernetic Theater. For filling the communication gap, both the audience member and the actor were able to communicate and locate each other in the theater by sending signals. Devices such as a pair of buttons, headphones or convenient earpieces, spring-loaded hand levers, rating buttons, tape recordings, etc., were used by the audience for expressing their approval or disapproval of the performances of actors in the play. Furthermore, the communication between the stakeholders was thought of in multiple forms, such as through hand signals and radio linkage, where verbal communication was possible. A flow diagram of this feedback loop that existed between the audience and actors was developed along with the diagrams showing *yes* or *no* signals of different colours sent by the audience to the actors and the seating plan of the audience. One of the interesting points that Pask makes in this proposal is of the participating audience member becoming *bored* when he observes that the actor is not acting in the manner as he voted for. Pask believed that a member of the audience is only reinforced or motivated to participate if his response and chosen actor behave in a synchronised manner, and any disparity between this would lead to a change in the identification of the audience member on the following stage in the system. This system seemed to be a little dull, Pask assumed, and consequently, audience members were expected to behave in a rather experimental or mischievous fashion. Only statistically well-defined and coordinated attempts were to pose problems for the system, and this was not considered to be the concern, as Pask argued, "[t]he trouble may be with the participant who becomes bored because he does not feel he is participating and influencing his agent [chosen actor on stage] and he is passably defined by our pedestrian model."[9]

To overcome the difficulty of boredom and many other uncertainties, Pask ultimately proposed that a feedback loop must be introduced so that the audience can be coupled more closely into the system. He proposed that if for a particular dramatic presentation none of these ergonomic and technical recommendations yield a satisfactory result, then a feedback loop must be introduced in response to preference choices. For this purpose, a meta-information channel would suffice, as it will couple the audience more closely into the system prior to the determination of any possible outcome. He defined meta-information:

[a]n important, but crudely realised, component of most dramatic presentations is auxilliary information, distinguished from the flux of discourse by such gambits as the "soliloquy" and the calculated "aside," which indicates the supposed thinking of some of the characters, (in anticipation of the actions they will later supposedly choose). Since this auxilliary information always describes a state of the actor, we shall call it metainformation[10] [emphasis in original].

Pask was concerned regarding the deliverance of the preference data received from the audience. Its purpose was of the selection and modification of operators or actors, as it was supposed to be a cybernetic system. This process was applicable to any of the feedback control or stabilisation procedures. And as in this dramatic presentation the operators were the actors, all this audience preference feedback was aimed to be ultimately delivered to them.[11]

Pask formed a cybernetics committee of which he himself acted as a chairman that helped to bring a variety of new ideas from different disciplines. A document titled *Fun Palace Cybernetics Committee* shows that specialists were appointed for supervision of different sections of the Fun Palace. Roy Ascott (born 1934), who was working at the Ipswich School of Art, then was responsible for form and amenities; Richard Goodman (untraceable), from the Brighton College of Technology, was responsible for operational research; A. R. Jonckheere (1920–2005) from the

University of London was responsible for psychology and experimentation; and A. G. MacDonald (untraceable) from the Scientific Advisors Branch, Home Office, was responsible for cybernetics and architecture.[12] Ascott – a renowned British artist whose work utilises cybernetics, digital, telematics, moist media, chemical or spiritual means and interactive and psychoactive technologies for creating art that addresses consciousness and connectivity – as a member of the cybernetics committee for the Fun Palace, supervised the division of form and amenities.[13] He stressed the need for an unrestrictive framework in which participants were supposed to act as a self-organising system through creative activities or group involvements. While presenting systems that he used in connection with visual art, he stressed avoidance of preconceptions that seemed *obvious* but could have been *insidious*.[14]

While on the one hand Pask was partially in favor of specific, definite and planned facilities such as restaurant facilities, etc., on the other hand, Ascott stressed the cybernetic view that was of letting the activities free and letting the Fun Palace learn from the feedback received from these free-flowing activities of its participants. In this way, interest and attention of participants was to be maintained by providing sufficient variety of the unspecific, indefinite and unplanned activities, Ascott suggested. Goodman – who was responsible for the operational research in the cybernetics committee – criticised the simple-minded mechanisation of the Fun Palace and suggested that people, as being the intelligent beings, cannot be tricked by an automation for a long period of time. Instead of making this program a *scientist's toy*, where intelligent human beings will not be able to enjoy themselves, he suggested that some tangible fixed activities or facilities must be introduced. Although his suggestion was also criticised, as it made a sheer distinction between educational and entertainment activities, and the committee feared that this practice would turn the Fun Palace in a mixture of a night school and a conventional fun fair. Price, Ascott, Clark, MacDonald, Goodman and Goldacre all agreed that novelty, innovation or creativity can be increased through interaction between fixed facilities or amenities. They suggested that straightforward communication can be enhanced by engaging participants in a number of activities through auditory or visual channels that can also be controlled by the operators.[15] John Clark from Bristol University, a committee member, suggested that the environment of the Fun Palace can be adaptively controlled which would encourage public participation and cooperative activity. Pointing towards systems and controls that at present are being enhanced by the technology of artificial intelligence, Clark suggested at that time that *magic doors* should be installed for admitting individuals of particular characteristics. Consequently, this idea was not implemented, as it seemed vague to other members of the committee.[16] He also suggested a list of some seventy projects for the Fun Palace, presenting some of the most fascinating and interesting activities for its participants (Table 2.1).

There were some characteristics that made Fun Palace a cybernetic system – an artificially intelligent architecture – and presented it as different from the conventional collection of entertainments, educational facilities, modern amenities and

*Table 2.1* "A List of 70 Projects for a Fun Palace" by Dr. John Clark.

| | | |
|---|---|---|
| The tower of dancing light | The scholarly staircase | The terrace amid the tree-tops |
| The flying men | The camera lucida | "An overhead carriage awaits." |
| The bubbling wall | The maze of silence | The glories of musical steam |
| The inhabited universe | Professor Piaget's pavilion | The cryptic chromosomes |
| The sensitive speedway | The cybernetic cinema | The Tower of Babel |
| The art-machine | Count-down at Cape Kennedy | The puppets rehearse |
| The elusive topiarist | Play the horses! | The gallery of coloured vistas |
| Why not try a trip around the moon in our realistic space-capsule Simulator? | The mathematical colonnade | The portico of enthusiastic myths |
| The tactful tango-teacher | Up periscope! | "Be a racing driver!" |
| The ladies of fashion | A curious getaway | A tower amid attendant delights |
| Astro-navigation over the polar ice-cap | The musical cloister | Ski down the forest path |
| The puzzling pavilion | The fantasy generator | The city barge welcomes sporting clientele |
| The counter-point computer | The glittering science | The waves are only 50 feet tall in mid-Atlantic |
| Captain Nemo's cabin | The craftsmen reveal much of their art | The hill-soarer |
| The five senses of travel | Aerobatics for all | Try your hand at Japanese paper-folding |
| "I would like to meet." | You may career down the Cresta run at breath-taking speeds – yet without the slightest danger | The reliable breeze |
| The palace of illusions | Climb the tree of evolution | The "domain of Arnhem" or a visit to Mr. Poe's own Fun Palace |
| The forest of violet twilight | Take a sleigh-ride through wolf-infested steppes | The deceptive flicker |
| The paradoxical pier | The waiting world | Mr. Friese-Greene presents a novel invention to the public |
| The grotto of kaleidoscopes | The maze of mechanism | Climb the rock pinnacle! |
| Would you like to land at Shannon by night? | "What is it like to be a." | A canoe journey down the river Dee |
| The deceiving corridor | The signposted library | In the steps of Monsieur Montgolfier |
| The fiery pagoda | "Put the elegant electron through his paces!" | The calligraphic cavern |

*Source*: Stanley Mathews, "Appendix D: John, Clark, "A List of 70 Projects for a Fun-Palace,"" in *From Agit-Prop to Free Space: The Architecture of Cedric Price* (London: Black Dog Publishing, 2007), 274–275.

covered enclosures. The committee unanimously agreed that this distinction rested upon a couple of features:

(1)  The organic and developing character of the system itself[;] and
(2)  Its organic relation to the external environment.[17]

The organic and developing character of the system was achieved through the developing character of fixed amenities, such as cinemas, theaters, restaurants or novel arrangements in the mixing regions. These were considered as adaptive catalysts or enzyme systems in an analogous biological system. These facilities acted as objects satisfying a need in conventional or arbitrary interconnected events, but in Fun Palace, they were supposed to act as operations that *catalysed* further activities. These activities were either pre- or participant-defined, cooperative or creative. While elaborating on the organic relation of the Fun Palace to the external environment, it could be said that its job was of stimulating the imagination and providing its users with a fresh perspective on the world, thus opening up new vistas. R. Pinker from Goldsmith's College, who was a member of the cybernetics committee, stressed that the aim of the Fun Palace was to educate its visitors in general and not in the specific senses, as it was aimed for people who already had rejected official educational facilities. He also warned against the dangers of moralising.[18]

The other most significant project by Price outlining the characteristics of artificially intelligent architecture was the Oxford Corner House (OCH) project – a feasibility study (1927–67, predominantly between 1965–66) conducted for his client, a British mega-catering company then called as J. Lyons and Company Limited.[19] The client owned an old building called as the OCH (probably from 1930s', construction date untraceable) that was initially used as the Lyons Corner House at Oxford Street/Tottenham Court Road and comprised of a food hall, hairdressing, teashops and restaurants, and specifically, each facility was equipped with its own resident musicians (Figure 2.2). The client approached Price in 1960s' for the regeneration of OCH in order to make it profitable again. Although the idea behind Price's Fun Palace project and OCH feasibility study remains the same – that is, of modifying their users through artificially intelligent architecture but OCH remains a bit different from the Fun Palace, as it was first a regeneration project – the external structure was retained, and Price played with the interior only, and secondly, as the client had a catering business, interactions of users over tea and cake were a major factor and supposed to be facilitated through advanced communications technologies. Classifying the OCH project as an artificially intelligent architecture, Price called it as the *People's Nerve Centre, a City Brain or a Self-Pace Public Skill and Information Hive* and explained its purpose in a textual record titled *OCH Feasibility Study*, dated September 23, 1965. He defines its purpose as to serve its clients as a pleasure place with ever-changing facilities for self-participatory leisure activities ranging from eating, drinking to self-pace learning and involvement with world news. It should provide "the excitement, delight and satisfaction that a 20th century metropolis should offer," Price proclaimed.[20]

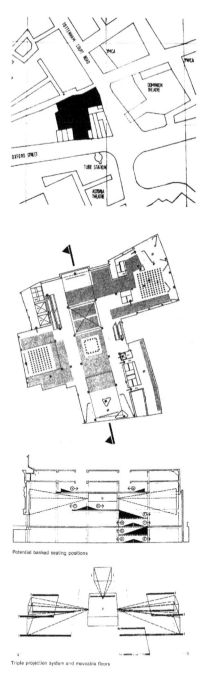

*Figure 2.2* Site and Ground Floor Plans and a Section showing details of the Eidophor projection system in combination with the hydraulic movable floors in a proposal for the regeneration of the Oxford Corner House by Price. These movable floors facilitated the triple projection system for the large Eidophor screens, and viewers were seated as in theater-like arrangements.

*Source*: Cedric Price, "Self-Pace Public Skill and Information Hive," *Architectural Design*, May 1968, 237–239. Copyright © John Wiley & Sons, Ltd. All rights reserved. Used with permission.

Price called the OCH project as a *Self-Pace Public Skill and Information Hive* and explains it as the most flexible centre in Central London, where the public regardless of their involvement attitude being passive, active or both can gather being single, regular or intermittent, be of any age group, tradition, scholastic, economic, academic backgrounds or regardless of any class restrictions were provided with facilities, systems, tools and equipment so that an individual can find any information he wants to as a result of "the determination of the intent, appetite and [his] free-time capacity."[21]

The kind of information that users were allowed to reach, use and research was both the internally generated, housed or processed within OCH or externally approached via electronic links with the central and local government authorities including education, health, technology, economic affairs and housing, police, telecommunications, railways and airlines departments, etc.[22] The OCH was supposed to be equipped with one of the most advanced computer systems of the time. According to Price, spare storage capacity was planned for the use of a new computer that was intended to be used for OCH. For the input and storage of information, other exciting facilities on-site were to be utilised as well in order to reduce the amount of on-site hardware requirements and links.[23]

The character of OCH was similar to that of a town hall, the labor exchange or the official letter in which lots of information can be found, as Price explains, but he strictly distinguishes it from the established information modes of a library, exhibition hall, conference room, etc. The intention of distinguishing the character of OCH with any of the existing information facilities was the fact that Price wanted OCH to be completely welcoming to all the newcomers, without any financial or involvement responsibilities. In an undated handwritten textual record called the *Capacity of Building – Activities*, Price states the suggestion of Sol Cornberg – who was communications consultant for the OCH – regarding the project's noncompetitive nature from the established modes of information. Cornberg suggested that if OCH in any case competes with these established modes of information, it would probably spoil the unique and vital service which was its potential.[24] However, he also suggested that some relationship must be present between these established modes of information and the activities of the OCH so that these would be uncertain and unpredictable. OCH would be both a bad theater and bowling alley, Price said, the capacity of the building was to be determined in terms of its containment value for continually changing social appetites. He further clarified that on this basis, "its capacity for safety in case of emergency and flexibility in case of change is likely to be the controlling factor of its content."[25]

Price suggested visual and audio aids to be scattered throughout the OCH information hive so that when a pedestrian passes through this centre, he subconsciously collects and processes information, thus positively encouraging intellectual participation. Price suggested this intellectual participation of users through the utilisation of information in an undated handwritten document titled *Extent of ex-site Static Communications possible: Internal Communication & Exchange potential – Static Communications*. The aim of Electronic Audio-Visual Equipment and Techniques (EAVET) was to create a centre for "the ingestion, digestion and regurgitation of Information, on demand – information for and available to, specific purpose, space-place and time." This on-demand processing of information included its selection, display, distribution, storage, feedback, retrieval, evaluation and comparison. This processing of information was made available to all members of the society, Price said. Their total and imaginative use was aimed at introducing a new dimension to the enjoyment of metropolitan life. This technology eliminated the need for movement and physical separation while achieving individualistic goals, and in doing so, it yielded unimagined relationships between users and their activities.[26][27]

One of the most important aspect of the OCH feasibility study is the handling of information: the selection, display, distribution, storage, feedback, retrieval, evaluation and comparison through multiple technologies that existed and were futuristic in the 1960s', such as carrels fitted with audio, video and print-out information facilities of teleprinters, International Business Machines (IBM) Corporation (an American multinational technology company that was responsible for designing the computer system or display stations for this project, CCTVs, Eidophor projection system, etc.). Price proposed the Eidophor projection system for broadcasting information on the large screens in the OCH. A newspaper clipping (unknown newspaper, undated) stated that a projection system has been developed by Ueto Scott and explained its details:

> [a]n image being projected on to an outdoor television screen during a demonstration at Croydon of a recently developed Eidophor projection system claimed to make possible the showing of programmes on large screens in full daylight . . . . the Eidophor throws high intensity light through a system of mirrors on to the screen.[28]

Another account on the Eidophor projection system states:

> Peto Scott Electrical Instruments photograph showing a television image projected by Ediphor [Eidophor], in the full glare of daylight, onto a 20 ft [feet] wide specially treated vinyl plastic screen. This breakthrough in outdoor television projection was successfully completed by Peto Scott technicians this morning.[29]

Price utilised this Eidophor projection system in combination with the hydraulic movable floors that were proposed to be installed in OCH. These movable floors facilitated the triple projection system for the large Eidophor screens, and viewers were seated as in theater-like arrangements. Price describes this set-up in detail in a flow diagram titled *Static communications network in the hive, providing audio, video and print-out information facilities.*

Keith Harrison – the information systems consultant for this project – explains a network of static communications in an undated handwritten document called the *Static Communications*. He suggested that transmission of information and its display were the major concerns for OCH, and this was to be achieved through two basic operations – transmission path and fitting the feasible equipment within the building. The transmission of information was to be achieved through the selection of right kind of medium and having agreements for renting time on an annual basis with the General Post Office (GPO) which was the state postal and telecommunications carrier at the time and was until 1969. For the equipment to be fitted within the building, for example, teleprinters, monitors, graphic panels, etc., the aim of displaying of information was to be achieved. Harrison believed that once these two basic ingredients were in operation, the users of OCH were able to utilise these services in a great manner of ways. Keeping in view the dynamic state of information, parameters regarding conditions and services were kept as in an ever-changing mode with transmission path and terminal equipment being static. News, education, local sort, and many other forms of information were considered for display purposes. Both internal and external users were welcomed for utilising information to their advantage, as Harrison confirmed. These requests were also to be catered from the following:

> industrial, business, commercial organizations and the Government who may wish to retrieve some of the information on display via the normal public telephone network. The possibilities are limitless and will be forever changing but the services will be of great use not only to those using the building but also those outside.[30]

In a memorandum to IBM dated June 21, 1966, Price and Harrison explain the purpose of almost 400 carrels that were proposed to be placed in the OCH. Each carrel was to support multiple range of activities, for example, users participating in conferences or 400 people retrieving hundreds of different kinds of information by utilising these carrels at a time. The memorandum classifies the nature of communication media in a carrel into Words, Speech, Still and Moving Pictures, etc. Words were to be displayed on a monitor, and hard copies were to be printed using teleprinter and facsimile equipment that were placed centrally and controlled by the Director of Communications Department situated within the OCH. It was supposed to be provided to each carrel using the pneumatic tube services. For Speech purposes, microphones were proposed aiming at voice retrieval from the computers and telephones for dealing information both internally and externally. Still Pictures service was directed at visual display on the monitors, and facsimile service via pneumatic tubes was suggested for printing hard copies. Teaching machines and language laboratories were also proposed to be integral parts of a carrel. The aim of Moving Pictures was the monitor display of live pictures and videotape recordings either by OCH's CCTV, the British Broadcasting Corporation (BBC), ITV or Pay TV, etc.[31] Price always thoughtfully considered the life cycle of his designs, and as has always been the case with his projects, he also suggested the demolition of the OCH project in ten years, and the cost of this demolition was also included in the total costings. He stressed flexibility as a prime factor in the life cycle of a structure that can also be witnessed in a handwritten textual record present in OCH manuscripts titled *Factors of obsolescence in relation to constituent parts: Extent of inbuilt flexibility required.*[32]

Generator – dates of creation are from 1959–95, predominantly between 1976–80 – has been widely appreciated as the first ever truly artificially intelligent architecture. The client Howard Gilman, who along with his brother, was in charge of a family-run business called the Gilman Paper Company and was interested in a design that could spark new ideas and creativity both for visitors and the staff on a site of 7,400 acres of White Oak Plantation located in Yulee, Florida. He sent Price a brief for this project through fax – a handwritten undated textual record that requested the following:

1   A building which will not contradict but enhance the feeling of beeing [sic] in the middle of nowhere.
2   Has to be of private and public access.
3   Has to create a feeling of intimacy conductive [conducive] to creative impulses – has to accomodate [sic] audiences.
4   Respect enviroment [sic] (jungle) – accomodates [sic] grand piano.
5   Respect history (with theatrical licences [sic]) – be innovative.[33]

What Price proposed as a response to the brief was a network of individual timber-framed cubes, 150 in number with a size of 12 × 12 feet that can be infilled with panels, claddings and screens. These cubes can be adjusted anywhere on a grid platform made up of concrete pads that were 4 × 4 feet in size with the help of cranes. Timber was selected as the structural material for these stiff-jointed frame cubes because of their repeated lifting and placing with the help of a crane on the concrete pads. Another factor was of easy fixation to the ground and manageable positioning and levelling. In case of a hurricane, these cubes were proposed to be tied down with inclined cables within the hurricane warning time.[34]

Price was of the view that unless and until people will not start using the Generator, they will not be able to understand its purpose. Its aim was to provide a space for "thinking, dreaming, working, talking, playing music, experimenting, not necessarily sleeping, for anywhere from one to 100 people." Its architecture served as a generator for the means and conditions that would enable its users to open up their minds and to enrich their lives through controllable simple enclosures and spaces. Thus, its sole purpose was to generate new thoughts in its users. Price reaffirmed and continued, "No one checks, there are no *demands* for a particular performance to be established. The only demand is that the architecture itself shall respond to the people's capacity to change their minds"[35] [emphasis in original].

Listing activities that are going to take place within the proposed structures have always been a unique characteristic of Price's design brief. As have been the case for the Fun Palace, compatibility questionnaires were prepared for the Generator as well in order to explore as many potential activities as possible to be carried-out within these cubes. Price requested respondents to answer questions such as "Over and above what you would normally expect, what would you like?" One of the most compelling points in the whole process of filling these questionnaires was of the *luxury sheet*. Price defines it as a *blank sheet*. He further explains that the aim of this sheet is to make people write and recall those things that they are desperately "aiming to miss." Price said:

> Over and above anything people could ask, you give people a chance to throw the system [b]ecause in relation to both research and cooperation, [Generator] . . . is aiming to miss something that is the tricky one, and may be the key to what we should be doing. The only example I give as a sort of quick example is: go to a fairground and start firing at a reasonable regular speed at the ducks and try not to hit one.[36]

Apart from everyday routine, some of the activities that were explored tend to be highly thought-provoking in one sense or the other. In order to give readers a crisp of the endeavors proposed, some activities are being listed:

> picking nose, making love, having a shit, ogling women, arguing with wife, smacking children, meetings (with eating) at invitation of individual, doing things you have never done – i.e. tree felling, landscaping (digger), reaping (the unexpected), constructing places, lazing in sun (day dreaming), putting on make up, ironing, listening to talking, learning a language, preparing food, knitting, watching people, lecture/live, audio/video large group, prototypes, meditate, contemplate, feed – human, sleep – private/communal rest, hide, hunt, service, information/reception, orientation, you are here.[37]

Among other characteristics, the fact that particularly renders Generator as an artificially intelligent architecture is the use of computer programs in such a way that it responds in accordance with the user's needs. Its fully responsive behaviour to a human being while he is busy performing different sorts of tasks, such as resting, changing his mind, having doubts, periods of quietness and great activity, etc., has been remarkable. It is through this responsive behaviour, Price states, that Generator aims to conserve the human spirit that is being killed by hard and boring work in this age of the microprocessor and silicon chip. With advancements in information and communication technologies, Price said, more and more people are going to be in a limbo to realise what their aim of life is and what their priorities are. With advantaged societal and economic circumstances, they will be having more free will, and it will be difficult for them to decide the usage of this unconsumed time. Stating his slogan of "Never look empty, never feel full," Price labelled it to be his design criteria for Generator and based on this presented a re-definition of architecture as "that which, through a natural distortion of time, place and interval, creates beneficial social conditions that hitherto were considered impossible."[38] Thus, the role of a computer in this case was to suggest re-arrangements of cubes based on the occupant's desires or the changes of their minds once the site was fully occupied and structures were in place. For a system that remained inactive for a considerable period of time, Price confirmed that "[w]e are also programming a method whereby if no one asks for anything else, the computer gets bored and suggests new arrangements."[39]

John Frazer (born 1945) and his professional and life partner, Julia Frazer (born 1945) – British architects, academics and software developers who wrote computer-aided design software – acted as the computer consultants and were in charge of developing computer programs for the Generator project. The Frazers also presented a working model of Generator that consisted of a Commodore PET computer, a plotter and a model made up of Plexiglas cubes on a platform that were controlled by the computer. Whenever cubes changed their positions in the model, the computer represented this layout on its screen and the plotter plotted it (Figure 2.3, 2.4).

The Frazers wrote a letter to Price dated January 11, 1979, in which they presented a classification system of the computer program they proposed for the Generator. This classification consisted of three levels in the ascending order of difficulty. Level 1 was for Architect or a Machine and was supposed to be interactive. Level 2 was designed for Client user or a Machine and was assumed to be interactive or semi-automatic. Level 3 was intended for User or a Machine and was

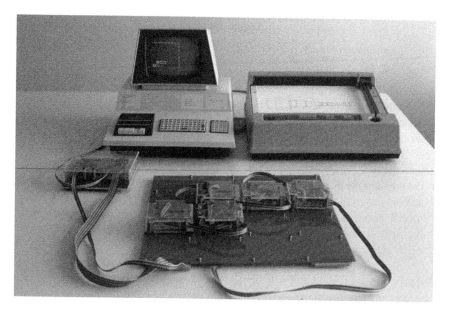

*Figure 2.3* John and Julia Frazer presented this model to Price. In an email message with the author on January 30, 2023, John Frazer stated that "a microprocessor should be embedded in every part of the building construction so that the building fabric could become 'intelligent' and generate its own configuration on a day by day basis. Working electronic model of small part of site with the plotter showing the configuration being generated[,] 1979–80" [emphasis in original].

*Source*: Image courtesy of John Frazer.

*Figure 2.4* In an email message with the author on January 30, 2023, John Frazer captioned
this photograph as "Working electronic model showing the electronic components proposed to be embedded in every part of the building fabric[,] 1979–80."

*Source*: Image courtesy of John Frazer.

fully automatic or generative.[40] Price was particularly interested in Level 3 that
consisted of automatic or generative functioning of Generator, and consequently,
the Frazers drafted their computer program in accordance to the Price's preference.
Level 3 of the computer program states:

> the site and the elements . . . should have a life and intelligence of their own
> and the program would start to generate unsolicited plans, improvements and
> modifications in response to users comments, records of activities, or even by
> building in a boredom concept so that the site starts to make proposals about
> rearrangements of itself if no changes are made.

The program was designed as heuristic and in-built with auto generation of the
strategies for site organisation based on the experience and feedback it received
from its users or participants. If a life was to be defined as a self-replicating information system, the Frazers said, then this program would be the one constituting
a self-replicating information system on-site, consequently providing itself with
appropriate intelligence.[41] The Frazers confirmed regarding their Level 3 proposal
that it incorporates a high possibility of machine intelligence and is far from being
straightforward. They confirmed that Generator must be equipped with an adequate

intelligence that learns, remembers and responds, and one should anticipate that "[i]f you kick a system, the very least that you would expect it to do is kick you back."[42] But Price still kept the Frazers in the mood of self-improvement, as he wanted something that he had not seen before from them, as John Frazer explained in a handwritten statement at the end of a letter to Price:

> [y]ou seemed to imply that we were only useful if we produced results that you did not expect . . . I think this leads to some definition of computer aids in general . . . I am thinking about this but in the meantime at least *one thing* that you would *expect* from any half decent program is that it should produce *at least one plan* which you did *not expect*[43] [emphasis in original].

The Frazers continuously revised their computer program and proposed an intelligent monitoring system which they called a *computing package* controlled via a computer for the responsive functioning of the Generator.[44] Each time in response to the changing needs of the users, the computer suggested a new arrangement, plotted it and handed it over to the crane driver, who then acted accordingly and moved the mobile cubes (Figure 2.5). Furthermore, small logic circuits were

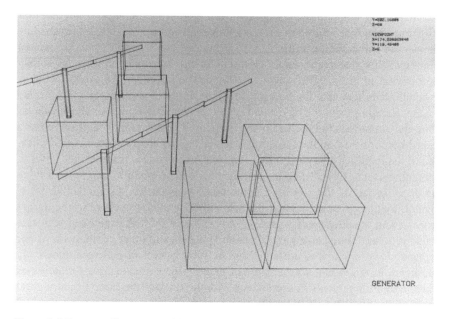

*Figure 2.5* In an email message with the author on January 30, 2023, John Frazer captioned this photograph as "Computer program by John and Julia Frazer for organizing the site on a day by day basis. Pen plot during development of the software[,] 1978."

*Source*: Image courtesy of John Frazer.

proposed to be installed in every nook and corner of the Generator's site so that each and every activity was recorded and transferred to and was controlled by the computer. In an email message with the author on January 25, 2023, John Frazer stated:

> we wrote [a design program] for Cedric Price using a Tektronix 4051. The program was able to generate layouts in response to requirements. . . . [T]he working electronic model [was] interrogated by a Commodore Pet (driving a plotter borrowed from the Tektronix system – the both used a GPIB interface) and its output including from the plotter. The crucial difference is that we proposed to Price that a single chip microprocessor should be embedded in every part of the building fabric and the parts of the building were to be interconnected so that the overall building could deduce its own configuration. It would then start proposing alterations to its own configuration. The model simulates the operation of a small part of the overall complex of units. So the drawings started to come from the model instead of from the 4051 . . . [The] old wireline non hidden line perspectives [produced by a design program that was written by using a Tektronix 4051] are of little interest to day! However it was a miracle to get even them in the late 70s![45]

The Frazers' computing package for Generator's functioning consisted of four programs. *Program 1* was designed as a perpetual architect acting as the schedule planner for the crane operator. All the necessary tools and information related to components placement and structural units was embedded in it so that it may reproduce it in the form of drawings as and when needed. *Program 2* acted as an intelligent diary that kept an inventory of all the activities being performed on-site. Ranging from the placement of components, equipment, future reservations and alterations to facilities being underused or overstretched, it served as a record keeper based on the feedback received so that an effective on-site utilisation of the facilities was performed. *Program 3* served as a maintenance advisor, reminding users of the Generator that they have to keep improving or modifying the organisation of the site on a continuous basis. Being an interactive interrogator, this program stimulated the users to be actively involved in the design process, and an *intelligent modelling kit* was also built that allowed to locate major structural units, changing of cladding panels and other components as per demand. *Program 4* was presented as the most powerful and technologically intelligent program that was capable of making recommendations for activities and site re-arrangements in accordance with the rules of the crane lift, structural spans and circulation. It was able to accept responding data from Program 2 and criticisms and users' comments from Program 3 in order to suggest better organisation and utilisation of spaces. This program was also embedded with action against boredom such that if the users didn't suggest any re-arrangements for cubes or spaces for a considerable period of time, it generated unsolicited plans and improvements.[46] The Frazers stressed in their computing package that although the aim of Generator is to facilitate the active and changing use of the site that has been achieved through physical components, at the same time, Generator must not entirely be dependent on its users for reorganisation and for avoiding the boredom. Instead, they proposed:

> [Generator] should have a mind of its own. The computer program is not merely a passive computer aided design program nor is it just being used to assist with the organization of the site, but is being used to actively encourage continual change and adaptation to changing requirements. This is made possible by the embodying of logic circuits into the structural elements themselves. In a sense the building can be described as being literally "intelligent."[47]

## Richard Saul Wurman: processing of information through visual data centres

Richard Saul Wurman (born 1935) – a renowned American architect and graphic designer who made the collection and sharing of information an architectural practice – introduced the idea of an *Urban Observatory* in 1967 and published it in 1971. Wurman defines it as a visual data centre of the city and region with the purpose of communicating information very clearly and straightforwardly to the public so that they can understand and take considerable actions on it. Wurman also refers to the Urban Observatory as the *Museum of the Living City*. His aim of presenting this proposal was to correct the working style of the City Planning Commission, Department of Streets and Department of Public Property. Information was the sole entity that was stressed and allocated supreme significance, and it was supposed to be delivered and communicated to the public for whom it was intended, no matter in whatever form it may be. He believed that the institutions and public meeting places of our cities are natural extensions of a street. A street is a necklace of rooms that changes its character from one block to another due to varied needs. He further exemplified a street with a room by saying that "[t]he street is a room with a stupendous ceiling – the sky. Its windows are the windows of all the buildings that frame its space, and the measure of its quality is the measure of the city itself."[48]

This Observatory was conceived as a working, educational centre for the development and dissemination of information, a new kind of museum where the city and its man-made environment along with its sociological, economic and political realities were described clearly to the people living in it. It was intended initially for displaying the growth of the region from the Seventeenth Century to the present through movies and models and was supposed to suggest futuristic growth patterns in population, land coverage, city plans and proposals, higher education and recreation facilities, etc., so that people coming from all walks of life, such as starting from school children to those looking for renting a house, can easily find, compare and understand various relationships and correlations among any kind of information they were looking for all gathered under one roof in a building. The information that was supposed to be presented was to be gathered from each and every aspect of life, such as displays showing the size and cost of industrial land and plant facilities, location of the unemployed, substandard housing, personal income levels, tax assessments, age and population density, etc. Listings locating public amenities, such as medical and social agencies, were also incorporated.

Wurman suggested Philadelphia's city hall as an ideal space for his Urban Observatory. The reason behind selection of the city hall was its historical significance and geographical positioning. Being symbolically and functionally the most prominent centrally located structure in the city, it possessed urban spatial characteristics of Campo of Siena, governmental symbolism and physical prominence of the Eiffel Tower. Facing a busy plaza incorporating major vehicular, pedestrian and mass transit routes, it was owned by the city with availability of unspecified space that can be utilised for this Urban Observatory.[49] The information was arranged for the public according to the floor levels of the building. Ground or first floor acted as the Observatory's nucleus, where all urgent information was to be displayed. Second floor was composed of a library containing material related to the current events and acted as the city's waiting room and an urban theater of news. Above these floors, an area was reserved for accommodation of special guests of the city. Acting as a nucleus, the Observatory was proposed as extending a supplemental network throughout the city in the form of major nodes located on the ground floor of all public buildings, where city officials were responsible of explaining the information on all matters of the city to the public.

Wurman presented characteristics of the Urban Observatory embedded in the conditions of time as *formation* narrating the past, *situation* focusing on the present and *aspiration* pointing towards the future. *Formation* tended to be the historical determinant of the region and focused on its political, social, economic, scientific and historical events. Its essential aspects, as Wurman identified, were simultaneous growth and change in a particular frame of time, where time was of the essence. *Situation* presented the current condition of the region. It included but was not limited to the annual, seasonal, daily life, events happening in the schools, institutions, in the lives of the people, the way utilities were being used, such as money, land, air, water, etc. It was also concerned with the way people managed their living, location of housing types, state of urban renewal and further extended to all the movement systems knitting the city together. This section of the Observatory was supposed to be a live and working centre of information, where comparisons, relationships and correlations between different entities of current information were to be discovered by the public but with the help of city officials. In this section, for example, the interrelationship between a highway program and residential development or between a school and the school-age population were to be sorted out by the public. Wurman also proposed this section as an ideal location for the urban gaming centre. *Aspiration* was concerned with the futuristic prospects of the people and city they inhabit. It focused on the short- and long-term goals of all public and private institutions operating within a city. "This section of the museum becomes the public forum for the display and public testing of ideas," said Wurman, with the intention of updating and educating the citizens so that they could be able to comprehend "what might be, what should be, what could be" done to their lives and their city. The first and foremost aim of the Urban Observatory, according to

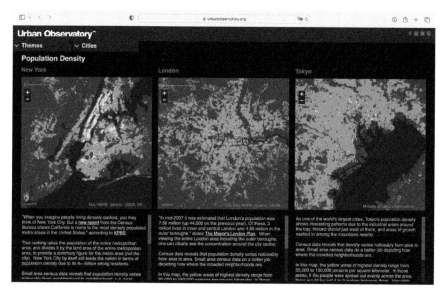

*Figure 2.6*  The Urban Observatory's City Comparison App enables its users to compare and contrast cities against a number of themes.

*Source*: Richard Saul Wurman, RadicalMedia and Esri, Urban Observatory (website), Esri, Richard Saul Wurman & RadicalMedia, accessed March 10, 2023, www.urbanobservatory.org/. Permission granted by Richard Saul Wurman.

Wurman, was to fill the enormous gap that existed between the public communication of information that was necessary for the running of everyday tasks. This lack of information coordination among the public was highlighted by the city government institutions of Chamber of Commerce, the Office of the City Representative and the Philadelphia Industrial Development Corporation. This Observatory was thought to revive Philadelphia's leadership in urban thought and development.[50] Furthering this approach, Wurman in collaboration with RadicalMedia and Esri launched a web-based platform in 2013 for urban data visualisation called *Urban Observatory: A Live Museum with a Data Pulse* (Figure 2.6). They stated its aim:

> an interactive exhibit that gives you the chance to compare and contrast maps of cities around the world – all from one location. It aims to make the world's data both understandable and useful. [Its creators believe] . . . it is the first exhibit of its kind.[51]

## Nicholas Negroponte: responsiveness, individuality and excitement as significant components of fully automatic, self-organising architecture

Nicholas Negroponte (born 1943) is a world-renowned technology visionary having deep understanding of the technology of artificial intelligence with respect to architecture in particular and the influence of technology on the business and society in general. He is credited for founding the *Architecture Machine Group* at the Massachusetts Institute of Technology (MIT) in collaboration with Leon B. Groisser (biography untraceable). Groisser was Professor of Structures and Executive Officer at the Department of Architecture, MIT. The Architecture Machine Group functioned from 1967–85 after which it was combined with other disciplines and renamed as the *Media Lab*. This group extensively experimented with the technology of artificial intelligence, particularly regarding its role in contemporary architecture. It was truly multidisciplinary in nature as along with the technology of artificial intelligence, the group also researched different aspects related either directly or indirectly with artificial intelligence – such as cognitive psychology, computer science, art, film, human-computer interaction, etc. The group frequently collaborated with the MIT's Artificial Intelligence Lab, and these experiments proved to be of considerable importance, as they were successful in receiving large fundings from national defense forces of the United States of America, such as the Defense Advanced Research Projects Agency (DARPA) and the Office of Naval Research.

Negroponte defines artificially intelligent architecture as possessing the characteristics of responsiveness, individuality and excitement. This intelligent architecture machine acts as a designer, becomes an equal partner of the user and understands its environment. He has been an ardent believer that architecture machines do need a personality like human beings in order to experience the same as we humans do. He expressed his concerns:

> [d]oes a machine have to possess a body like my own and be able to experience personally behaviors like my own in order to share in what *we* call intelligent behavior? While it may seem absurd, I believe the answer is *yes*[52] [emphasis in original].

With the help of these qualities, an architecture machine then becomes habitable, as Negroponte stresses that these machines must be designed in a way so as to solicit information from the real world by utilising their internal computation mechanisms and without the intervention of any human designer. And the most feasible method of achieving this sophistication is to make these machines interact with the real world, as Negroponte said, "if machines are given the faculty for sophisticated interactions with the real world (people, places, pictures, and so forth), they can learn to develop their own design methods and methodologies, perhaps better than our own."[53]

Joseph Carl Robnett Licklider, known as J. C. R. Licklider (1915–90) – a renowned American psychologist and computer scientist – introduced the idea of a *thinking centre* in his well-received paper *Man-Computer Symbiosis* (1960). Similar to Negroponte, he also suggested a successful partnership of a man and his computer system as an important component of a thinking centre, in other words, artificially intelligent architecture machine. Licklider states that aim of the man-computer symbiosis is of computers facilitating the formulative thinking of the user and to enable men and computers cooperation in making decisions for unexpected problems together. He said that if clerical or mechanical office work problems can be solved in an efficient manner by the symbiotic relationship between a man and his fast information-retrieval and data-processing machine, then it shows that this cooperative interaction would also be greatly enhancing the thinking power and creative abilities. On the basis of these facts, Licklider projected that it would be extremely difficult to segregate the contributions of human operators and their information storage and retrieval equipments in an assignment.[54] Elaborating the role of this equipment, Licklider said that its job is to convert hypotheses into testable models and to evaluate them against that data which human operator designates it. This equipment will answer the questions, simulate the mechanisms, carry out the procedures, transform data, plot graphs, convert static equations, logical statements into dynamic models, etc., and consequently display all of these results to its operator so that he may analyse these and conclude any results. In short, this equipment was designed to show its operator all the alternatives if he is not sure of the possible options. As Licklider said, this equipment will "interpolate, extrapolate, and transform, . . . [thus carrying out] the routinizable, clerical operations that fill the intervals between decisions." Further explaining his idea of a thinking centre by linking it to the functions of a library, Licklider said that "[i]t seems reasonable to envision, for a time 10 or 15 years hence, a 'thinking centre' that will incorporate the functions of present-day libraries together with anticipated advances in information storage and retrieval and the symbiotic functions suggested" [emphasis in original]. He further elaborated that there will be a network of such centres linked by wide-band communication lines and also to individual users by leased-wire services. As such endeavors were expensive when Licklider proposed them, he said that the cost of gigantic memories and sophisticated programs would be distributed among its users.[55]

In the *Epilogue: An Allegory* section of his book *Soft Architecture Machines*, Negroponte explains the characterisation of the applications of computers to architecture. It can also be viewed as a very brief historical narrative outlining the artificially intelligent architecture. He approaches this problematic by dividing it into four consecutive eras. *Era 1* aimed at finding all the possible solutions to a problem and then selecting the best. *Era 2* focused on letting the designer do what he was good at and let the machine perform what it was good for. Negroponte classified *Era 3* as of the 1970s' in which all the efforts were directed towards finding out what the human could bring to the design process and, as he said, "who that human should be." *Era 4* is of a special purpose, fully automatic, self-organising, artificially intelligent architecture machine that Negroponte calls as a "string-and-ring machine" for architecture.[56]

An exhibition called *SOFTWARE – Information technology: its new meaning for art* held at the Jewish Museum in New York from September 16 through November 8, 1970, exhibited Architecture Machine Group's artificially intelligent architectural project known as the *Seek* (1969–70). The exhibition catalog includes an article by the MIT's Architecture Machine Group, *Life in a Computerized Environment*, that explains about this project in detail. While looking simply at the Seek, it seems like an arrangement of numerous toy cubes that are stacked,

*Figure 2.7* Spectators observing the Seek (1969–70).

aligned and sorted within a large glass box by a robotic arm hanging above them (Figure 2.7). There are in fact 500 two-inch-sized cubes that are also metal plated. Interestingly, in order to make this project as close to a real-life community as possible, the large glass box has also been filled with gerbils. The hanging robotic arm stacks, aligns and sorts these two-inch-sized cubes in a strict rectilinear arrangement whenever the gerbils disturb their arrangement according to their desires and wishes while playing up and down on these small toy cubes. The glass box is sized 5 × 8 feet. Negroponte states that this project's aim was to train a machine for handling real-world scenarios. In order to achieve continuous disruption, gerbils were introduced as a community due to their unresting nature and curiosity so as to challenge the strictly rectilinear arrangement of the machine (Figure 2.8). Any minor dislocation or disarrangement was to be realigned by the machine, and the resulting scenario was a continuously changing architecture.[57]

According to the Architecture Machine Group, Seek was a device controlled by a small general-purpose computer that senses, affects and in turn attempts to control the unexpected events within the physical environment. Negroponte further

*Figure 2.8* Gerbils were introduced into this computerised environment in order to challenge the strictly rectilinear programming of the machine.

elaborates that this device was a homemade sensor or effector consisting of multiple attachments, such as magnets, photocells, markers, etc., which it was able to position in three dimensions under computer control. It was believed that the system was able to pile blocks, carry TV cameras and observe colours, etc.[58] Its 5 × 8 feet superstructure supported a carriage having three dimensions of freedom. It was composed of an electromagnet, micro-switches and pressure-sensing devices. This artificial part received its guidance from an Interdata Model 3 Computer having 65,536 single (yes/no) bits of memory[59] (Figure 2.9). Furthermore, all the actions that Seek performs are remembered and stored in its computer's memory. Seek keeps on performing its duties according to these stored actions, but when the gerbils disturb these pre-stored actions by performing new tasks, Seek's computer readjusts and modifies itself, as the Architecture Machine Group states that "[i]n the process, *Seek* exhibits inklings of a responsive behaviour inasmuch as the actions of the gerbils are not predictable and the reactions of *Seek* purposefully correct or amplify gerbil-provoked dislocations"[60] [emphasis in original].

Seek was truly a transdisciplinary artificially intelligent architectural project, where people from a number of disciplines collaborated. The Architecture Machine Group comprised of a number of undergraduate and postgraduate students along with their professors who worked on the Seek. This project was sponsored by the Ford Foundation and was carried out within the MIT Urban Systems Laboratory.

*Figure 2.9* Negroponte (left) with Interdata Model 3 Computer that was responsible for managing the intelligent behaviour of the roaming electromagnet hung overhead in the Seek.

*Source*: Shunk-Kender, *Nicholas Negroponte (left) with Karl Katz and Steven Gregory*, September 1970, photograph. Copyright © The Jewish Museum, New York. All rights reserved. Used with permission.

Along with Negroponte and Groisser, Randy Rettberg and Mike Titelbaum, who were students in electrical engineering, were in charge of the electronics particularly focusing on the interface and controller aspects. A graduate student, Steven Gregory, from the School of Architecture and Planning was also in charge of the programming. Construction of the device was carried out by Steven Peters and Ernest Vincent.[61]

Seek was designed to respond to the unpredictable nature of people, and in this experimental set-up, it played with the restless nature of gerbils (Figure 2.10). It is due to these characteristics of sensing, storing, affecting and controlling the environment that Seek was able to possess a responsive behaviour, a quality that particularly makes Seek an artificially intelligent architecture. In other words, Seek attempted to generate, degenerate, fix, straighten, find and detect the error. The Architecture Machine Group stated regarding this responsive behaviour of Seek:

[i]f computers are to be our friends they must understand our metaphors.
If they are to be responsive to changing, unpredictable, context-dependent

*Figure 2.10* Seek's intelligent response to the unpredictable actions of gerbils proved it as capable of exhibiting responsible behaviour.
*Source*: Shunk-Kender, *Uncaptioned*, September 1970, photograph. Copyright © The Jewish Museum, New York. All rights reserved. Used with permission.

human needs, they will need an artificial intelligence that can cope with complex contingencies in a sophisticated manner (drawing upon these metaphors) much as *Seek* deals with elementary uncertainties in a simple-minded fashion[62] [emphasis in original].

## Conclusion

Fun Palace (1961–85) was a collaboration between Price and radical English theater director Joan Littlewood (1914–2002) that resulted in an adjustable and flexible framework presenting activities of its participants. A huge steel frame integrated movable, modular components of portable stairways, pivoting escalators, moving walkways, projection units, mobile gantry cranes for placing ceiling, floor modules and other pneumatic structures, etc., in compliance with the activities of the participants. Pask (1928–96) in his *Proposals for a Cybernetic Theatre* presented a theater for Fun Palace in which the audience was able to control the performance of the actors through a feedback loop. He introduced a feedback loop in the system so that an audience member must not become *bored*. Unspecified, indefinite and unplanned activities were promoted, and the public was supposed to enter it as *Input of Unmodified People* and leave as *Output of Modified People*, presenting a self-organising cybernetic system that processed and feedbacked information. Dr. J. Clark from Bristol University, who was a member of the Fun Palace Cybernetics Committee, also suggested installation of magic doors so that individuals of particular characteristics were to be admitted in the Fun Palace. This system is similar to the artificially intelligent facial recognition systems of today. Fun Palace can said to be artificially intelligent on the basis of the following two characteristics. First, it was organic, and the character of the system was self-organising. In ordinary conditions, Cinemas, Theaters and Restaurants act as objects that satisfy a need, but in the Fun Palace, they functioned as operations promoting further activity. Secondly, it had an organic relation to the external environment. Its job was of stimulating imagination and presenting people with a new perspective on the world around them and opening up new vistas.

Oxford Corner House (1965–67) was to be regenerated for a British megacatering company called as the J. Lyons and Company Ltd. The aim was to modify the users while interacting over tea and cake through advanced information and communications technologies. Price proposed the Oxford Corner House as *People's Nerve Center, a City Brain or a Self-Pace Public Skill and Information Hive*. Carrels were fitted with audio, video and print-out information facilities containing teleprinters, IBM display stations, CCTVs and Eidophor projection systems that were to be used in combination with hydraulic movable floors. Electronic Audio-Visual Equipment and Techniques (EAVET) were utilised in order to make information accessible on demand, for specific purposes and at any space, place and time. Through this exercise, information and communications were selected, displayed, distributed, stored, feedbacked, retrieved, evaluated and compared.

Generator (1976–80) aimed to spark new ideas and creativity on a site of 7,400 acres located at the White Oak Plantation site in Yulee, Florida. Price proposed a network of timber-framed cubes that could be adjusted on a grid platform with the help of cranes. Generator used a responsive computer program that suggested site re-arrangements according to user's desires, and if a user remained uniform, the program got *bored* and suggested revisions. John and Julia Frazer presented a working model of Generator that comprised of Commodore PET computer, a plotter and a model of Plexiglas cubes on a platform that were controlled by the computer. Whenever cubes changed their positions in the model, the computer represented this layout on its screen and the plotter plotted the layout. The Frazers also presented a three-level computer program for Generator. Level 1 consisted of architect-machine interaction and was called as interactive. Level 2 comprised of client-use and machine interaction and was labelled as interactive or semi-automatic. Level 3 is of significance to this study, as it was based on the user-machine interaction and was called as automatic or generative. This level stated that the site and its elements should have a life and intelligence of their own. The computer program should act as a self-improving and self-replicating information system that generates plans, re-arrangements and modifications based on user experience and feedback. This system incorporated a high possibility of machine intelligence. On the basis of this program, the Frazers concluded that in a sense, the Generator could be described as being literally *intelligent*. They proposed that it must also be equipped with adequate intelligence that learns, remembers and responds. This system with machine intelligence was supposed to be highly complicated. They also proposed an intelligent computing package that was controlled via a computer. Small logic circuits were proposed to be installed in every corner of the Generator's site so that every activity was recorded and transferred to and was controlled by the computer.

Negroponte defines characteristics of an artificially intelligent architecture machine as those of responsiveness, individuality and excitement. He states that in this intelligent architecture machine, computer acts as a designer and an equal partner of the user and understands its environments and makes this machine habitable. He states that we are living in an era of exploring the role of humans and computers as equal partners, and the next stage will be of special-purpose, fully automatic and self-organising machines for architecture. In his project Seek (1969–70), he experimented with a device controlled by a small general-purpose computer that sensed, affected and in turn attempted to control the unexpected events within the physical environment.

Likewise, Wurman's Urban Observatory (1967–71) was a visual data centre of the city and the region that attempted to communicate clear and straightforward information to the citizens. It was a museum relating at different levels sociological, economic and political realities. He proposed Philadelphia's city hall as an ideal location for this purpose and suggested that this Observatory should act as a nucleus and an extension of supplemental network scattered throughout the city and must be located on the ground floor of all public buildings. This Observatory was to present different time frames, for example, formation section displaying past, situation section displaying present and aspiration section exhibiting future.

## Notes

1  Cedric Price, "Fun Palace, *ARK*, Spring 1964," in *Cedric Price Works 1952–2003: A Forward-Minded Retrospective, Vol. 2, Articles & Talks*, ed. Samantha Hardingham (London: AA Publications, 2016), 21.

2  Joan Littlewood, "Non-Program: A Laboratory of Fun by Joan Littlewood, Head of Project Committee," in *Cedric Price Works 1952–2003: A Forward-Minded Retrospective, Vol. 2, Articles & Talks*, ed. Samantha Hardingham (London: AA Publications, 2016), 97.

3  Cedric Price, "Research and Cooperation, Architectural Association, 7 June 1984: A Talk Given by Cedric Price to Celebrate Cedric Price Works II, an Exhibition and Catalogue," in *Cedric Price Works 1952–2003: A Forward-Minded Retrospective, Vol. 2, Articles & Talks*, ed. Samantha Hardingham (London: AA Publications, 2016), 372.

4  Cedric Price and Joan Littlewood, *Fund-Raising Brochure for Fun Palace*, 1964, DR1995:0188:525:001:023, Fun Palace Project, line/mechanical/tool-aided drawing,

36.2 × 59.8 cm, Cedric Price Fonds, Canadian Centre for Architecture, Montréal, accessed September 29, 2020, www.cca.qc.ca/en/search/details/collection/object/378822.

5 Littlewood, "Non-Program," 96.

6 Ibid., 95.

7 Gordon Pask, Proposals for a cybernetic theatre, ca. 1964–74, DR1995:0188:525:001:009, Fun Palace Project, Cedric Price Fonds, Canadian Centre for Architecture, Montréal.

8 Ibid., 4–5.

9 Ibid., 15.

10 Ibid., 3, 16.

11 Ibid., 21.

12 Joan Littlewood, who was the client for the Fun Palace project, also indicates names of other cybernetics committee members (including herself) in her autobiography. They include Chester Beatty (from Research Institute), Stafford Beer (Sigma), Richard Bowdler (Fun Palace), Asa Briggs (Sussex University), R. Chesterman (Goldsmith's College), J. Clark (Bristol University), Tom Driberg MP, F. George (Bristol University), R. Goldacre, Richard Gregory (Cambridge University), Brian Lewis (Systems Research Ltd), Mr. and Mrs T. R. McKinnon Wood, Ian Mikado MP, R. Pinker (Goldsmith's College), Cedric Price (Architect), Gerry Raffles (Theatre Workshop), G. Slot, J. H. Westcott (Imperial College) and M. Young (Institute of Community Studies). There are, however, two names with the same surname of Chesterman that have been listed in the sources as R. Chesterman (Goldsmith's College) and G. Chesterman. Also, sources indicate different spellings of the same name of "Mikado" and "Mickardo." Gordon Pask, Fun Palace Cybernetics Committee: Minutes of the Meeting held at the Building Center, Store Street, London W.C.1, January 27, 1965, DR1995:0188:525:001:001, Fun Palace Project, Cedric Price Fonds, Canadian Centre for Architecture, Montréal, folio 8r; Joan Littlewood, *Joan's Book: The Autobiography of Joan Littlewood*, 4th ed. (London: Bloomsbury, 2016), 498.

13 Details regarding Ascott's cybernetic artistic endeavors can be found in a collection of his papers published as Roy Ascott, *Telematic Embrace: Visionary Theories of Art, Technology, and Consciousness*, ed. Edward A. Shanken (Berkeley: University of California Press, 2003).

14 Gordon Pask, *Fun Palace Cybernetics Committee: Minutes of the Meeting held at the Building Center*, Store Street, London W.C.1, January 27, 1965, DR1995:0188:525:001: 001, Fun Palace Project, Cedric Price Fonds, Canadian Centre for Architecture, Montréal, folio 12r.

15 Ibid., folio 12r–16r.

16 Ibid., folio 15r.

17 Ibid., folio 16r–18r.

18 Ibid.

19 Price also refers to *Oxford Corner House* as the *Oxford Circus Corner House*, London. Cedric Price, "Self-Pace Public Skill and Information Hive," in *Cedric Price Works 1952–2003: A Forward-Minded Retrospective, Vol. 2, Articles & Talks*, ed. Samantha Hardingham (London: AA Publications, 2016), 104–107.

20 Cedric Price, OCH Feasibility Study, September 23, 1965, DR1995:0224:342:002, OCH Feasibility Study Folio, Cedric Price Fonds, Canadian Centre for Architecture, Montréal.

21 Cedric Price, OCH handwritten notes: User Watershed, undated, DR1995:0224:342:002, OCH Feasibility Study Folio, Cedric Price Fonds, Canadian Centre for Architecture, Montréal.

22 Price listed a number of external agencies that were supposed to cooperate and contribute to the running of the OCH on a hire basis. These public agencies were "Central Government – including Ministry of Education, Health, Technology, Economic Affairs, Housing: Local Government. Local Authorities – G.L.C. [Greater London Council – a

local government administrative body that operated from 1965–86.], Greater London Boroughs, I.L.E.A [Inner London Education Authority], L.T.E [Long Term Evolution – a wireless data communications technology], British Rail, C.O.I.D [untraceable], Metropolitan Police, B.E.A [British European Airways – a British airline that operated from 1946–74], B.O.A.C [British Overseas Airways Corporation that operated from 1939–74]." Regarding private agencies, Price stated that they are "subject to further programming considerations (To be discussed at meeting 28.1.66.)." Cedric Price, OCH handwritten notes: Nature of Co-operation with outside bodies, undated, DR1995:0224:342:002, OCH Feasibility Study Folio, Cedric Price Fonds, Canadian Centre for Architecture, Montréal.

23 Price, "Self-Pace Public Skill and Information Hive," 107.

24 Cedric Price, OCH handwritten notes: *Capacity of Building – Activities*, undated, DR1995:0224:342:002, OCH Feasibility Study Folio, Cedric Price Fonds, Canadian Centre for Architecture, Montréal.

25 Ibid.

26 Cedric Price, OCH handwritten notes: Extent of ex-site Static Communications possible: Internal Communication & Exchange potential – Static Communications, undated, DR1995:0224:342:002, OCH Feasibility Study Folio, Cedric Price Fonds, Canadian Centre for Architecture, Montréal.

27 Price, "Self-Pace Public Skill and Information Hive," 107.

28 Cedric Price, *Newspaper Clipping about the Eidophor Projection System from Unknown Newspaper*, ca. 1965–66, DR1995:0224:342:001:002, OCH Feasibility Study Folio, newsprint, 16.8 × 15.5 cm, Cedric Price Fonds, Canadian Centre for Architecture, Montréal, accessed September 29, 2020, www.cca.qc.ca/en/search/details/collection/object/417905.

29 Peto Scott Electrical Instruments, *Breakthrough Outdoor Television Projection*, July 27, 1966, 1983–5236/30319, ink and paper fiber product, dimensions unstated, Daily Herald Archive, National Science and Media Museum, Bradford, accessed September 29, 2020, https://collection.sciencemuseumgroup.org.uk/objects/co8621936/breakthrough-outdoor-television-projection-photograph.

30 Keith Harrison, OCH handwritten notes: Static Communications, undated, DR1995:0224:342:002, OCH Feasibility Study Folio, Cedric Price Fonds, Canadian Centre for Architecture, Montréal.

31 Keith Harrison and Cedric Price, O.C.H. Feasibility Study: Memorandum to IBM, June 21, 1966, DR1995:0224:342:002:001, OCH Feasibility Study Folio, Cedric Price Fonds, Canadian Centre for Architecture, Montréal, accessed September 29, 2020, www.cca.qc.ca/en/search/details/collection/object/433397.

32 Cedric Price, OCH handwritten notes: Factors of obsolescence in relation to constituent parts: Extent of inbuilt flexibility required, undated, DR1995:0224:342:002, OCH Feasibility Study Folio, Cedric Price Fonds, Canadian Centre for Architecture, Montréal.

33 Howard Gilman, "Generator Brief Sent as a Fax from the Client to Price," in *Cedric Price Works 1952–2003: A Forward-Minded Retrospective, Vol. 1, Projects*, ed. Samantha Hardingham (London: AA Publications, 2016), 456.

34 Cedric Price, *Plans and Perspectives of Typical Cubic Units for Generator*, ca. 1976–79, DR1995:0280:621, Generator Project Folio, photomechanical reproduction: Red ink and blue crayon, 41.6 × 29.5 cm, Cedric Price Fonds, Canadian Centre for Architecture, Montréal, accessed September 29, 2020, www.cca.qc.ca/en/search/details/collection/object/322582.

35 Cedric Price, "Technology is the Answer, But what was the Question? Prerecorded Talk, Pidgeon Audio Visual, 1979," in *Cedric Price Works 1952–2003: A Forward-Minded Retrospective, Vol. 2, Articles & Talks*, ed. Samantha Hardingham (London: AA Publications, 2016), 330.

36 Price, "Research and Cooperation," 372–373.

37 Compatibility questionnaires resulted in a variety of activity proposals for Generator, and the potential activities as listed by Price included "picking nose, gardening, accounting, writing, watching TV, making love, cleaning floors, drawing, having a shit, tending pets, conversation, filing, listening to radio, cooking, painting pictures, washing up, drinking (alcohol), radio repairs, eating big dinner, taking a bath, rapid transit passenger [stay], reading, telephone calls, driving car, listening to car radio, mowing lawn, writing letters, ogling women, attending meetings, walking in country [side], dreaming (during day), running, arguing with wife, kicking a football, smacking children, smoking cigars, having haircut, swimming, having a shower, walking (alone), sitting (alone), eating (alone), meetings (with eating) at invitation of individual, boating, working (alone), working (with others), keeping in touch – teleprinter/TV/radio/films etc., doing things you have never done – i.e. tree felling, landscaping (digger), photography (dark room), singing/instrument (practice), singing/instrument (performance), gardening/landscape, decorating, English snooker, table games, physical games (tennis, squash, football), reaping (the unexpected), constructing places, shopping, playing the piano, putting on make up, ironing, traveling by train, listening to music, listening to talking, learning a language, preparing food, praying, household cleaning, knitting, shooting, visiting friend, visiting doctor/dentist, watching people, lecture/live, audio/video large group, rehersal [sic]/music, drama, dance etc., read/library (books, slides, tapes), poetry debate, workshop/machine materials, sets, prototypes, studio/paint, draw, script, also – sound studio, film/active, edit, photography, develop, print, cinema/passive, look, sit, exhibition/space, gallery, show, meditate/worship, contemplate, feed – human, horse/train, race, house, show, kitchen, cook, snacks, drinks (soft), canteen, sleep – private/communal rest, land activity/landscape work, hide, hunt, vehicle/private, service, river/water, boat, explore, swim, resource, gymnasium, yoga, field sports, bar, club, alcohol, entertainment, animals/captive/free range/observe/eat/sell, ablutions/bath, wash, WC, sauna, shower, information/reception, orientation, you are here, group discussion, no more than (or equal to) 20."
   Cedric Price, *Generator: Activity Compatibility Chart*, May 1977, DR1995:0280:651: 004:010, Generator Project Folio, ink with ink stamp over electrostatic print on paper, 29.8 × 21.1 cm, Cedric Price Fonds, Canadian Centre for Architecture, Montréal, accessed September 29, 2020, www.cca.qc.ca/en/search/details/collection/object/470938.
   Cedric Price, *Chart of Activity Compatibility for Generator*, 1977, DR1995:0280:651:004:005, Generator Project Folio, photocopy on paper with porous point pen and stamp pad ink, 29.7 × 21 cm, Cedric Price Fonds, Canadian Centre for Architecture, Montréal, accessed September 29, 2020, www.cca.qc.ca/en/search/details/collection/object/396769.
   Cedric Price, *Activity Compatibility*, ca. 1977, DR1995:0280:651:004:007, Generator Project Folio, ink over electrostatic print on paper, 30.4 × 21.1 cm, Cedric Price Fonds, Canadian Centre for Architecture, Montréal, accessed September 29, 2020, www.cca.qc.ca/en/search/details/collection/object/461618.
   Cedric Price, *Activity Compatibility Chart for Generator*, May 1977, DR1995:0280:651:004:008, Generator Project Folio, ink and ink stamp over electrostatic print on paper, 29.69 × 20.64 cm, Cedric Price Fonds, Canadian Centre for Architecture, Montréal, accessed September 29, 2020, www.cca.qc.ca/en/search/details/collection/object/461619.
38 Price, "Technology is the Answer, but what was the Question?" 331.
39 Ibid.
40 John and Julia Frazer, Letter to Cedric Price, January 11, 1979, DR1995:0280:651:005, Generator Project Folio, Cedric Price Fonds, Canadian Centre for Architecture, Montréal.
41 Ibid.
42 Ibid.

43  Ibid.
44  The document is undated, but in the handwriting of Price, a note has been stated in the end that reads "See Frazer Letter 20/3/80 [March 20, 1980]." John and Julia Frazer, Example 5 – Generator [Description of Computer Programs], undated, DR1995:0280:651:001, Generator Project Folio, Cedric Price Fonds, Canadian Centre for Architecture, Montréal.
45  John Frazer, email message to author, January 25, 2023.
46  Frazers, "Example 5 – Generator," Ibid.
47  Ibid.
48  Richard Saul Wurman, "Making the City Observable," *Design Quarterly*, no. 80 (1971): 75–76, accessed August 12, 2020, https://doi.org/10.2307/4047376.
49  Ibid., 76.
50  Ibid.
51  Richard Saul Wurman, RadicalMedia and Esri, Urban Observatory (website), Esri, Richard Saul Wurman & RadicalMedia, accessed March 10, 2023, www.urbanobservatory.org/.
52  Nicholas Negroponte, *Soft Architecture Machines* (Cambridge, MA: MIT Press, 1975), 49.
53  Ibid., 48.
54  J. C. R. Licklider, "Man-Computer Symbiosis," *IRE Transactions on Human Factors in Electronics* HFE-1, no. 1 (March 1960): 6, https://doi.org/10.1109/THFE2.1960.4503259.
55  Ibid., 7.
56  Negroponte, *Soft Architecture Machines*, 155.
57  Ibid., 46–47.
58  Nicholas Negroponte, *The Architecture Machine: Toward a More Human Environment* (Cambridge, MA: MIT Press, 1970), 104–105.
59  Architecture Machine Group, M.I.T., "Life in a Computerized Environment: Seek 1969–70," in *SOFTWARE – Information Technology: Its New Meaning for Art*, ed. Jack Burnham (New York: The Jewish Museum, 1970), 23, accessed September 29, 2020, https://monoskop.org/images/3/31/Software_Information_Technology_Its_New_Meaning_for_Art_catalogue.pdf.
60  Ibid.
61  Ibid.
62  Ibid.

## Bibliography

This chapter has benefitted from the archives of Cedric Price Fonds at the Canadian Centre for Architecture in Montréal. This bibliography only lists the name of the collection that has been consulted instead of the specific items. It is in accordance with the guidelines of *The Chicago Manual of Style*, 17th ed. (Chicago: University of Chicago Press, 2017) and for more details, section 14.222 can be consulted. The details of specific items have been listed in the notes. Unless otherwise noted, all translations are by the author.

Architecture Machine Group, M.I.T. "Life in a Computerized Environment: Seek 1969–70." In *SOFTWARE – Information Technology: Its New Meaning for Art*, edited by Jack Burnham, 20–23. New York: The Jewish Museum, 1970. Accessed September 29, 2020. https://monoskop.org/images/3/31/Software_Information_Technology_Its_New_Meaning_for_Art_catalogue.pdf.

Ascott, Roy. *Telematic Embrace: Visionary Theories of Art, Technology, and Consciousness.* Edited by Edward A. Shanken. Berkeley: University of California Press, 2003.

Fun Palace. Cedric Price Fonds. Canadian Centre for Architecture, Montréal.

Generator. Cedric Price Fonds. Canadian Centre for Architecture, Montréal.

Gilman, Howard. "Generator Brief Sent as a Fax from the Client to Price." In *Cedric Price Works 1952–2003: A Forward-Minded Retrospective, Vol. 1, Projects*, edited by Samantha Hardingham, 446–469. London: AA Publications, 2016.

Licklider, J. C. R. "Man-Computer Symbiosis." *IRE Transactions on Human Factors in Electronics* HFE-1, no. 1 (March 1960): 4–11. http://doi.org/10.1109/THFE2.1960.4503259.

Littlewood, Joan. *Joan's Book: The Autobiography of Joan Littlewood*. 4th ed. London: Bloomsbury, 2016.

Littlewood, Joan. "Non-Program: A Laboratory of Fun by Joan Littlewood, Head of Project Committee." In *Cedric Price Works 1952–2003: A Forward-Minded Retrospective, Vol. 2, Articles & Talks*, edited by Samantha Hardingham, 97. London: AA Publications, 2016.

Mathews, Stanley. "Appendix D: John, Clark, "A List of 70 Projects for a Fun-Palace"." In *From Agit-Prop to Free Space: The Architecture of Cedric Price*, 258–284. London: Black Dog Publishing, 2007.

Negroponte, Nicholas. *The Architecture Machine: Toward a More Human Environment*. Cambridge, MA: MIT Press, 1970.

Negroponte, Nicholas. *Soft Architecture Machines*. Cambridge, MA: MIT Press, 1975.

OCH Feasibility Study. Cedric Price Fonds. Canadian Centre for Architecture, Montréal.

Price, Cedric. "Fun Palace, ARK, Spring 1964." In *Cedric Price Works 1952–2003: A Forward-Minded Retrospective, Vol. 2, Articles & Talks*, edited by Samantha Hardingham, 21. London: AA Publications, 2016.

Price, Cedric. "Research and Cooperation, Architectural Association, 7 June 1984: A Talk Given by Cedric Price to Celebrate Cedric Price Works II, an Exhibition and Catalogue." In *Cedric Price Works 1952–2003: A Forward-Minded Retrospective, Vol. 2, Articles & Talks*, edited by Samantha Hardingham, 372. London: AA Publications, 2016.

Price, Cedric. "Self-Pace Public Skill and Information Hive." In *Cedric Price Works 1952–2003: A Forward-Minded Retrospective, Vol. 2, Articles & Talks*, edited by Samantha Hardingham, 104–107. London: AA Publications, 2016.

Price, Cedric. "Technology is the Answer, But What Was the Question? Prerecorded Talk, Pidgeon Audio Visual, 1979." In *Cedric Price Works 1952–2003: A Forward-Minded Retrospective, Vol. 2, Articles & Talks*, edited by Samantha Hardingham, 327–331. London: AA Publications, 2016.

Wurman, Richard Saul. "Making the City Observable." *Design Quarterly*, no. 80 (1971): 1–96. Accessed August 12, 2020. http://doi.org/10.2307/4047376.

# 3 Kenzo Tange and Arata Isozaki
## Cybernetic environments

*(In Japanese, the surname comes before the given name. But this chapter treats the names "Kenzo Tange" and "Arata Isozaki" in the name order of English, assuming that the given name precedes the surname. It also cites these names as per primary literature consulted.)*

Kenzo Tange, one of the most significant architects of the twentieth century, and his disciple, Arata Isozaki, another most prominent architect from Japan, both came to fame through their involvement in the remarkable *Metabolism* movement in architecture but followed extremely diverse trajectories afterwards. This chapter case studies projects designed by both Tange and Isozaki and attempts to find out how their designs, particularly from the decade of 1960s', incorporated characteristics of the artificially intelligent architecture. Emphasis have been placed on their cybernetic designs and, consequently, the information and communications handling within it. Furthermore, the Japan World Exposition Osaka 1970 and, particularly, its Festival Plaza have been case studied as their collaborative project in order to trace their ideologies regarding artificially intelligent architecture.

### Kenzo Tange: communications as the cement of society

The headquarters building of the *World Health Organisation* (WHO) Geneva and *Massachusetts Institute of Technology (MIT) Boston Harbor* projects were proposed by Tange in 1959 but, unfortunately, were not executed. The ideas developed in these projects were carried over to another of his project *A Plan for Tokyo* (1960–61). Tange argued that a person exercises his control at two discrete levels of individuality and collectivism. In individuality, he attempts to practice his freedom and spontaneity through different expressions conforming but not limited to the houses, gardens, streets and plazas he lives in. On the level of collectivism, he and many others like him are controlled strictly by technology, thus determining and forming the systems of his era. In other words, Tange stresses, these short- and long-term cycles contradict each other, and this contradiction is

DOI: 10.4324/9781003401858-3

increasing at a very rapid pace that he attempts to control as an architect. "The important task facing us is that of creating an organic link between these two extremes and, by doing so, to create a new spatial order in our cities" he said, and in order to achieve this spatiality, he designed and presented the spatial structures of the Kurashiki Town Hall, WHO, MIT and A Plan for Tokyo projects to provide a sense of individualistic freedom within a more systematic, technologically controlled environments.[1]

A sense of individualistic freedom enclosed and invisibly incorporated within a more systematic technologically controlled structure was achieved by the technique of visually communicating spaces that Tange called as *core spaces* – virtually in the process of information and communication discourse.[2] Facing both Lake Geneva and the Alps, his proposal for WHO headquarters presented two office blocks leaning towards each other, presenting recessed terrace structures and finally culminating as one mass at the apex. In between these two leaning office blocks, there was a tentlike, infinite, open-sided space that acted like an arena. This proposal was also an initial step by Tange towards the development of a relationship between an office cell and a huge public hall. Similarly, as was the case with the proposal of the WHO headquarters, he and his team proposed MIT Boston Harbor project – a residential unit – while he was teaching there in the winter of 1959, and its spatial structure presented the same recessed terraces. Under Tange's guidance, the team comprised of George Pillorge, Edward Haladay, Ted Niedermann and Gustave Solomons at the MIT. This proposal presented the building and road as one single entity, and in theory, these recessed terrace structures or leaning residential units were not conceived as a definitive, self-contained design but can be easily extended anytime when needed. This project eliminated the differences between residential, work, recreational and commercial functions by placing private living and community facilities in a naturally organised context. Furthermore, this whole structure was also conceived to be situated on a man-made island.

Tange developed a proposal titled *A Plan for Tokyo* in 1960–61 in collaboration with Sadao Watanabe, Koji Kamiya, Moriaki Kurokawa, Heiki Koh and Arata Isozaki. Isozaki was in charge of this project under Tange's leadership and used the joint core system that aimed at expanding architecture to an urban scale and reconsidered building types through the incorporation of urban factors into the architectural planning. Isozaki also utilised the same structural and urban design elements for his series of projects called *City in the Air*.[3] In this plan, Kenzo Tange Team proposed that a growing city, like Tokyo, is in fact like an organism that cannot be explained through any fixed planning concept in the sense of a master plan and suggested gradual reconstruction of the existing city and its expansion into the Tokyo Bay for a population of more than 10 million. For the reconstruction, among other points, the team adopted a top-down approach that proposed a new urban order of an open system – linear development instead of the existing radial centripetal system – and the spontaneous mobility of contemporary society that ultimately resulted in the organic unity of the city structure, transportation system and urban architecture. The Tange Team suggested the following basic aims for the redevelopment of Tokyo in their proposal:

1  A remarkable shift from a radial centripetal to linear development urban planning.
2  Unifying the city structure, transportation system and urban architecture into an organic entity.
3  Formulating an urban spatial order reflecting the open organisation and spontaneous mobility of the contemporary society.[4]

Regarding preference of the linear instead of radial centripetal urban development, Tange argued that linear development is a significant representative of the biological principles. He said that evolution and growth patterns indicate that radial forms unfold themselves during the evolutionary processes into linear formations as have been the case with the amoeba and asteroid patterns. But vertebrates possess linear bone structures emitting parallel radiations. While exemplifying this evolutionary process of radial to linear transformation through spine and arteries, he said that the hatching of an egg is a representative of a gradual approach towards a linear development. Situating the urban planning principles of a city on this linear biological developmental pattern, he argued:

> [i]f the various functions of a great city were distributed along a line, communication linking them could be carried out in a minimum of time by movement along that line. Nothing could be simpler or quicker. The entire movement of a city of 10,000,000 would be sustained by this communication[5] (Figure 3.1).

In order to justify the unity of city structure, transportation system and urban architecture, Tange said that in the early twentieth century, the architectural pioneers devised pilotis as a means of liberating the ground from all the life for movement of the automobiles and transferring the men and their work to the first floors. Thus, pilotis area was meant to serve two purposes: first, to act as a link between the ground and the first floor and second, to privatise the first floor, thus restricting the vehicular automobiles to the ground. But in the A Plan for Tokyo 1960, he said, his team unified these two discrete concepts by merging the vehicular automobiles and people of the city together. The solution they sought was to replace the columns with the core of the buildings, thus eliminating the columns as a whole and re-defining the area thus reclaimed as *columnless pilotis under the buildings*. This area on the ground was merged with the transportation system of the vicinities. At nodes where multiple modes of transportation systems overlapped, multi-level parking spaces were proposed. People were supposed to enter these multi-level parking spaces in their cars, getting to the vertical cores and rising up using the elevators situated within these cores of the buildings. The result was an intermeshed system presenting an amalgamation of the unit urban area and highway system,

*Figure 3.1* According to Tange, when the functions of a city with 10 million people are
distributed along a line, the communication linking them can be carried-out in a
minimum of time. The linear pattern development or open organisation in *A Plan
for Tokyo* (1960–61) results in a central civic communications axis (diagonal) or
the vertebrate's linear bone structure emitting parallel radiations.

*Source*: Akio Kawasumi, *A Plan for Tokyo, 1960: Toward a Structural Reorganization*, 1970, photograph. Copyright © Akio Kawasumi. All rights reserved. Used with permission.

Tange said, thus allowing the "spatial order as well as a speed hierarchy linking,
first, streets, interchanges, parking space, and buildings and, second, high speed,
low speed, human speed, and immobility. Urban space would be restored to life."[6]

Within this linear, organically unified and open urban spatial order, particular
emphasis was on the processing of information in this metropolis (Figure 3.2).
Tange suggested that it is people who carry this information from one place to

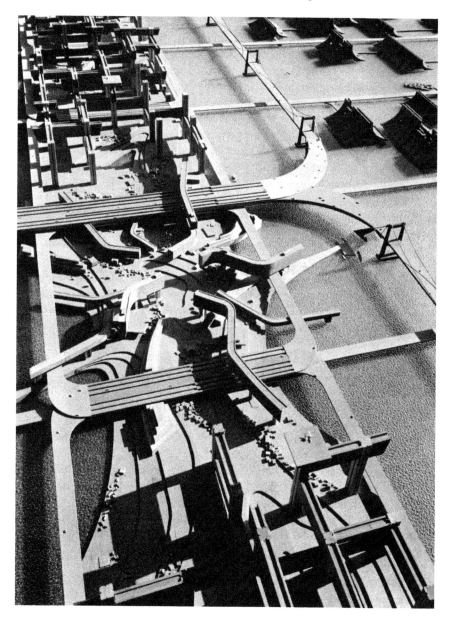

*Figure 3.2* A perspective of the central civic communications axis from *A Plan for Tokyo* (1960–61) showing the communal axis and the community facilities (left) and the residential area (right).

*Source*: Akio Kawasumi, *A Plan for Tokyo, 1960: Toward a Structural Reorganization*, 1970, photograph. Copyright © Akio Kawasumi. All rights reserved. Used with permission.

another – a process he classified as *communication*. This communication can exist between a man and man, man and function and/or function and function. These different varieties of communication were proposed by Tange in 1960, but these are being put to use these days under different names. For example, communication between man and man can be through a video call via a mobile phone. Communication between man and function can be a communication between a man and his laptop, commonly referred to as communication via graphical interface. An example of communication between a function and a function can be the internet of things, where two different functions communicate with each other with the help of artificial intelligence and other established and emerging technologies. This interaction through different mediums results in a communication taking place through different mediums, such as the railways, motor vehicles, mails, telephone, radio, television, portable and video telephones, etc., and these indirect interactions then produce a greater demand for direct communication.

Tange stressed that when men carry messages from one person to another, they are in fact formulating linkages that in turn result in an urban organisation.[7] He defines this *urban organisation* as a great city in which invisible linkages of information and communication system continuously transform it into an open entity that is a representative of culture and society of the twentieth century. It is a reversal of the fixed, immovable enterprises and closed cities of the Middle Ages. This organisation comprises of a mobile population resulting in the formation and dissolution of conferences at several levels and fields. It is this organisation that necessitates a man to create wisdom, produce values and stay connected with the world. If a man is associated with this organisation, he is not alone but in a wider network performing significant tasks while simultaneously being identified as a constituent of the whole. It is for these reasons that people gather in cities to formulate linkages by utilising this organisation.[8] The words *conference* and *organisation* have been used by Tange as of interchanging meanings as he said that as individuals have a lesser authority of decision-making in this age of organisation, groups meeting as in the conferences thus take decisions on our behalf. This can said to be another incidence of a direct communication between men.[9]

Furthermore, he proposed that this contemporary communication has released the city from the bonds of a closed organisation and is rapidly changing the societal structure of the city itself. The role of the metropolis of Tokyo with 10 million people is then to act as a *brain centre* that performs countless invisible tasks for promoting the economic development and cultural activities of Japan. "Above all, communication is of the essence, for all the various functions are interrelated – politics with finance, finance with technology, technology with culture, culture with journalism, journalism with politics and government," Tange said. While elevating Tokyo as the generator of values, ideas and maintaining liaison with the rest of the world, he said that it is an open organisation, where functions communicate with each other, resulting in a cumulative function. "What gives this organization its organic life," he said, "is the flowing movement of the 10,000,000 people who are engaged in the communication of functions."[10]

In a research article, *Tokaido-Megalopolis: The Japanese Archipelago in the Future*, Tange refers to rapid and ever-increasing development of modern communication methods as the Second Industrial Revolution made possible by information processing. He refers to tremendous development – in both theory and practice – of information, technology and communication systems including computers as the second great advancement of the contemporary society, first being the advancement in energy that resulted in tremendous production techniques. Mankind receives infinite mass of information every day through the mass media, such as publishing, radio, television, telephone, telegraph, teletype, etc. Humans are being stifled by the overload of this information. It is only with the help of electronic computers and man-made brains that humans are being able to cope with this information bombardment. Tange further argued in this regard that "our electronic computers and man-made brains absorb millions of bits of information, remember them, arrange them, compile them, sift them, and otherwise dispose of them in such a way as to help us to make decisions and take actions."[11]

This information revolution has completely changed and modified "the relationship between man and man, between man and material object, and between man and nature itself," he said.[12] Again by referring to nature as inspiration, Tange emphasises that information revolution has enabled man to extend the functions of his nervous system to the whole society. This extended nervous system then results in the metabolic functions that are resultant of the First Industrial Revolution. The metabolic functions then lead to the control functions that are a product of the Second Industrial Revolution. Thus, metabolic functions, while being highly active, have given way to energetic communication that was representative of the ancient society based on fixed classes or ranks. A progress in this energetic communication then produced a more advanced, complete and intricate system of control functions that are transforming the society as a whole into an organised organic system. These control functions then result in the informational coupling or communication. With these control mechanisms, Tange negated the perception that a small group of elitist members of the society controlling it with their influence but an ever-growing and expanding brain power comprising of dynamic informational coupling that particularly advances the civilisation, cultural creation, freedom and constant choice of the Japanese and the world as a whole. A city of the twentieth century is thus conceived as a physicalisation of this dynamic organisation. "I think the city must be endowed with freedom, with diversity, with mix, with mobility, and with unlimited choice," Tange added.[13]

"Norbert Wiener, the creator of cybernetics, has described communications as the 'cement of society,'" Tange quoted and argued that it is an informational coupling that links the cells of an animal together and involves a nervous system that controls actions by sending and receiving information that can said to be the mutual exchange or feedback of information [emphasis in original]. This phenomenon can be witnessed in the process of a human speech. This sending and receiving of information resulting in communication is not a new concept at all, but humans have been performing it since unknown times, but the point that is of significance here is the fact that these processes are now being mechanised or in other words, being simulated on rather advanced levels. "[S]ome of the most important techniques for transmitting, exchanging, and storing and treating information have taken place in the twentieth century," he said by further adding that "[w]e are, in effect, undergoing a great revolution in the science and technology of communication, and as a result, the whole organization of contemporary society is being transformed." By exemplifying the evolution of plants into animals and animals into men, he said that our society is evolving into an advanced state – a higher organic composition by further adding the following:

> We have begun to create a new nervous system in society using the advanced communications technology that will enable the social brain to function more effectively. . . . In large contemporary urban complexes, communications networks twist and interwine [sic] into a complex which must be something like the nervous system of the brain. Large metropolitan areas or megalopolises in our day are becoming the brains for the body of modern society. Whirling around in these brains are the people, and the information. The citizens are like electrons flowing in an electronic "brain"[14] [emphasis in original].

In 1963, Hideo Yoshida (1903–63) – a Japanese advertising firm Dentsu's fourth president – commissioned Tange to design the headquarters for his advertising firm. Starting from the design of the headquarters building and expanding to the whole district, Tange proposed a regeneration project for a district of about 300,300 square meters in area and with a working population of about 100,000 situated in Tokyo between the Ginza and the port called as the *Tsukiji Project in Tokyo* (1963). This project can said to be an extension of A Plan for Tokyo (1960–61), as many of the ideas that were initially developed in A Plan for Tokyo (1960–61) have been carried over and extended in the Tsukiji Project. The Tsukiji Project also consisted of an open system – a linear development comprising of a central civic axis that acted like a spinal cord that emitted many arteries – resulting in the spontaneous mobility of the district at different levels. Tange applied the same line of thought in this project that a straight central civic communications axis makes the processing of information within the city rapid, smooth and well-balanced. He made an analogy between this central civic communications axis and that of a factory's conveyor system in order to explain the rapid processing of information. The manufacturing system of the factories is going through a major transformation in which centralised machinery is being broken down into its constituents as the functions are being divided and nothing called *all-purpose* is being left. However, the work these smaller constituents are carrying out is being unified with a linear movement of a conveyor system. Adapting this approach of demassification to the cities, he said that "[i]f the various functions of a great city were distributed along a line, communication linking them could be carried out in a minimum of time by movement along that line. Nothing could be simpler or quicker."[15]

The organic unity among the city structure, transportation system and urban architecture was also intelligently achieved in this regeneration project but rather on a reduced scale in comparison with his A Plan for Tokyo (1960–61). Tange incorporated the same bridge-like architecture being serviced by utility shafts in this project. Unfortunately, the Tsukiji project was never realised, reason being that the president of the Dentsu firm – Hideo Yoshida – who commissioned Tange and was passionate supporter of this project, passed away in 1963, and the succeeding president abandoned this project. Furthermore, the headquarters building that was completed in 1967–68 was also greatly altered, and only twelve floors were constructed out of the proposed twenty-one floors. This headquarter building was constructed in isolation and holds no relationship with the Tsukiji Regeneration Project. A proposal for the Dentsu building and a regeneration project for the Tsukiji area in Tokyo were extensions of the Tokyo Plan (1960–61). The Dentsu building can said to be the physicalisation of Tange's theories of information and communications, as in this design, vertical cores were responsible for carrying people, information and energies in vertical directions. These vertical cores acted as benchmarks and could be constructed as per need so that buildings could be suspended between these cores as large-span bridges. In this three-dimensional, latticelike system, the bridge building typologies were researched and designed to be suspended at the height of 120 meters. The structural engineer Yoshikatsu Tsuboi and his associates were responsible for the design of these suspended bridge-like structures at extreme heights, and Tange's team drew up working drawings and budgeting analysis. Although this research and design studies proved this latticelike system to be highly feasible both technically and economically, due to the death of the president of Dentsu organisation, Hideo Yoshida, this project was ultimately not constructed. As a result, this whole study was carried over to the redevelopment plan for the Tsukiji area.[16]

In a research article titled *Function, Structure and Symbol* written by Tange in 1966, he attempts to find the definition of space in the age of information and communications. He states that space is not a static entity, and its definition has changed from time to time. For example, he explains that space has considerably been changed from the period of 1920–60 till the period starting from 1960 onwards. From 1920–60, the relationship between function and space was static, deterministic and decisive. Each function was associated with a specific space, for example, eating at a table, relaxing on a sofa, working on a desk, etc., and this approach further extended to urban design, for example, a recreational space was used for recreation, a street was used for transportation, etc. This approach was essential at the earlier stage of modern architecture. Space was less static, decisive and less compulsory during this span. Thus, the space from this period can said to be *energetic*. But since 1960 onwards, this relationship between function and space has become more pluralistic, elastic, selective and more spontaneous. In other words, since 1960, space has become informational. Based on the classifications proposed by the creator of cybernetics, Norbert Wiener, Tange labels these elastic and selective couplings as informational and static and decisive as energetic ones.

Further, he quotes Wiener regarding the co-existence of informational and energetic schemes that "an organization is not connected so tightly that it is impossible to change one aspect without destroying the specific features of all other aspects, nor so loose that anything can happen without any relation to other things."[17] There are two reasons behind the change in interpretation of space in these two periods, Tange explains. First is the fact that the huge and ever-increasing power of modern society is changing the physical appearance, such as urban design and architecture of the city. Second factor is the rapid development of organisations due to the modern communication system, informational technology and their reflection on the spatial organisation of urban design and architecture of a city.

Tange further elaborates his hypothesis of the information and communications theory by expanding it to the architecture and city. He believed that in a modern civilised society, space acts as a communication field that is gradually transforming itself into a more organic entity with the rapid development of information and communication systems. "Tactual, auditory, and visual communication, communication by walking and transportation, and informational communication – these means of communication are expanding the communication field into cosmic space," he said. Thus, physicalisation of an architecture and a city is, in other words, "a process of making the communication network visible in a space." So architecture and city of this age must be conceived as of physicalising a communication network that is ever-growing and changing as a living body in space. As an addition to the *functioning* of spaces, care must also be given to their *structuring*. And it is this system of structuring that Tange said to be the basic theme of urban design in the age of information and communications.[18]

Tange defined communication as a thing that gives structure to space through continuous mobility, flow of people and things and visual display, and he rejected the abstract definition of space that considers it as a place to live or a place to work only. Furthermore, he also presented notion of a space as a communicational field when it is considered in a purely symbolic sense. There are different invisible channels of communication that act as a foundation based on which the functional units of cities or vast, complex buildings are structured, he said. He further continued in the same line of thought by stating that communication gives structure to a space. Normally, communication is only associated with the flow of people or things, but in case nothing really moves, we can have the notion of a visual communication. "The process of formalizing the communicational activities and flows within spaces is what we mean by giving structure to architectural or urban spaces."[19]

*The Yamanashi Communications Center* (1964–67) situated on a site measuring about 4,000 square meters in Kofu is a project that acts both as an urban and architectural design at the same time and thus incorporates the ideas presented in A Plan for Tokyo (1960–61) and information and communications theories put forth by Tange. The centre incorporates three different divisions related to the communications field – a newspaper printing plant, a radio station and a television studio – and comprises two substructural and eight superstructural floors. By combining similar functions, such as office space, production area and studio space, Tange presented a kind of a complex, an open spatial structure that can be extended as needed. Printing plant with all of its installations was placed on the first floor, the studios in windowless blocks were placed on the upper floors and the offices of all of the three divisions were combined and enclosed with glass walls. The building is supported on sixteen vertical shafts, each having a diameter of about five meters. These shafts incorporate service rooms, stairwells, lifts, air-conditioning plant, freight lifts and sanitary facilities. These vertical shafts incorporate all the facilities while clearing the floors to be used for multi-purposes. All the internal functions, such as offices, studios and production rooms, are clearly legible in the external design, like a city where different functions are clearly visible. The flexibility provided by the floors that can be extended as and when needed makes this Communications Center an organic structure resembling a city. Tange introduced a number of vertical shafts in this project that served as *communication shafts*. With each of these shafts serving a number of functions placed within them, the result was a luxurious free space around these vertical roads that could be utilised for a number of purposes. These unoccupied voids were also able to offer extra space for expansion. "In this sense," he said, "the building is at once a single spatial type capable of change and growth and a space established within a three-dimensional communications grid. This is a proposal for both a single building and for urban design."[20]

Tange's *Plan for Skopje* (1965) can said to be an application of the ideas he developed in his A Plan for Tokyo (1960–61) and Yamanashi Communications Center (1964–67). The multi-level traffic unit's systems from the Tokyo Plan and vertical communication shafts from the Communications Center were the carried overs from his previous design studies for the reorganisation and reconstruction of the city of Skopje. Skopje is the capital of the Republic of North Macedonia that was part of Yugoslavia in 1965. This city was almost 65% destroyed by an earthquake in 1963. In 1965, the United Nations organised a restricted urban design and architectural competition and invited four Yugoslav and four foreign urban planning and architectural firms for participation. The participants from Yugoslav included Slavko Brezorski, Aleksandar Dordevic, Radovan Mishevic, Fedor Wenzler and Eduard Ravnicar. Foreign firms included Van den Broek and Bakema from Holland, Luigi Piccinato from Italy, Maurice Rotival from USA and Kenzo Tange from Japan. Tange's submission received 60% of the first prize, while the remaining 40% was awarded to the Yugoslav team of Radovan Mishevic and Fedor Wenzler of Zagreb, Croatia. The jury consisted of representatives from the United Nations and included Adolf Ciborowski (representative project manager), Ljube Pota (director of the Town-planning Department of Skopje) and Risto Galic (director of the Institute for Town-planning and Architecture).

Tange's team for the Plan for Skopje (1965) included Arata Isozaki, Sadao Watanabe, Yoshio Taniguchi and earthquake specialists Kiyoshi Muto and Toshihiko Hisada, who worked in collaboration with Yugoslav architects. Isozaki recalls his membership of Tange's team for the Skopje project and said that "[i]n 1965, I spent several months in Yugoslavia, coordinating work on the plan for the reconstruction of Skopje on which I had assisted Kenzo Tange."[21] The Greek firm Doxiadis Associates and a Polish group presented a regional plan for the Skopje district, leaving blank the city centre space of about 2 square kilometers that was further designed by Tange and his team. The designing of the Skopje district progressed in first, second and the final third phase that presented concrete architectural and urbanist proposals covering the entire Skopje district and key architectural complexes. The plans and structures became more simplistic and less complex from the first to the third phase of the project. Among these structural reorganisational elements, the *City Gate* and the *City Wall* were the most important focal points around which all the district has been meaningfully organised. Tange emphasised that it is communication that gives structure to a space, and in the case of the Plan for Skopje (1965), he utilised the technique of *visual communication* between the space and its observer. Elements such as the City Gate and City Wall were used for visual communication. The City Gate term was used in order to continuously remind people of the area of an entrance to the city that not only acted as a visual vocabulary but also as an element of grandeur and significance. It was made sure that the design also followed and incorporated these characteristics; otherwise, people could have rejected this gate's purpose. Similarly, the City Wall immediately gained fame among the people of the area, and when concerns emerged of not implementing it as it was considered to be obstacle, people of the area opposed this argument and said that "[t]he City Wall is familiar to us and in our imagination it has already become the symbol of the city centre. We can no longer give it up." Tange emphasises that through these experiences, he and his team learned the significance of symbolic processes that emerged during the operation of structuring.[22]

The City Gate not only acted as a source of visual communication for the citizens but was also proposed as a communications and business operations hub by Tange and his team. All the major transportation systems, such as rail, motor, bus and pedestrians, converged at this point, thus making communication a key element of this convergence. The buildings adjoining the City Gate centre were composed of office high-rises, a library, banks, exhibition halls, three cinemas, a hotel, shops and restaurants all connected with transportation and pedestrian systems. As have been the case with the Tokyo Plan (1960–61) and the Tsukiji Project in Tokyo (1963), Tange and his team also proposed an open system – a linear development consisting of a central civic communication axis that was in fact a spinal cord of the plan that further emitted several arteries. Starting from the City Gate and running towards the West in parallel to the Vardar River, the central civic axis of the Skopje Plan comprised of the republic square with two museums, the house of the Communist Party, court, tourist district, city square with the city hall, municipal library, cinemas, municipal university, assembly hall and the people's university. Furthermore, in addition to this central civic axis, other facilities proposed on the opposite bank of the Vardar River included the liberty square with two museums, opera, ballet theater and a ballet school, church, hotel and a school. On the north, Charchia district was proposed with museums, folklore centres, shops, restaurants and departmental stores. This area also incorporated those parts of the city that survived the earthquake and furthermore featured the national university. The City Wall comprised of high-rise residential blocks reminding of the Yamanashi Communications Center (1964–67) featuring the vertical communication shafts. These residential blocks were located in slanting angles both on the north and south of the central civic communication axis acting as the City Wall. The Skopje (1965) project exhibits Tange's enthusiasm for implementing the information and communications discourse not only in theory but also practically on an urban as well as architectural grounds. This plan explores the importance of communications not only on a symbolic but also on programmatic levels.

Almost two decades later in 1987 at the Pritzker Architecture Prize's acceptance speech, Tange continued in the same line of thought and expressed that a shift in Japan from materialistic industrial to the non-physical information and communications society has majorly been due to the energy crisis of the 1970s'. He emphasised that the need for intelligent buildings is natural, and this phenomenon is going to expand itself to the whole districts and cities, consequently resulting in intelligent or smart districts and cities. Advanced technological equipment that finds its applications in the exterior of buildings today will be incorporating itself into the concealed interior of these structures. This approach further points our attention towards the relationship between architectures, in other words, inter-architectural relations. These inter-architectural relations are going to be a significant aspect of architecture and a city in informational or communication society. While an industrial society placed strong emphasis on budget and functionality of individual buildings, a society having great stress on communications demands inter-architectural relationships as well as the functional sufficiency of the structures. He had a firm belief that these conditions are going to yield a new style of architecture that was in its infancy at that time and needed further in-depth research and study, as he said that "further consideration of those views will help us find a way out of the current impasse, and reveal to us the kinds of buildings and cities required by the informational society." Further stressing the importance and need of intelligent buildings, he expressed that the following three prominent elements will decide what kind of buildings and cities we are going to have in an information and communications society:

1 Human, emotional, and sensual elements.
2 Technologically intelligent elements.
3 Social-communicational structure of the space.[23]

Tange stressed the re-evaluation and improvement of urban design and architecture from industrial to information and communications society at many accounts. The inter-architectural relations that he stressed are being served by the interconnecting technologies of artificial intelligence, big data and internet of things. In due course, back in the 1960s', he said:

> a completely new way of structuring or system of urban relationship [is needed]: a relationship between a region and another region, between a city and another city, a relationship between highways, streets, parking areas,

plazas, buildings; between traffic systems and buildings; between stations and buildings; between one building and another building; and between each building and its component parts.[24]

Similarly, on another account, he stressed:

> a necessary condition to the maintenance of organic life is the establishment of a rapid, smooth, and well-balanced system of links among and between areas of various sizes – the city block, the urban district, the geographical region – and by area, I mean not only the physical area, but the organizations that exist within it and the functions these organizations perform.[25]

### Arata Isozaki: cybernetic environments where functions lose their meaning and are covered by an information membrane

Isozaki explains that constant movement due to the rejection of fixed images, diffusion, infinite advertising and noise are hallmarks of daily life in Tokyo existing in complicated, diverse and confused forms as well as the same goes with the modern cities of the United States but on a far lesser severity. By pointing towards the unique and completely contradicting concepts that exist regarding the definition of an urban space in Japan and in the Western world, he argues that searching this urban concept particularly from the reference of Japanese cities has always been intriguing for him. Regarding the precedents of this unique urban design of Japanese cities, his ideals were totally erased and burned to ashes by the B-29 incendiary bombs of World War II. But it is a fact that Japanese cities that were once completely erased rapidly managed themselves to be rebuilt in a post-war period even on a far larger scale than ever before.

As Isozaki was a team member for A Plan for Tokyo (1960–61) under the leadership of Tange, he explains that the rapid population explosion after the war, particularly of Tokyo, not only posed severe problems but also astonished Japanese, as no one ever wondered that this could also happen. He states in this regard:

> immediately after the war, estimates offered little reason to hope that the plan of restoring Tokyo to a population of three million could be realized. But, before anyone knew what had happened, there were ten million people living there. It is said that in the past five years, more money has been spent in Tokyo on construction than in the whole preceding century. Just after the war, no one would have believed this could happen.[26]

By walking in the footsteps of Tange, Isozaki also explains a city with reference to cybernetics creator Norbert Wiener as an informational and communications system, an organic entity that is in a constant state of reproduction, division and feedback in which only the process – that he calls as a *software* – holds importance instead of the physical appearances that are referred to as *hardware*. This continuous motion of a cybernetic system then influences the architecture of a city, as Isozaki said that "[e]ven something fixed, like a work of architecture, when set down in the constantly metamorphosing city, is part of growth, change, and metabolism."[27] Although both Tange and Isozaki presented the concepts for *architecture of growth* but in their own different ways. Tange defines the architecture of growth by linking it with metabolism, while on the other hand, Isozaki defines it by associating it with the cybernetic environments. Characteristics of a cybernetic environment that Isozaki outlines in his article *Invisible City* (1966) can well be traced back to his previous article titled the *Theory of Process Planning* (1963).

Isozaki presented his *Theory of Process Planning* in 1963. His design for Library at Oita, Kyushu, presents implementation of this theory. In this library, he deliberately avoids the completeness in architecture and lets it remain incomplete, empty or in other words, evolving, so that it may remain in the continuous process of growth. Provision has been given for future extension. This kind of architecture can only be observed at a particular point in time. There is no complete or finished stage of this architecture, as it presents itself as a part of a process. This ever-evolving growth with incompleteness as its inherent quality presents a system of architecture, a theory that Isozaki calls as the theory of process planning. He states regarding this theory that "[a]s we are never able to foresee the ultimate totality of the building, the section under construction at Oita implies, in its detail syntax, the appearance of something which is 'under way', of the unfinished"[28] [emphasis in original]. This theory of process planning can be understood with his planning process for Library at Oita, Kyushu. Let us consider three components of a control desk, reading table and book stack. These three components have been called as elements by Isozaki, and these elements, while acting on their own and maintaining their individuality, also belong to a system as a whole. These elements are kept free of any constraints; thus, they are permitted to be in ever-evolving growth. There are some principles that these elements within a spatial system yield:

1  Function: is defined with reference to its content. In case of Library at Oita, Kyushu, a control desk, reading table and book stack – elements – are functions within a library.
2  Self-identity: of elements and their own inherent laws must be appreciated.
3  Interchangeability: of elements must be achieved, thus resulting in greater flexibility of elements and their functions.
4  Growth: of functions, elements and of their self-identities, interchangeable characteristics and flexibility is inevitable once the points 1, 2 and 3 have been achieved.
5  Skeleton: comprises of relationships that are developed among different elements in a given setting. In case of a library, different functions and purposes resulting in relationships between a control desk, reading tables and book stacks are called as skeletons.
6  Open-character: must be allowed for each skeleton as it facilitates the growth-process and flexibility of the elements and system as a whole.
7  Medium: such as a mechanical or structural must be selected in order to enclose a spatial system.

8  Dual-character: as inherent in this architecture must be appreciated.
9  Limitless Development: of this architectural system is unavoidable.[29,30]

Isozaki argues that the fluidity of the urban environment is on increase. While viewing the city through the lenses of *time axis of transformation*, it is in a constant organic reproduction and division. Quoting Norbert Wiener – the pioneer of cybernetics – and restating Tange, he explains that a city is neither too tightly bound nor too loosely knighted together that any sort of disruption may not be influencing the other stakeholders. Witnessing the fragmentation of cities in the process of flux, where fragments keep on constantly shifting into the succeeding phases, he quotes that "Wiener is describing the world of process, the world that lacks both the rigidity of quantum-physics images and the ultimate entropy or extinction of heat in a state of undulation in which no truly new things can be born." Furthermore, he adds that "[i]n a city of this kind, where exterior appearances move and change without cease, process alone is trustworthy."[31]

Isozaki refers to the city of today as a virtual image, a space of imagination just as a human brain acts as an organic entity or the modern urban structure accommodates communications networks. In this imaginary city, "[t]hough distance is lost, though material objects have lost their meaning, we must nonetheless search for a new surveying method to come to grips with the invisible objects confronting us," Isozaki suggests.[32] Space becomes a code-sprinkled schema, and thus, a city is reorganised as a system model having cybernetics as the basis of this reorganisation. Tange argued that the definition of space has considerably changed from 1920–60. In this period, space was static, deterministic and decisive. And further from 1960 onwards, space has become more pluralistic, elastic, selective and spontaneous. Similarly, Isozaki also defines 1920s' as the honeymoon period of modern urban planning, and in the successive fifty years, rapid technological developments have fundamentally changed the urban situation. He idealises the 1920s' as being inspired by the mechanical technologies and states some of the most important visionary plans from that period as Antonia Sant'Elia's Città Nuova, Bruno Taut's Alpine Architecture that gleamed like a crystal on the top of the Alps, Frederick Kiesler's Space City possessing infinite development possibilities, Iakov Chernikhov's Constructivist City spanning immense horizontal and vertical structures and Theo van Doesburg's Transportation City designed on multi-levels.[33] By referring to machine and its component parts, he suggests that urban planning of the 1920s' was focused on functions of daily life, work, relaxation and circulation and the reassembling of these functions into a whole. Ford Motor's assembly line and Taylor system were completely introduced into architecture, reason being the industrialisation fueling mass production. Consequently, Isozaki classifies urban design into the following four stages:

1  Substantial: in which direct connections were made between architectural and urban forms.
2  Functional: based on abstract principles developed by Congrès internationaux d'architecture moderne (CIAM), or International Congresses of Modern Architecture, that was formed in 1928.

3 Structural: that was first noticed in the 1950s'.
4 Semiotic or Symbolic: which we are only beginning to develop now.[34]

Isozaki suggests that as the functionalist and structuralist stages were linked with mechanical production theories, so the semiotic stage that we are just beginning to develop has evolved from the electronics' theories. Computers are making the feedback process possible, thus replacing the disorganised, fragmentary products of the assembly line by simulation. He defines simulation as a city model based on infinite abstract systems that are then compared with reality, thus generating hypothetical conditions.[35] This simulation is ultimately going to change urban design by enhancing senses of the humans, thus making the development of a *City on the Sea, in the Air, Labyrinth City or a City for the Dead*, etc. possible. He then presents a comparison of electronic music with the traditional one by Marshall McLuhan. McLuhan said that electronic music has made it possible to listen to any tone, with any intensity and for any duration of time. While on the other hand, traditional symphony orchestra was an organic unification of multiple individualistic components working hard to achieve synchronisation. Electronic music has eliminated this need of hard-achieved synchronisation on behalf of individual participants and directly achieves this height of perfection as soon as a listener starts playing it on his electronic device. Consequently, as traditional music's goal was to achieve this organic unity, electronic music already finds itself at this achievement and must find some other goals to achieve. Isozaki says that as this electrification of music has transformed its goals completely; thus, the achievables of art have also been altered. To this state of rupture between traditional and electronic music, he argues, very similar is preceding for the semiotic or symbolic stage of thought on urban design.[36]

Edward Twitchell Hall – American anthropologist – suggests environment as a space for the transmission of different forms of communication and information processes that support modern culture, quotes Isozaki. McLuhan perceives environment as a phenomenon that at once involves human beings from different perspectives, such as systems engineering to events embodying transforming systems. Allan Kaprow – American painter, assemblagist and pioneer of concepts regarding performance art – defines an environment as a system that must incorporate all people without any preconceived notions. These definitions conclude an environment to be a "place of active relations arising among human beings and their surroundings." These kinds of experiments have shed light on the work being done in order to explore the invisible segments of the city. Cybernetics can said to be as the foundation of these environments, and the space it yields can be called as a cybernetic environment, Isozaki concludes.[37] On the basis of these arguments, Isozaki concludes the characteristics of a cybernetic environment:

1 The environment will be enveloped in a protective membrane for the sake of preserving definite, balanced conditions.
2 Spaces will be extensively interchangeable.
3 The environment will include a wide variety of movable equipment.

4  A man-machine system will be developed.
5  This system will possess a self-instructing feedback channel.[38]

Isozaki participated for the first time in his professional career in an overseas exhibition, *Electric Labyrinth: 14th Triennale Di Milano* in Milan, Italy (1968), and states that this project not only summarised his studies of the past fifteen years but also made way and acted as an inspiration for the Japan World Exposition Osaka 1970s' Festival Plaza's cybernetic environment.[39] According to Isozaki, the basic theme of his proposal for this exhibition was the inherent contradiction in the idealistic or logical planning concepts and the irrational impulses of men. He is of the view that only when a man realises that the opposites of construction and destruction, planning and extinction are synonymous, then the meaningful spaces come into being.[40] The exhibit consisted of two portions. First portion consisted of a group of sixteen curved, revolving panels. The second portion consisted of a large panel that displayed the ruined structures of a future city montaged on the scorched earth of Hiroshima (Figure 3.3). By making this as a background, countless images of the radiant and optimistic future cities proposed by Japanese architects in the early 1960s' were displayed. Isozaki explains the composition of the mini-cybernetic environment that he created through a group of sixteen curved, revolving and signal-sensing panels as an Electric Labyrinth. He attempted to make this exhibit a cybernetic environment through the central four panels that were able to turn automatically by sensing sounds electrically through the infra-red beams. The rest of the twelve panels were to be turned freely by using hands. His intentions were to display to the world the thoughts and images that the humans of highly densified urban areas of Japan possessed within themselves. These senses, experiences, emotions and memories were not necessarily to be positive but represented ill will of Japanese people, such as images portraying the "depictions of hell, *ukiyoe* from the end of the shogunate, corpses from the atomic bombing, famished demons (*gaki*), and ghosts, etc."[41] [emphasis in original].

Exploring the cybernetic environments and figuring-out their characteristics on both macro and micro scales, *Arai House* (1968–69) presents his experimentations, although on a much smaller scale and with simple mechanisms. In this responsive house, Isozaki aimed at presenting a model of a technologically advanced residential module that was maximally responsive in a way that allowed its occupants to change internal layouts as and when needed with the utilisation of simple domestic devices, such as Japanese *shoji* screens. Furthermore, these technological advancements were not achieved with high-profile hardware gadgets but with everyday mechanisms, such as butterfly hinges.[42] The plan of the house fundamentally depends on the behaviour of its occupants. He describes this house as "a simulation model translated into physical form."[43] The structure comprised of a cube and a sphere that was suspended from the cube in order to cancel and absorb the vibrations of the overall structure (Figure 3.4). Three movable partitions were proposed for making changes in the interior spaces as per need. Isozaki called these three movable partitions or walls as three *primitive domestic robots*. First

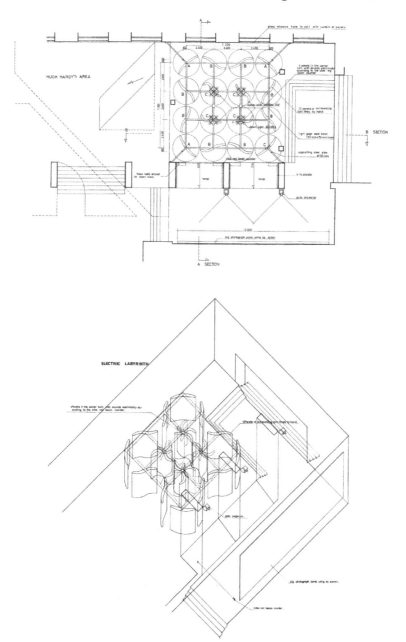

*Figure 3.3* Floor plan and axonometric of the exhibit *Electric Labyrinth* (1968). A micro-cybernetic environment was created by Isozaki by making these panels revolving. The central four panels were made automatically turnable by sensing sounds electri-cally via infra-red beams and the rest of the twelve panels were turnable by hands.

*Source*: Arata Isozaki, *Electric Labyrinth: 14th Triennale Di Milano, Milan, Italy*, 1968, floor plan and axonometric. Copyright © Estate of Arata Isozaki. All rights reserved. Used with permission.

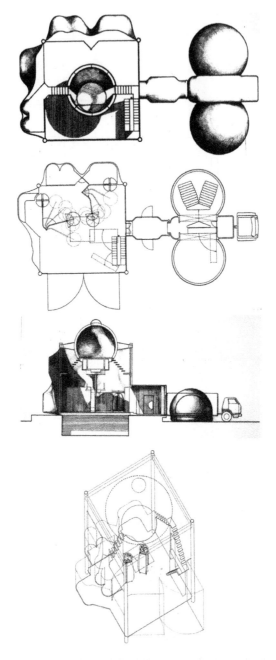

*Figure 3.4* The *Arai or Responsive House* (1968–69) was a cybernetic house that responded
to the behaviour of its occupants. Changes can be made with the help of simple
mechanisms, such as butterfly hinges and casters. It comprised of a static, immobile house (left) and a mobile, detachable camper (right). The hanging sphere
canceled and absorbed the vibrations of the overall structure.

movable partition acted like a stairway, and with rotation, it served as a study corner. Second and third movable partitions are parts of the mechanical system unit
for the built-in wall, such as formation of a dining table, etc., through casters and
two butterfly hinges. The responsive house not only consisted of a fixed structure
but also contained a camping wagon as its component so that its residents were able
to form an instantaneous environment anywhere they wanted to. An elastic heat
insulator with a translucent and weatherproof membrane was used as the bound-
ary of this house. Furthermore, various electrically operated mechanical systems
were also introduced in this house, such as a terminal for a data bank, a television
set, a telephone, video, facsimile and speakers for playing back information, thus
approaching a cybernetic environment. These mechanical systems were suspended
from the ceiling. Isozaki states regarding the information processing in this house
that "[e]veryday one swims in the waves of information received and transmitted.
. . . This is used only for purposes that are meaningless, in other words, for meta-
physical reasons."[44] Isozaki calls the fixed and static portion of this house as *stabile
house* and the movable portion as the *mobile house*. He said that a female-male
relationship exists between these two parts, as they are attached through an airlock
on the wagon.

In 1970–72, just after the Festival Plaza of the Japan World Exposition Osaka
1970, Isozaki presented a proposal called *Computer Aided City* as an extension of
the computer-aided environment of the Festival Plaza and suggested that information processing in a city by a supercomputer can somewhat lead to the idea
of an artificially intelligent architecture on a city-scale (Figure 3.5). This completely computerised city was proposed for the Makuhari area, Chiba, that was
to be reclaimed from the Tokyo Bay. Isozaki presented this information city as a
dystopia, where technology exercised a greater share and control over the human
efforts. He labelled the information-processing supercomputer as the *brain of the
city* and quoted the computer-aided space of the Festival Plaza as its example.
He further added regarding this proposal that "such a concept, when extrapolated
into the future, approaches what might be called 'cable city,' where information
is exchanged by means of a network of coaxial cables" [emphasis in original].
In this cable city, information was to be sent and received in both the incoming
and outgoing formats. This two-way communication was against the television and
radio systems in which communication was only limited to one-way messages. In
order to avoid this system of becoming a mere cable television, he suggested that
if supercomputers are introduced in the process of sending and receiving large
volumes information with the utilisation of the coaxial cables, then this exchange,
processing and storage of information can begin to serve as *the brain* of the city
(Figure 3.6). By classifying the density of information distribution as a measure of
a city, Isozaki said:

> [i]f there is a constant and heavy flow of perceptual information, then it will
> be natural for a machine to take over its processing. If humans dealt with
> only non-routine work involving intellectual judgement, then all the compo-
> nents of the city, including human beings, could be reduced to signs.[45]

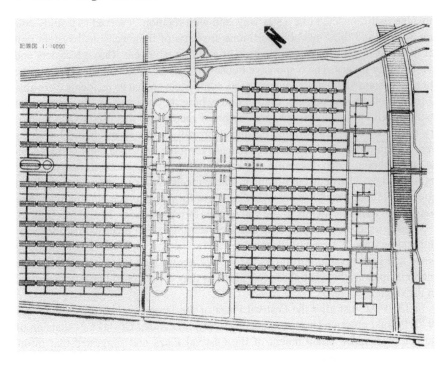

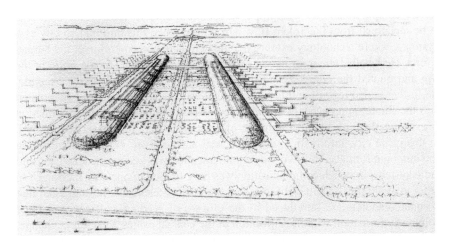

*Figure 3.5* The Computer Aided City deployed supercomputers acting as brain of the city as
they exchanged, processed and stored information (1970–72).

*Source*: Arata Isozaki, *Computer-Aided City: Makuhari, Chiba, Japan*, 1972, site plan and perspective.
Copyright © Estate of Arata Isozaki. All rights reserved. Used with permission.

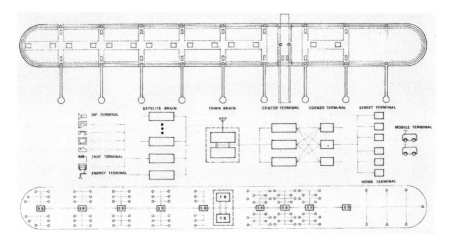

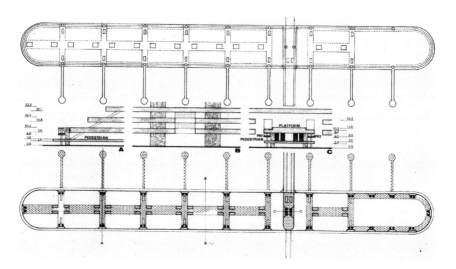

*Figure 3.6* Terminologies such as satellite brain, town brain, centre, corner and street terminals, mobile terminals, home terminals and information, traffic and energy
terminals were used in order to indicate the processing of information and communications within this brain of the city.

*Source*: Arata Isozaki, *Computer-Aided City: Makuhari, Chiba, Japan*, 1972, floor plans. Copyright ©
Estate of Arata Isozaki. All rights reserved. Used with permission.

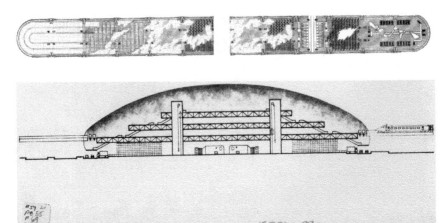

*Figure 3.7* The two rows of buildings in the city centre consisted of layers performing multiple functions, such as a hospital, laboratory, office and shopping complexes,
local community centre, convention hall, etc.

*Source*: Arata Isozaki, *Computer-Aided City: Makuhari, Chiba, Japan*, 1972, floor plan and section.
Copyright © Estate of Arata Isozaki. All rights reserved. Used with permission.

The information network system using light fibers was proposed to be incorporated in the city's infrastructure, and due to the limitations of technology at
that time, it was impossible to implement such a futuristic idea, and thus, this
proposal – Isozaki's Computer Aided City – was discarded. Isozaki recalls and
explains the shortcomings of this project. One of the miscalculations that he
confesses he made was the installation of a supercomputer in the centre of the
city in order to process the flow of all sorts of information. These days, routine
computer systems that are being put to use are of the dispersed and personal
computers, and the notion of centralisation of such systems is not being promoted. Although coaxial cables are able to carry huge volumes of information
and maintain the accuracy of the systems, the network as a whole is not centralised but instead functions as multicentred. This cable network then connects and
unifies multiple different centres together. He argues that he made an effort to
break the centralisation of the buildings in his proposal by designing two rows
of buildings in the city centre, but this multiplication of buildings was to back
up each other (Figure 3.7). This backup system was to be prioritised instead of
viewing this design scheme was a method of breaking away with the centralisation themes. The mere significance of this Computer Aided City rests in a single
factor, Isozaki states, and explains in this regard:

> [i]f this imaginary proposal has any significance, it is in its anticipation of
> the destruction of building types from which cities hitherto have been assem-
> bled, once the information system becomes the infrastructure of the city.

City hall, hospital, school, stadium, art museum, office building, shopping center – all these would then be linked by the information processing system and would lose their individual facades and be enveloped by one membrane. This prediction is gradually coming true, albeit in a guise different from that of the proposal.[46]

In an article titled *From Manner to Rhetoric, and now . . .* written by Isozaki in 1976, he classifies his work into the seven systems of amplification, projection, transferal, response, slicing, chessmen and packaging. The first four items represent the automatic operations that are observable through visual systems, and the last three items represent intervention methods for the previously listed four elements. Here, the intention is to define "an architecture that is akin to an autonomously operating machine," states Isozaki.[47] This operating machine is not based on the structural principles, like a ship or an airplane, but is rather a black-box mechanism. Being transdisciplinary in nature, Isozaki defines this autonomously operating machine as "a weaving together of diverse systems."[48] He defines the characteristics of this autonomously operating architecture:

1   A manner [operating system] generates more than one system in the visible domain.
2   What is intended is an independent style that is nevertheless a projection of the architect's ideas.
3   A manner causes catabolic action, such as visual transformation and annihilation, to take place in ordinary material objects or space.
4   The generation of individual meanings as a result of these catabolic operations is permitted within the domain defined by a system. This shows the distribution of signs within a given place.
5   The imprint of the individual is eliminated as much as possible in the process of architectural design.
6   The reduction of a manner to clear procedural techniques or diagrammatic methods is desirable.
7   Concepts or original images that represent the initial forms of concepts are assimilated by style through the generation of a non-individualised manner.[49]

Similarly, in another article titled *Architecture of Quotation and Metaphor* (1977), Isozaki elaborates a transition from the visible to invisible architecture. He states that architects of the Modern Architecture Movement in the 1920s' used machine as a metaphor. That machine was composed of individualistic, simple compositional elements that were unified into an object in order to perform a specific task. The algebraic function of these individualistic components let to the introduction of a mechanistic philosophy. Since then, this machine has been viewed and exemplified as a visually achieved extension of man's tool, as McLuhan also argues. But with the changing times, this machine has concealed its mechanism away from our eyes, somewhere outside of this visualised world. With the advent of this information and communications age, we are living an invisible environment where machines are performing their operations in a soundless, invisible manner. We can only witness their existence and visual presence through the outside covering of packages, Isozaki states. He said in this regard:

> [t]he machine has become a kind of playmate; sometimes it even performs the role of a clown. It disturbs our established daily life and gives rise to inexhaustible, meaningless activity. By favoring machines it is possible to uncover in their cool, sharp expressions a kind of erotic stimulation.[50]

### The Festival Plaza: the Japan World Exposition Osaka 1970 as experimental grounds for Tange and Isozaki's cybernetic environment theories

In Paris on September 14, 1965, at a meeting of the board of directors of Bureau International des Expositions – an inter-governmental organisation responsible for overseeing and regulating world expos – Japan was selected as a site for the 1970s' world exposition. In order to organise the Japan World Exposition Osaka 1970 (Expo '70) from March 15 till September 13, 1970, almost 330 hectares of Senri Hills in Osaka Prefecture were cleared to make way for the seventy-seven participating countries. In 1965, a Theme Committee was formed under the chairmanship of Seiji Kaya, and in October 1965, *Progress and Harmony for Mankind* was chosen as the theme for the Expo '70. Tange explained the reason behind the selection of this theme that since the modern scientific and technological progress at a very rapid pace, it has become extremely difficult for man to grasp and cope with this transformation in the society. As a result, a lot of problems that this rapid advancement has generated are still unsolved. While optimistically viewing this scenario of the swiftly changing world, Tange said that as a nation, Japan believed that man possesses the wisdom to tackle this tricky situation, and his light of wisdom will illuminate each and every place that he inhabits. He further added:

> [i]f all the various wisdoms of mankind effectively flowed together and mutually stimulated each other, a wisdom on a higher plane would result, and this new wisdom would make possible mutual understanding and tolerance of differing traditions and harmonious growth toward a better way of life.

It was this wisdom from all over the world that Tange and the organisation team of the Expo '70 intended to display exhibiting the achievements of people of different proud nations and thus resulting in the "plaza of human contacts."[51]

Tange being a member of the Theme Committee represented the field of architecture and planning. In October 1966, he and Uzo Nishiyama, who were appointed as the master planners for the Expo '70, presented their final proposal. In January 1967, Tange was appointed by the Expo '70 association for preparing the master plan and the design for the trunk facilities. Tange further invited twelve architects, thus forming a group for the designing of the trunk facilities. This group, while working from February to October 1967, presented a master plan for the Expo '70 and a three-dimensional master design of the trunk facilities. The architects, designers and their responsibilities under the leadership of Tange are presented in Table 3.1.

*Table 3.1* The architects, designers and their responsibilities for Expo '70 under Tange's leadership.

| | |
|---|---|
| Asao Fukuda, Koji Kamiya | Space-frame roof and theme space |
| Atsushi Ueda | Festival Plaza's seating facilities – main viewing stand, elevated viewing stand, VIP seating and café terrace |
| Arata Isozaki | Festival Plaza's mechanical, electric and electronic installations – robot[s], movable seating stand, movable stage and trolley |
| Kiyoshi Kawasaki | Art museum |
| Machio Ibusuki | Expo theater |
| Masato Otaka | Main gate |
| Kiyonori Kikutake | Expo landmark tower |
| Koichiro Nezu | Headquarters building (Nezu joined the group quite later and his design was selected through competition) |
| Koichi Sone | Moving pedestrian ways and sub-plazas |
| Kunio Kato | Sub-gates |
| Kunikazu Hikotani | Guests' reception hall |
| Taro Okamoto | Theme pavilions, including the following: |
| | 1. Celestial theme pavilion by Koji Kamiya. |
| | 2. Subterranean theme pavilion by Koji Kamiya. |
| | 3. Theme towers – Tower of the Sun, Tower of Motherhood and Tower of Youth by Taro Okamoto and Ken Yoshikawa. |

*Source*: Kenzo Tange, "EXPO '70: The EXPO '70 Master Plan and Master Design," in *Kenzo Tange 1946–1969: Architecture and Urban Design*, ed. Udo Kultermann (London: Pall Mall Press, 1970), 282. Yutaka Shikata, ed., "Symbol Zone (master design producer: Kenzo Tange): Space Frame, Festival Plaza, Theme Pavilions, Expo Tower, Expo Museum of Fine Arts, Expo Hall, Main Gate," *The Japan Architect: Reprint Edition Expo '70* 113 (Spring 2019): 22.

The master plan of the Expo '70 was divided into North and South sections because of the presence of a highway that runs through the site. The Northern part was reserved for the pavilions, and the Southern section contains recreation and administrative facilities (Figure 3.8). As have been the case with Tange's previous projects – such as A Plan for Tokyo (1960–61), Tsukiji Project in Tokyo (1963), Yamanashi Communications Center (1964–67) and Plan for Skopje (1965) – he focused on a central civic communications axis for the master planning of the Expo '70 which he called as the *Symbol Zone*. 150 meters wide by a 1000 meters long and spanning from North to South of the site, this Symbol Zone intersects with the highway and forms a Gate for entrance and exit for the Expo '70 venue. It is not surprising to note that the introduction of a Gate for Expo '70 was proposed in 1966, while in 1965, a gateway was also proposed for the Skopje project by Tange. It may be assumed that Tange was heavily inspired by the idea of a Gate in those days that acted as a symbolic as well as organisational element in structuring the civic communications axis of a large-scale planning as have been the case with both of his Osaka Expo '70 (1966–69) and Skopje (1965) projects.

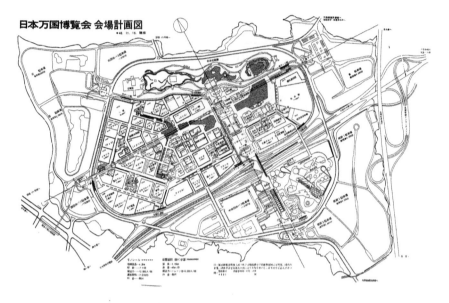

*Figure 3.8* The master plan of the Osaka Expo '70 (1966–69). As have been the case
with Plan for Tokyo (1960–61), Tsukiji Project in Tokyo (1963), Yamanashi
Communications Center (1964–67) and the Plan for Skopje (1965), Tange
focused on a central civic communications axis for the master planning of the
Expo '70 which he called as the Symbol Zone (diagonal). This Symbol Zone in
collaboration with the moving pedestrian walkways then formed the basic trunk
facilities. He also introduced a Gate in this master plan as a visually communicating symbolic device as he did for his Skopje (1965) project.

*Source*: Arata Isozaki, *The Expo '70 Master Plan and Master Design*, 1966, master plan. Copyright ©
Estate of Arata Isozaki. All rights reserved. Used with permission.

Four sub-gates located at North, South, East and West directions were connected with the Symbol Zone through moving pedestrian ways that also helped in
controlling and regulating the flow of pedestrians throughout the site. These moving pedestrian walkways prevented extreme freedom of movement of pedestrians
by segregating them into smaller groups, thus ultimately avoiding any confusion
that would have risen. These walkways acted as a physical tool for the functional
and visual integration of different pavilions into a unified whole. "Relying on them,
the visitor can move at will among the pavilions and exhibitions and still feel sure
of reaching whatever goal he has set," said Tange.[52] The Symbol Zone and these
moving walkways formed the basic trunk facilities. What did Tange mean by these
*trunk facilities*? Being of communal service for all pavilions, they provided a space
for information. By referencing this exposition as a tree with pavilions as its flowers, he appreciated the individuality and variety of types of this tree and its flowers,
but he also insisted that in order to grant this tree order and harmony, branches and
a trunk are required. So in order to fill this gap, he proposed trunk facilities.

By filling these roles functionally, visually and psychologically the Symbol Zone (the trunk) and the moving pedestrian ways and the sub-plazas (the branches) provide organic order and total harmony. On the basis of this analogy, we call these trunk and branches trunk facilities.[53]

The colour and form of the trunk and associated facilities that were named as trunk facilities were kept neutral. Simple basic forms were preferred for these facilities with their colour being white. The reason behind the selection of white colour for these secondary facilities acting as a linkage between different pavilions was to assign prominence to the individual and impressive colourful pavilions.

The presence of these trunk facilities not only granted order and harmony among all of the activities of the Expo '70 but also conveyed a strong symbolic message regarding spatial harmony and order within diversity. Tange references the Great Exhibition of the Works of Industry of All Nations, also known as the Great Exhibition or the Crystal Palace Exhibition, that was organised in the Hyde Park, London, from May 1 to October 15, 1851. He notes that in this exhibition, the huge glass roof of the Crystal Palace granted a unity and harmony to all of the exhibits underneath by first being a kind of a monument and, secondly, sheltering all under one roof. In expositions afterwards, pavilions expressed themselves in greater form and order, thus liberating themselves from the unified approach and thus becoming prone to the loss of order and harmony. Tange confesses that he did not aim to control the diversity within the exposition grounds that would just be operating against the nature of such endeavors. But he said, "[o]n the contrary [the aim] . . . is to evolve spatial harmony and order within diversity." In order to achieve this spatial harmony within the diversified grounds, he utilised the trunk facilities as for granting unification to the whole. While explaining the significance of these trunk facilities, he classified them as a space for eating, drinking, rest and lavatory facilities, in short, a communal structure. He furthermore said that almost 50 million people were projected to visit this exposition during the span of six months. On weekends, this number was projected to be increased by some 400,000. This site was projected to become a living city with 400,000 daytime population. "The Symbol Zone, with its vast spaceframe covering, the sub-gates, and the elevated moving pedestrian ways will form the trunk facilities and then become both the ordering and harmonizing elements in a city," he said.[54] From the security point of view, a step-shaped headquarters building was designed on the Southern part of the site in proximity to the landmark tower. With a height of 120 meters, this tower acted both as an observation platform from where the whole site was visible and a control tower for site operations. This tower was directly linked to the headquarters building and functioned as a command point for transmitting and receiving antenna signals.

Tange realised his ideals of an information and communications society while acting as a master design producer for the Expo '70. First, he questioned why this mega-event was especially organised in Japan in the decade of 1970s', and second, he attempted to figure out the reason behind this classic representation of an industrial society through technological display in this mega-event, especially when Japan was entering the age of a communications society. He expressed that this second point had a direct influence on both the design of the main theme and the Festival Plaza. In this case, he presented the trunk facilities as a central civic communications axis controlling all of the other branches of the Expo '70, and the Festival Plaza acted as the focal point of these trunk facilities. He argued that these kinds of expositions have had greater significance in the cultural and economic development of nations in the past. These expositions helped in advertising the physical aspects of the industrial society at large whether these were the techno-logical artefacts or results of scientific technologies. But on the other hand, it held much lesser significance for a nation like Japan that was entering the age of infor-mation and communications society at that particular point in time. Tange stressed and continued:

> There is now more meaning in displaying an environment connected with software than in displaying the purely physical hardware of culture, [i]n other words, it is more important for people to get together to exchange non-physical aspects of their culture, wisdom, and traditions; but under these circumstances the exposition becomes more a festival. As a result of this conclusion on our part, the Festival Square became the central feature of the grounds at the earliest planning stage.[55]

Tange designed a vast space-frame roof for covering the theme spaces and the Festival Plaza, thus controlling the harsh climatic conditions for visitors. Artist Taro Okamoto was responsible for designing the theme space. He divided the space into three levels, thus representing three different symbolic representations. The underground level expressed the past, the surface level denoted the present and the elevated space-frame section presented the future. For the designing of the spaces of the future in the space frame, Tange and Okamoto further invited Noboru Kawazoe, Fumihiko Maki, Koji Kamiya and Noriaki Kurokawa for the task. The three towers called as the *Tower of the Sun, Tower of Maternity and Tower of Youth* designed by Okamoto also presented the aforementioned periods of time, and all of these were situated within the space-frame roof of the Festival Plaza. As in the Plan for Skopje (1965) Tange utilised the technique of visual communication between space and its observer, he treated the Tower of the Sun in the similar fashion and said that it acted as "a central communications organ . . . [symbolically represent-ing] to the viewer tales of past, present, and future and [aimed] to preside over the Festival Plaza as a divinity of festivities."[56]

The Festival Plaza acted as an artificially intelligent environment. It was situ-ated north of the theme space and at the back of the Tower of the Sun. It comprised of special guest's seats and fixed stands arranged in the form of a flat area and a stair step peripheral terrace looking down to the flat area. $100 \times 150$ meters in area and with a ceiling height of approximately 30 meters, the Plaza accommodated a different number of seating as per the requirements of 1,500, 5,000 or 10,000, thus consequently leading to a maximum of 30,000 seating capacity. The space was multi-functional, and this functional versatility was supported by an extensive array of mobile equipment. This mobile equipment included movable seats, stages, tower cranes containing stage machinery and robots that were able to re-adjust themselves as the scale, position and direction of the event demanded. Special purpose lights, speaker systems installed in the ceiling and floor systems supported the staging of events by enhancing the musical performances through synchronised sound and illuminations. This equipment including lights and sound were made artificially intelligent, as they were pre-programmed. Scores were fed to the memory storage units of computers beforehand in order to make this system entirely self-operable. Furthermore, the glass-enclosed and floating stages of the theater were unified with the environment of the Plaza through electronic and motion-picture techniques. Kunisuke Ito was the producer in charge for the performing arts department for this exposition. A man-machine symbiosis was successfully incorporated and achieved through the artificially intelligent environment of the Festival Plaza. The performing arts particularly depicted this man-machine symbiosis and led the spectators experience this harmony too. The artificially intelligent music and environmental performances also invited spontaneous participation of the visitors. While classifying these events as *software monuments*, Tange said, "[t]hese unforgettable experiences of the environmental events of Festival Plaza will be the one sort of software monuments which will be compatible to the hardware monuments like Eiffel Tower."[57]

Although the whole concept of the Expo '70 was to be a festival where people can meet, shake hands, accord minds and exchange wisdoms, according to Tange, this festival was intended to be for software rather than being a mere exposition of the hardware as have been the case with the predecessors of the Brussels and Montreal expositions. Being right in the centre of the Expo '70 grounds, the Plaza was connected with other theme displays and thus supported contents of the Expo's basic theme. The Festival Plaza thus acted as a direct expression of a soft environment that is composed of information and communications reacting constantly to a mutual feedback process. The entire Expo '70 from the master plan to individual pavilions aimed at enhancing the communication between human beings and their environment. The Festival Plaza was one of the most direct manifestations of this soft environment, Tange confessed, by further elaborating that still it remains difficult to think about how this environment will look like if it is physicalised. He said:

> [s]till the problem of how to give this kind of environment concrete physical form, or in other terms, how to create an environment permitting spontaneous human participation, is one of our most pressing topics. EXPO '70 seems to me to be the first step toward[s] a solution.[58]

It has not been the case that Tange wanted only to focus and emphasise on some particular aspects, but he was interested in and expressed a desire for a balance between the hardware or physical aspects and the software or non-physical characteristics of an information and communications society as well. He explains his gradual ideological shift from hardware to software that can also be witnessed in his master design for the Expo '70 and in his architectural designs. He states that the ideology behind the physicalised forms of the master design of Expo '70, such as the tree trunk and its branches representing the basic facilities, was a soft environment. Since the 1960s' and till the middle of this decade, Tange perceived cities in terms of structure by designing quite hard enclosures for their urban designs. This approach is well-evident from his Tokyo Plan (1960), but since the middle of the 60s', he started thinking and diverting his approach more towards the softer aspects of the environment, thus minimising the hardware components. He tried to implement his ideals for soft environments fully in the network of the Expo '70s trunk facilities and amenities. He has been of the view ever since Expo '70 that he could have designed more freer and softer structures either as in the case of individual buildings or for his urban design proposals.[59]

Isozaki was the member of a group responsible for designing the trunk facilities under the leadership of Tange, and his responsibilities included the Festival Plaza's mechanical, electric and electronic installations, including robots – Deme and Deku – mobile seating stands, stages and trolleys (Figure 3.9). Shuichi Fujie, Koukichi Shioya, Yasuhiko Yamamoto, Yoshio Tsukio, Yushi Morioka, Takahiro Nakamori and Noriyuki Miura were his team members for the designing of the Plaza.[60] Regarding his role, Isozaki states that he spent his late thirties and up to five years on this project. This project went through the three stages of designing of the master plan, siting of facilities and consequently the final design. He participated in these stages in the roles of a planner, designer and producer. As he worked under Tange's leadership, he being appointed as a subproducer of the Expo '70 on an immediate basis was no surprise. This position carried a huge responsibility of, first, preparing a preliminary proposal for the master plan and, second, drifting through the complex political considerations in order to get the approval of the organising committee, as they had the final say. Isozaki states:

> It was necessary to maneuver one's way through many different centers of authority such as the central government and local governments, agencies in conflict within the government, eastern and western national universities engaged in a struggle for hegemony, and opinion makers of the financial world.[61]

In addition to proposing and designing the mechanical equipment of the Plaza, his role was also to provide assistance if the event was stalled in any case by technical shortcomings.[62] He also received a special prize by the Architectural Institute of Japan in 1970 for the mechanics and electronics of the Plaza and defines it as the focal point of the Expo '70, acting as its main thoroughfare, base for transportation and a place for gatherings.[63]

This space acted as a multi-purpose venue that accommodated different performances and activities from morning till late at night. Activities were divided into

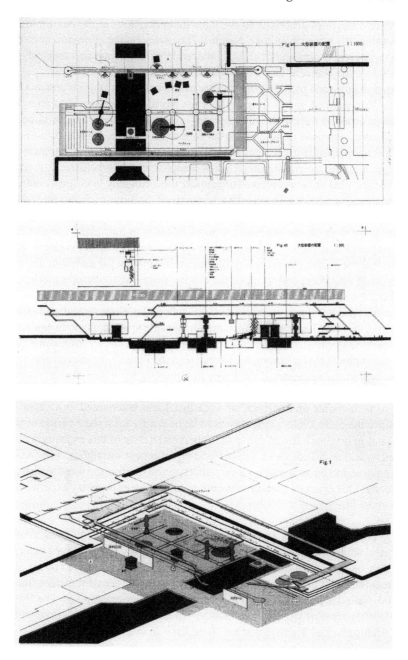

*Figure 3.9* Robot cranes were designed by Isozaki for the Festival Plaza for lifting and re-arranging of movable seating stands, stages and trolleys. These robot cranes were capable of moving across the railways and performed multiple functions.

three main categories according to the three main divisions of the day timings. In the morning, it was reserved for a National Day event, in the afternoon, it acted as a meet-and-greet piazza and at night, it housed large-scale pageants and shows. In the morning, the National Day event was celebrated in the Plaza. It was a day that was reserved for each participating country to celebrate its traditions and modernities. As distinguished guests from all over the world were supposed to attend this day, so in order to follow the international protocol, all the activities to be performed were organised to be in a formal format. Therefore, these activities grant the Plaza an exalted festival significance. In the afternoon, the Plaza transformed itself into a public square or piazza, where people can rest, stroll freely, meet and greet friends, chat or have a relaxed time under the artificially intelligent controlled environmental conditions. During the afternoon, all the mobile equipment had been removed and stored away from this space. Finally, at the end of the day, this Plaza was installed with all the necessary fixtures in order to host elaborate and large-scale pageants and shows.[64] Thus, the aim of this space was "to create a spatial quality that facilitates the evocation of these three moods [of morning, afternoon and evening activities] and to make the change from one to the other technically possible," Isozaki states.[65]

Isozaki outlined the characteristics of a cybernetic environment in his essay *Invisible City* (1966) and argued that interchangeable spaces, movable equipment, man-machine symbiosis and a self-instructing feedback channel results in a cybernetic environment that he attempted to realise in the Plaza.[66] In order to explain the reason behind the selection of the Plaza for applying his ideals of the cybernetic environment, Isozaki said that Expo '70 was an ideal space in order to "experiment with 'invisible architecture,' an idea that I had entertained in a vague way ever since the early 1960s', since it was to be held only for a short period of time" [emphasis in original]. It was due to the ephemeral nature of this exposition that he wanted to realise his ideals of a cybernetic environment through it. The facilities were supposed to be arranged for a very short period of time and were to disappear eventually. This event as a whole was conceived to be a momentary experience, he states and adds:

> [b]y putting together a series of such experiences it might be possible to expand what we take to be architecture. . . . Behind my proposal for a central facility on the exposition grounds called the Festival Plaza where large-scale ceremonies and performances could be held was the idea of transforming a solid, spatial architecture into a momentary and experiential place. The "Fun Palace" scheme of Cedric Price and the "Electro-Responsive Environment" of Archigram had been suggestive[67] [emphasis in original].

Regarding a feedback process from the spectators in the Festival Plaza, Isozaki wanted to achieve a performer-spectator-machine symbiosis so that it must give the audience "the psychological sensation of taking place in the performance . . . [so that as a result] the plaza becomes something truly unique."[68] In order to make this

Plaza functionally as versatile as possible, the equipment was to be conceived and designed as a highly creative and artistic endeavor. The space was conceived as an *elastic* notion so that it was able to simultaneously limit and expand the boundaries of the events it contained and supported. The space was also designed to contain multiple focal points for a variety of events, and reversely, it was also supposed to be accommodating several focal points at once. In order to balance the superhuman scale of the Plaza, the movable equipment was designed in such a way so that it was capable of approaching the maximum extent; thus, an interaction was made possible between an individual or a group of performers and the spectators. Isozaki compared the mood of this environment with a television studio and added that the festivity, equipment and spectators were balanced as a whole with the help of intricate programming and planning of the ground equipment (Figure 3.10). This cybernetic environment of the Festival Plaza was achieved with the help of pre-planned and controlled computer programs. These programs helped in synchronising the flashing lights, spotlights, projections on screens, sounds and time-space music, etc. The entire area under the Great Roof of the Plaza and the exhibition deck was covered by these tremendous light and sound effects. Isozaki mentions that the intention behind the program planning of this huge space was not to promote the visual aspects but "instead to employ flickering media to suggest a vast environment."[69]

The possibilities of experimentation and realisation of his ideologies regarding cybernetics environment was the force that compelled Isozaki for participation in the Expo '70 as he said that "[t]he introduction of modern architecture into Japan after the war and its development over the subsequent 25 years had their splendid culmination in the exposition."[70] But once after the design and implementation of the cybernetic environment of the Plaza, in other words, his dreams were realised, and consequently, he started poking fun at and criticising it.[71] The space-frame structure acting as the roof of the Plaza was 30 meters high, and it was for the very first time that such kind of an expansive covering was levitated at such a great height and presented an urban scale. Isozaki states that only these kinds of incentives forced him to participate in this Expo. He further adds that "[t]he word 'experiment' had enticed me. . . . Even so, the lure of the possibility that I could finally realize something that I had dreamt about for years was irresistible" [emphasis in original]. If he could have stayed out from this project, he would have developed a rational argument objecting that he had not taken part in this grand exercise, he confesses. "I became absorbed in it as if seized by a fever, however, and emotion overruled reason. And thus I gave in," states Isozaki.[72] But after this enthusiasm subsided, the account of his participation that he wrote remains ambivalent. His statements regarding what he felt while the design and execution of the Plaza under the leadership of Tange were ridiculed to a considerable extent. For example, his statement that "I felt as though I had participated in executing a war" was highly criticised. This Expo '70 was a celebration of Japan's economic boom, presenting an incredible success story that no one believed could happen, even such that *Time Magazine* also declared in its

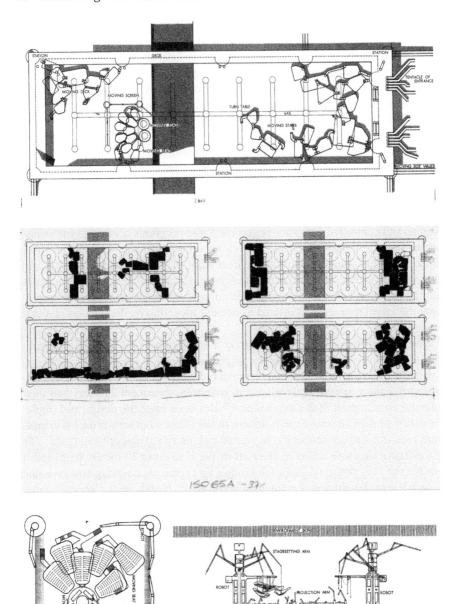

*Figure 3.10* The Festival Plaza's mobile apparatuses, including seating stands, stages and trolleys, made numerous festival arrangements possible with the help of robot cranes.

*Source*: Arata Isozaki, *Mobile apparatuses of the Festival Plaza, Expo '70 Osaka Suita, Osaka*, 1967–70, master plans and a section. Copyright © Estate of Arata Isozaki. All rights reserved. Used with permission.

March 1970 issue that "No country has a stronger franchise on the future than Japan." Furthermore, this article stated:

No developed nation is growing faster. Its economy quadrupled in the past decade, and will triple again in the next. Powered by a boomu (the word is a typical Japanese neologism) that has been picking up speed for a full ten years, Japan whistled past Britain in gross national product in 1967, then France in 1968. Last year it surpassed West Germany. With a G.N.P. that is expected to reach $200 billion this year, Japan now ranks third in the world, be hind only the U.S. ($932 billion) and the Soviet Union ($600 billion). U.S. Commerce Secretary Maurice Stans says that Japan "could very well" move to the head of the class in the next 20 years. Says economist Peter Drucker: "It is the most extraordinary success story in all economic history"[73] [emphasis in original].

Isozaki considered Expo '70 as both of a political and festivity venue. While explaining the dual character of this exposition, he said that this celebration emblematically announced to the world that Japan has fully recovered after a quarter of a century from its defeat in the war. He further added:

[t]he reason why both the terms "*seiji*" (political affairs, 政事) and "*saiji*" (festivals, 祭事) are read as "*matsuri-goto* (政事・祭事)," is because politics are visualized through festivals. Plazas were prepared as the site for such festivals. This happened at Moscow and Beijing, and Munich and Nuremberg, before moving onto Berlin. The existence of the Festival Plaza at Expo '70 thus made sense, and its naming by the architect Nishiyama Uzō proved to be fitting.[74]

He was of the view that at this kind of international events, hidden aims and objectives of authorities reveal themselves. Although he was contributing to this exposition only in the capacity of a designer and organiser of some of his creativities, he constantly found himself bound by these hidden, intricately woven webs of constraints imposed by the competing authorities. The decade at the culmination of which this exposition was organised already had been full of revolts and protests, such as the international moment of youths and Cultural Revolution in which hippies were also contributors, Isozaki states. Being unhappy and discouraged for pursuing a career as a professional planner, he realised that his duties were merely limited to the design of "organized spaces and made them perceptible in a way that was advantageous to the Establishment." He firmly believed that as a professional, if his job could had been in accord with his social concerns and ideologies, he would have been much more contented with his choice of profession. Considering this whole as a period of contradiction, he again puts forth his point:

[t]hough I was taking part in the production of that festival, I was not happy. In fact I wanted to stop and destroy it. It was as if I has been helping to carry out a war but at last had emotionally dropped out.[75]

Due to overwork, Isozaki suffered from a severe back pain, and as he was assigned the duty of operating the Deku robot, so he planned to view the opening ceremony of the Expo '70 through the window of this robot and consequently was not able to attend it. Instead, he watched the live television broadcast resting in a hotel room and stated that "the announcer's commentary irritated me to no end. Then they aired the Expo '70 theme song, *Hello from the Countries of the World*. It was only at that moment when I finally awoke from my fever"[76] [emphasis in original]. Tange emphasised on the software aspects – interactions among people – in the Festival Plaza instead of the mere display of technological artefacts that he called as hardware. In the similar but rather provoking fashion, Isozaki also rejected and criticised the hardware display of the Expo '70 by saying that "[t]echnology was merely converted into toys for entertainment – the robots were what Pokémon are today."[77]

Isozaki states that he was influenced by the term *environment* particularly in the 1960s', as it was being promoted due to avant-garde art movements at that time. His interest can be witnessed through his experimentations of environments – cybernetics being one of them – at different platforms. The term *environment* (環境) gained popularity in post-war Japan due to avant-garde art movements such as *Fluxus* and the intermedia and environmental art practices.[78] In the mid-60s, with the advent of the pop art, new media and emerging developments in the realm of *art and technology*, different technological devices were being experimented with. Being inspired by these emerging trends of the period, he thought of expanding the concept of architecture to incorporate this movement, and the specialism he inspired to pursue was to be *art, architecture and technology*, he states.[79] It was this interest in these experimental art and environmental exhibitions that led him to distinguish his architectural ideas from his metabolism predecessors. He also designed a studio set depicting a strange black-coloured or blank space with glass partitions that reflected the actors in motion for the movie *The Face of Another* that was released in 1966. *The Face of Another* (他人の顔) was an experimental movie based on Kōbō Abe's 1964 novel with the same name. It was directed by Hiroshi Teshigahara, who was Isozaki's friend and invited him to design a studio set of a psychiatrist's office for a character of this movie. This movie follows an engineer whose face gets severely burnt in an industrial accident, and he gets a new one from a doctor. Then this engineer seduces his wife with the help of this new personality, and the story revolves around this platform.[80] This studio set also portrayed Isozaki's interest towards physicalising the cybernetic environment. He states that it was the *Environment Society* that resulted in the designing of the Plaza and the foundation of his company for this purpose called as the *Environmental Planning* that he founded in collaboration with Katsuhiro Yamaguchi. The Environment Society also organised an experimental exhibition called *From Space to Environment* (1966) that invited participants from different disciplines, such as architecture, painting, sculpture, photography, music, etc., and as a result formulated many of the ideas that Isozaki later implemented in the design of the Festival Plaza.

By confessing that the spectators were surrounded by hidden products of technology, mechanisms or apparatuses under the Grand Roof of the Festival Plaza, Isozaki presented the giant *Deme and Deku robots* as devices that would aid the presentation of the events (Figure 3.11). He decided to call these robots as mere

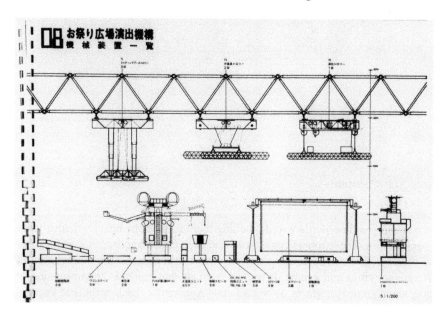

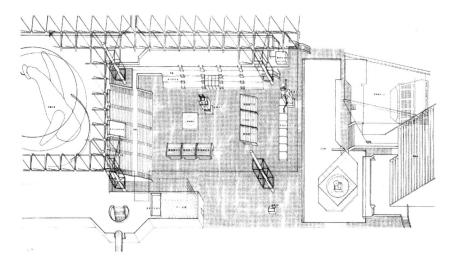

*Figure 3.11* Isozaki was influenced by science fictions while designing the cybernetic environment of the Festival Plaza. He mentions his visit to NASA at Houston, watching a rocket launch at Cape Kennedy and Stanley Kubrick's *2001: A Space Odyssey* (a movie released in 1968). The culture of the time can also be witnessed through the display of the USA Pavilion at the Osaka Expo '70. In an effort to make the environment of the Plaza as a control room of a space station, he designed a set of performance robots. Deme (pop-eyed) was one of them that housed projector rooms inside its two plastic spheres.

*Source*: Arata Isozaki, *Deme and Deku at the Festival Plaza, Expo '70 Osaka Suita, Osaka*, 1967–70, elevations and views. Copyright © Estate of Arata Isozaki. All rights reserved. Used with permission.

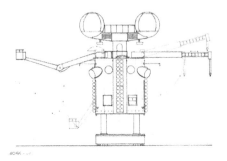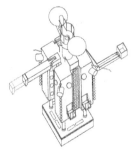

*Figure 3.11* (Continued)

*mechanisms* just in order to avoid labelling them as with the heavily loaded word of *architecture*. These robots could have also been called *apparatuses*, as he states that the objective was to develop devices that would assist in the presentation of different activities and events. It was an exercise that marked the termination of heavy technological artefacts, as he said that "Apparatuses such as those in Festival Plaza marked the end of a period of giant technology. They have disappeared except in photographs and records just as 'invisible architecture' was supposed to"[81] [emphasis in original]. These robots were manufactured by a train car factory. He explains the difficulties he faced during the production and implementation of these robots. Although he thought that technology was available in Japan for the production of these robots, as due to rapid economic growth, the automation of production lines was taking place, he was to some extent misled. He proposed a number of proposals for the installation of these robots in the Plaza but was stuck when no manufacturer was willing to take the production orders. He recalls this process of finding a suitable manufacturer:

> Manufacturers that supplied automobile plants were bound to production line schedules, and they did not seem to have any idle time for taking part in our trivial amusements. Then we met an eccentric character at a train car factory. Train cars are not mass-produced. They are all custom-made and production is begun from scratch each time. It was in such a factory that the one-of-a-kind, useless robots of the Festival Plaza were built. The fact that flatcars were available there was of key importance, as the robots were much too unsteady to walk on two feet. They had to ride in wheelchairs.[82]

Another problem that the team faced was of providing these robots with the power supply, as batteries were not able to power such enormous machines. The only solution that was available was to supply the power by cables. "Unable to move without cords, the robots were like performing monkeys on leashes," recalls Isozaki whimsically.[83]

The giant Deme and Deku robots were designed to move around the Plaza while blowing steam. Isozaki resembled them with the *a-un* guardian warriors further being a derivation from the figure of Hercules. Deku robot served as the control station for stage performances, and he was to ride inside it, controlling the stage activities. The reason these robots were named as Deme and Deku rests in the fact that the robot that housed projector rooms inside two plastic spheres was named as *Deme* (a Japanese word meaning pop-eyed) and the other that served as the control station was named as *Deku* (a Japanese word derived from *deku-no-bō*, meaning literally in English as *good for nothing*). It was good for nothing, as it was not able to perform any significant tasks but was able only to move from one side to another.[84] Fact being this robot also housed an information collection and processing centre. A control room was housed in its head. Its body was designed to contain equipment for the collection of information, lights, sounds, etc. All of this information was to be sent to the main control room of the exposition for processing purposes. It was capable of emitting lights, sounds, smoke and bubbles into its vicinities if activated by the information. While elaborating the functionality of this robot for stage performances, Isozaki states:

> trunk section can move up or down 1.8 m. When it is in the up position, the resulting platform is at the same level as the stage and is therefore a suitable place for performance. When down, it becomes a moving dressing room. One arm can bend and extend to a maximum of 9 m; the other extends and retracts 7.5 m. Either human beings or sets can ride on the arms.[85]

Isozaki states that he was particularly interested in the centralised control room of the Expo '70 that controlled all of the operations (Figure 3.12). By considering this control room as a model, he believed that in general various social phenomena, such as city planning, can be controlled and operated at a much-complicated level, and he attempted to implement this idea on a much smaller scale at the Festival Plaza.[86] He was under the influence of science fictions, especially Stanley Kubrick's movie *2001: A Space Odyssey* (1968), dealing with the theme of artificial intelligence among others at the time of designing the Festival Plaza. This movie remains one of the most influential, epic science fiction films of the 60s'. The screenplay was jointly written by Stanley Kubrick and Arthur C. Clarke. The film presents a voyage to Jupiter with the sentient computer HAL, dealing with the themes of artificial intelligence, existentialism, human evolution, technology and prospects of the extraterrestrial life. Isozaki summarises his perception of the movie as some sophisticated, cosmic, transcendental and a God-figure-like being sent to the earth. In the story, it physicalises itself as a primary structure, a cuboid that resembles the Seagrams Building in New York. He calls it in Japanese as *go-shintai*, literally meaning in English as *a divine body*. In order to locate this divine being, a spacecraft is sent into the space that embarks on the Jupiter having a computer HAL in it. It happens that HAL, a simulation model, betrays its human masters. Another feature that Isozaki mentions in his account of Clarke's stories is the representation of an *Over-mind* that he says frequently appears in his movies. Quoting extra-vehicular pod that is portrayed to be a small, one-man maintenance vehicle equipped with robotic arms is a machine that fascinated him greatly. Projecting its

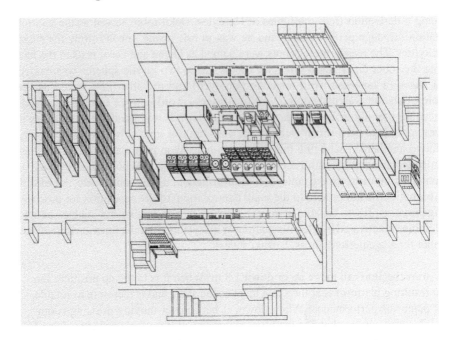

*Figure 3.12* The main control room of the Osaka Expo '70. As the system of the Expo
was controlled from this room, Isozaki believed that the whole city could be
controlled with such city brains.
*Source*: Arata Isozaki, *Expo '70 Osaka Suita, Osaka*, 1967–70, axonometric. Copyright © Estate of
Arata Isozaki. All rights reserved. Used with permission.

utility, Isozaki labels it as a pioneering vision and mentions that astronauts work
manually by space-walking these days, and as he wrote this account back in the
days of the Osaka Expo 1970, he projected that such kind of extra-vehicular pods
could prove to be extremely useful if large-scale spacecrafts are to be assembled
in space.

Isozaki was inspired by the science fiction film depicting extra-vehicular pods
and other technologically advanced devices that he was very keen to introduce to
the realm of architecture. He further adds in this regard that "I even visited NASA
at Houston to collect as much promotional material and video as I could, after
which I wasted more time by making a trip to Cape Kennedy just to observe a
rocket launch from a distance."[87] He emphasises this visit:

[i]n the past, religious architecture involved the expenditure of enormous
sums for the sake of symbolizing the slippery idea of divinity. Today super-
hangers devoted to the worship of the divinity of technology are the only
comparable structures on the globe.[88]

As a spaceship can be controlled from a control room located on earth, similarly,
he made the controls of the Festival Plaza to be located in the control headquarters

and also placed a sub-station in a moving tower.[89] After the failing of the Apollo 13 mission, its engineers, who as a result were unemployed, built a structure that can be controlled with a telephone system. This is what he believes was the beginning of an intelligent building. He states that after the military industry declines, the technology it produces is eventually utilised by the private sector. This is the reason why the architecture of the 1950s' in the United States of America is of highest quality and went into decline into the 1960s', as the war technology was not being transferred to the private sector in the peacetime, states Isozaki.[90]

In addition to the Deme and Deku performing robots, there were other equipment and control stations as well. A movable lighting installation, the *hanging robot*, was suspended from the Grand Roof. Criticising this hanging robot, Isozaki states that "[these] resembled the long-armed monkeys in Hasegawa Tōhaku's paintings. Alas, they were all monkeys."[91] Furthermore, a sub-control station in the form of a moving tower with a local control room in its upper section and a projection booth, light deck, dressing room and waiting area for the performers were also designed for the Plaza that controlled lights, sound and trolley equipment. The floor and the ceiling of the Plaza were outfitted with different kinds of performance equipment comprising majorly of fixed or movable lighting, sound, mechanical and control devices, etc.[92] The ceiling consisted of six hanging trolleys running on rails and handled lighting and a traverser that was used for switching a trolley from one set of rails to another. The floor equipment consisted of a movable stage, eight wagon stages, six movable stands and a movable robot capable of performing all kinds of tricks. Each of these performance equipment was connected with the control room, while at the same time, independent supervision and activities were possible through sub-control station. The main control room contained a computer, FACOM 270–30, for performing real-time control and tele-control operations. Furthermore, controls for general activities, such as lighting, sound, speaker switching, trolleys and input-output typewriters for the electronic information boards, were all available in the main control room. An electronic information board measuring $4 \times 11$ meters was also fixed in the Festival Plaza, displaying illuminated letters, diagrams and animated figures. Exhibiting the characteristics of artificially intelligent architecture, Isozaki explains that the artificially controlled environment of the Plaza was also dependent on some automated systems, as he indicates:

[i]t is by no means accidental that automatic controls are essential to handle the numerous kinds of equipment dispersed throughout a vast space and subject to contact surveillance and frequent change and alteration during the 184 days of the exposition.[93]

Thus, the control system of the Festival Plaza was further divided into the four sub-control mechanisms. First sub-control system was responsible for controlling individual performance equipment, second dealt with theatrical effects, third was responsible for the complete performance set-up of the entire Plaza and fourth dealt with lighting and sound equipment patterns. The first and second control systems were largely manual and depended on the main control room, the sub-station and wireless remote control. The third and fourth control systems that were responsible for controlling the entire artificial environment of the Plaza inherited the characteristics of an artificially intelligent architecture. The third control system was fitted with a pre-set computer program that handled direct and indirect down lighting, lighting booths, strobes, speaker matrix, etc. This computer program was capable of memorising a hundred different patterns for such arrangements. Using the technology of magnetic tapes, having the pre-set computer programs written on them were then fed into a computer, and a six-channel tape recorder controlled all of the performance activities in the Plaza. This equipment was able to control each of these components either individually or in a group. Even if alternations in the pre-defined patterns were to be made in the real time, provisions were provided for them as well. Finally, the fourth sub-control system was to be used in synchronisation with the display instrument's systematic programming language in order to control the lighting and sound equipment patterns. This whole system worked on pre-set patterns that were fed into the computer.[94]

Isozaki not only designed and implemented the Festival Plaza from the very start but also thought of its dismantling as well, as he said:

> the exposition seemed to me less like a huge festival and more like meaningless ruins. It all was to disappear in 6 months, but I had helped realize it from the start. My intention, in a sense, was to try to rush the modern architectural movement along to its logical conclusion in order to dismantle it. For me at least modern architecture had been in the process of being dismantled even before that, but now I was witness to its death.[95]

## Conclusion

Discussing Tange's projects first, the ideas developed in the World Health Organization (1959) and the Massachusetts Institute of Technology Boston Harbor (1959) projects led to the development of A Plan for Tokyo (1960–61). Visual communication spaces acted as core spaces and granted structure to the whole. In A Plan for Tokyo (1960–61), Tange and his team presented Tokyo as an organism, a growing city with 10,000,000 population for which linear development was suggested based on biological principles. Functions were distributed along a line to carry out fast information and communications. He emphasised on the processing of information and communications in this plan. He suggested that people carry information from place to place – a process he labelled as communication. This communication can exist between man-man, man-function or function-function. Although he suggested this phenomenon in 1960, it is being realised in the form of internet of things these days. He also stressed that Norbert Wiener – the pioneer or creator of cybernetics – has also described communications as the cement of the society.

In the Tsukiji Project in Tokyo (1963), he presented a regeneration proposal for a district. It was an extension of A Plan of Tokyo (1960–61) and presented a central civic axis of communication, or in other words, a conveyor system that acted like a spinal cord that emitted various arteries. Yamanashi Communications Center (1964–67) presented an open spatial structure that acted as an urban and architectural design simultaneously and incorporated ideas from A Plan for Tokyo (1960–61) and communications theories presented by Tange. He designed a three-dimensional communications grid as vertical communications shafts with different functions. Tange, while defining space in the age of information and communications, stated that space has become a continuously changing entity since 1960 onwards. The relationship between space and function has become pluralistic, elastic, selective and spontaneous. In other words, space has become informational possessing tactual, auditory, visual and transportation characteristics. It is a communication field that is gradually becoming organic with the development of information and communications system. Consequently, the aim of architecture has become to make communication network visible in a space.

In Plan for Skopje (1965), Tange carried over ideas from A Plan for Tokyo (1960–61), Yamanashi Communications Center (1964–67) and Tsukiji Project in Tokyo (1963) and proposed the vertical communication shafts and central civic axis of communication, etc. He designed this project in three phases so that plans and structures became less complex with the advancement of phases. City Gate and City Wall acted as visual communicative elements between the space and its observer. Tange also proposed elements of an intelligent building as of human, emotional and sensual (tactual, auditory, visual, etc.), technologically intelligent and social-communicational structure of the space.

Similarly, Isozaki also followed Norbert Wiener, as his mentor Tange did. Isozaki states that city has become an organic entity due to constant reproduction, division and feedback. Only the process or software has become trustworthy, neglecting physical artefacts or hardware. Space has become a code-sprinkled schema, and thus, a city has become a system based on cybernetics. Computers are making feedback possible through simulation. It is this semiotic or symbolic stage that has evolved from the electronics theories that we are currently living in. Consequently, on the basis of Wiener's theories, he defines characteristics of a cybernetic environment as of enveloped in a protective membrane, space with extensive interchangeability, a wide variety of movable equipment, man-machine symbiosis and a system with self-instructing feedback channel.

Isozaki attempted to implement these ideals of a cybernetic environment in a number of his projects. For example, in the Electric Labyrinth: 14th Triennial Di Milano (1968), he presented a mini-cybernetic environment with sixteen curved, revolving and signal-sensing panels. Central four panels were able to turn automatically by sensing sounds electrically through infra-red beams. He states that this installation acted as an inspiration for the Festival Plaza's cybernetic environment. Responsive House (1968–69) was a technologically responsive house with changeable layouts using butterfly hingers, etc. Isozaki called it a simulation model that was translated into a physical form. Computer Aided City (1970–72) was an extension of the computer-aided environment of the Festival Plaza and suggested information processing by a supercomputer leading to artificially intelligent architecture on a city-scale. Functions, such as city hall, hospital, school, stadium, art museum, office building, shopping centre, etc., lost their meaning, as they all were linked by an information-processing system and were covered by a single membrane.

Likewise, in the collaborative project of the Festival Plaza (1965–70) and the Japan World Exposition Osaka 1970, both Tange and Isozaki implemented their cybernetic ideals. As have been the case with A Plan for Tokyo (1960–61), Tsukiji Project in Tokyo (1963), Yamanashi Communications Center (1964–67) and Plan for Skopje (1965), Tange focused on the central civic axis of communication and technique of visual communication for the master planning of the Expo '70. Isozaki's responsibilities included Festival Plaza's mechanical, electric and electronic installations, including robots – Deme and Deku – movable seating stand, movable stage and trolley. He realised characteristics, such as interchangeable spaces, movable equipment, man-machine symbiosis and a self-instructing feedback loop, through this project. Tange called this set-up as a representation of a soft environment. Isozaki also mentions Fun Palace by Price and Electro-Responsive Environment by Archigram as inspirations for the Festival Plaza. He wanted to achieve a performer-spectator-machine symbiosis at the Plaza so that audience may experience the psychological sensation of participation in the performance through feedback, but unfortunately, these ideals were not completely executed. Furthermore, he was also interested in the centralised control room of the Expo '70. He believed that a city can also be controlled with a centralised control room, an idea that he presented in his Computer Aided City (1970–72) project. Isozaki also designed Deme (pop-eyed) and Deku (good-for-nothing) robots. He mentions that he was inspired by science fiction movies of the time, such as Stanley Kubrick's *2001: A Space Odyssey* (1968), that presented the theme of artificial intelligence for the designing of the Plaza. He also visited NASA at Houston and Cape Kennedy to watch a rocket launch. He states that after the failure of the Apollo 13 mission, its engineers designed a building that was controllable with a telephone system that he believes to be the beginning of an intelligent building design.

## Notes

Parts of this chapter have been previously published in *Journal of Architecture and Planning (Transactions of AIJ)* by the Architectural Institute of Japan (AIJ). Danyal Ahmed and Junichiro Higaya, "Figuring-out the characteristics of artificially intelligent architecture by re-visiting the cybernetic projects of Kenzo Tange and Arata Isozaki from 1959–1972," *Journal of Architecture and Planning (Transactions of AIJ)* 86, no. 787 (2021): 2358–2367, https://doi.org/10.3130/aija.86.2358.

1  Kenzo Tange, "A Plan for Tokyo, 1960: Toward a Structural Reorganization," in *Kenzo Tange 1946–1969: Architecture and Urban Design*, ed. Udo Kultermann (London: Pall Mall Press, 1970), 130.
2  Kenzo Tange, "Function, Structure and Symbol, 1966," in *Kenzo Tange 1946–1969: Architecture and Urban Design*, ed. Udo Kultermann (London: Pall Mall Press, 1970), 242.
3  Arata Isozaki, "City in the Air 1960–63," in *GA Architect 6: Arata Isozaki Vol. 1 1959–1978*, ed. Yukio Futagawa (Tokyo: A.D.A. EDITA, 1991), 27.

4 Kenzo Tange Team, "A Plan for Tokyo, 1960," trans. Charles S. Terry, *Ekistics* 12, no. 69 (1961): 10, accessed October 10, 2020, www.jstor.org/stable/43613534.

5 Tange, "A Plan for Tokyo, 1960: Toward a Structural Reorganization," 123–124.

6 Kenzo Tange Team, "A Plan for Tokyo, 1960," 14–16.

7 Ibid., 9.

8 Tange, "A Plan for Tokyo, 1960: Toward a Structural Reorganization," 118–119.

9 Kenzo Tange, "Tokaido-Megalopolis: The Japanese Archipelago in the Future," in *Kenzo Tange 1946–1969: Architecture and Urban Design*, ed. Udo Kultermann (London: Pall Mall Press, 1970), 154.

10 Tange, "A Plan for Tokyo, 1960: Toward a Structural Reorganization," 116–117.

11 Tange, "Tokaido-Megalopolis: The Japanese Archipelago in the Future," 153.

12 Ibid., 150–152.

13 Ibid., 157.

14 Ibid., 153–154.

15 Tange, "A Plan for Tokyo, 1960: Toward a Structural Reorganization," 124.

16 Tange, "Function, Structure and Symbol, 1966," 242.

17 Ibid., 240–243.

18 Ibid.

19 Ibid.

20 Ibid.

21 Arata Isozaki, "Festival Plaza, Expo '70 Osaka Suita, Osaka 1967–70," in *GA Architect 6: Arata Isozaki Vol. 1 1959–1978*, ed. Yukio Futagawa (Tokyo: A.D.A. EDITA, 1991), 86.

22 Tange, "Function, Structure and Symbol, 1966," 244.

23 Kenzo Tange, "Kenzo Tange 1987 Laureate: Ceremony Acceptance Speech," speech, Pritzker Architecture Prize Ceremony, Kimbell Art Museum, Fort Worth, May 2, 1987, accessed October 14, 2020, www.pritzkerprize.com/sites/default/files/inline-files/Kenzo_Tange_Acceptance_Speech_1987.pdf.

24 Tange, "Tokaido-Megalopolis: The Japanese Archipelago in the Future," 154.

25 Ibid., 157.

26 Arata Isozaki, "1966: Invisible City," in *Architecture Culture: 1943–1968, A Documentary Anthology*, ed. Joan Ockman with the collaboration of Edward Eigen (New York: Rizzoli International Publications, Inc., 1993), 403.

27 Ibid., 404.

28 Arata Isozaki, "Library at Oita," *Architectural Design* 34, no. 12 (December 1964): 612, accessed January 30, 2023, http://designtheory.fiu.edu/readings/kurokawa_architecture_of_action.pdf.

29 Arata Isozaki, "The Theory of Process Planning 1963," in *GA Architect 6: Arata Isozaki Vol. 1 1959–1978*, ed. Yukio Futagawa (Tokyo: A.D.A. EDITA, 1991), 30.

30 Isozaki presents his *Theory of Process Planning* (1963) in rather a more technical language that is difficult to understand for a nonspecialist. In the main text, this theory has been simplified for the convenience of the reader. Technical account is being presented here: In the *Theory of Process Planning* (1963), Isozaki defines architecture as a planning concept that can be implemented to situations where space is transformed at a tremendous speed by time. It is through this planning concept that the architecture of growth can be realised. He outlines certain parameters for achieving architecture at such a tremendous speed of transformation. Function is defined through its content so that it corresponds to a particular space; thus, function becomes an element. Any changes in this element due to variations in scale have been titled as a *vertical order*. Interchangeability and self-identity as in a form or an expression are possessions of each and every element, and they are capable of growth and diminution independently. General composition demands decisive changes at regular intervals, and Isozaki labels such conditions as *generative factors*, or *emergent qualities*. Mutual relationships are developed among different groups of elements, and it is the responsibility of the design

operation to give this bonding concrete meaning. He names this bonding as a *skeleton*. For a specific condition, a particular type of pattern exists that enables the self-identity and growth of this skeleton. A group of patterns corresponding to a stage of scale has been labelled as a *horizontal order*. It is extremely important for the overall structuring of the architectural space. A skeleton fixates the directionality of growth of each group of elements. As much as the regulations are clear, less likely the growth of that group of elements is to be hindered. If the scale fluctuates, so the transformation of spatial systems it is associated with. This exercise permits the transfer of a skeleton from one order to the higher as well as the discontinuous growth. Patterns are open, and an element can continue in a particular direction even though it may be complete. Patterns are open in principle, and an element is allowed to proceed in its chosen direction. A suitable medium, such as structural or mechanical, must be selected in order to enclose a spatial system. A purposeful space reveals its dual character, thus being a constituent of the totality. This architecture presents itself as an expression in transition from one condition to another. Limitless development presents the concept of totality for this architecture. A given point in time being examined gives us information regarding the specific directionality from a treasure of transitional processes taking place.

31  Isozaki, "1966: Invisible City," 403.
32  Ibid., 404.
33  Ibid., 405.
34  Ibid., 406.
35  Ibid.
36  Marshall McLuhan, *Understanding Media: The Extensions of Man* (New York: McGraw Hill, 1964), quoted in Isozaki, "1966: Invisible City," 406.
37  Isozaki, "1966: Invisible City," 407.
38  Ibid.
39  Arata Isozaki, "ターニングポイント、空間から環境へ," [Turning Point: From Space to Environment] interview by Naohiko Hino, in 磯崎新インタヴユーズ [*Isozaki Arata Interviews*] (Tokyo: LIXIL出版 [Publications], 2014), 118–119.
40  Arata Isozaki, "Electric Labyrinth: 14th Triennale Di Milano, Milan, Italy 1968," in *GA Architect 6: Arata Isozaki Vol. 1 1959–1978*, ed. Yukio Futagawa (Tokyo: A.D.A. EDITA, 1991), 92.
41  Ibid.
42  Arata Isozaki, "Responsive House 1968–69," in *Arata Isozaki: Architecture 1960–1990* (New York: Rizzoli International Publications, Inc., 1991), 142.
43  Arata Isozaki, "Arai House (Responsive House) 1968–69," in *GA Architect 6: Arata Isozaki Vol. 1 1959–1978*, ed. Yukio Futagawa (Tokyo: A.D.A. EDITA, 1991), 96.
44  Ibid.
45  Arata Isozaki, "Computer Aided City 1970–72," in *GA Architect 6: Arata Isozaki Vol. 1 1959–1978*, ed. Yukio Futagawa (Tokyo: A.D.A. EDITA, 1991), 100.
46  Ibid.
47  Arata Isozaki, "From Manner to Rhetoric, and Now . . . 1976," in *GA Architect 6: Arata Isozaki Vol. 1 1959–1978*, ed. Yukio Futagawa (Tokyo: A.D.A. EDITA, 1991), 181–182.
48  Ibid., 182.
49  Ibid.
50  Arata Isozaki, "Architecture of Quotation and Metaphor 1977," in *GA Architect 6: Arata Isozaki Vol. 1 1959–1978*, ed. Yukio Futagawa (Tokyo: A.D.A. EDITA, 1991), 216.
51  Kenzo Tange, "EXPO '70: The EXPO '70 Master Plan and Master Design," in *Kenzo Tange 1946–1969: Architecture and Urban Design*, ed. Udo Kultermann (London: Pall Mall Press, 1970), 284.
52  Ibid., 294.
53  Ibid., 286.
54  Ibid.

55 Kenzo Tange and Noboru Kawazoe, "Some Thoughts about EXPO '70: Dialogue between Kenzo Tange and Noboru Kawazoe," *The Japan Architect: Reprint Edition Expo '70* 113 (Spring 2019): 16.

56 Tange, "EXPO '70: The EXPO '70 Master Plan and Master Design," 289.

57 Ibid., 289–293.

58 Tange and Kawazoe, "Some Thoughts about EXPO '70," 18.

59 Ibid., 17.

60 Arata Isozaki, "Selected Buildings and Projects: The Festival Plaza, Expo '70," in *Arata Isozaki: Architecture 1960–1990* (New York: Rizzoli International Publications, Inc., 1991), 286.

61 Isozaki, "Festival Plaza, Expo '70 Osaka Suita, Osaka 1967–70," 86.

62 Arata Isozaki, "Recalling the Days of Expo Art (?) (2001)," trans. Machida Gen, *Review of Japanese Culture and Society* XXIII (December 2011): 73.

63 Arata Isozaki, *GA Architect 6: Arata Isozaki Vol. 1 1959–1978*, ed. Yukio Futagawa (Tokyo: A.D.A. EDITA, 1991), 4.

64 Arata Isozaki, "Festival Plaza," *The Japan Architect: Reprint Edition Expo '70* 113 (Spring 2019): 53.

65 Ibid.

66 Arata Isozaki, "『空間へ』《お祭り広場》『日本の都市空間』　一九六〇年代における都市論の方法をめぐって," [To Space, Festival Plaza, and Urban Space in Japan: Towards the Urban Theory of the 1960s] interview by Naohiko Hino, in 磯崎新インタヴューズ [*Isozaki Arata Interviews*] (Tokyo: LIXIL出版 [Publications], 2014), 52.

67 Isozaki, "Festival Plaza, Expo '70 Osaka Suita, Osaka 1967–70," 86.

68 Isozaki, "Festival Plaza," 53.

69 Ibid.

70 Isozaki, "Festival Plaza, Expo '70 Osaka Suita, Osaka 1967–70," 86.

71 Isozaki, "Recalling the Days of Expo Art (?) (2001)," 73.

72 Ibid.

73 Unknown Author, "World: Toward the Japanese Century," *Time*, March 2, 1970, accessed February 9, 2023, https://content.time.com/time/magazine/article/0,9171,904215,00.html.

74 Isozaki, "Recalling the Days of Expo Art (?) (2001)," 79.

75 Isozaki, "Festival Plaza, Expo '70 Osaka Suita, Osaka 1967–70," 86.

76 Isozaki, "Recalling the Days of Expo Art (?) (2001)," 73.

77 Ibid., 73–74.

78 Isozaki, "ターニングポイント、空間から環境へ [Turning Point: From Space to Environment]," 108.

79 Isozaki, "Festival Plaza, Expo '70 Osaka Suita, Osaka 1967–70," 86.

80 Isozaki, "ターニングポイント、空間から環境へ [Turning Point: From Space to Environment]," 111–114.

81 Isozaki, "Festival Plaza, Expo '70 Osaka Suita, Osaka 1967–70," 86–87.

82 Isozaki, "Recalling the Days of Expo Art (?) (2001)," 77.

83 Ibid.

84 Ibid., 72–73, 77.

85 Isozaki, "Festival Plaza," 54.

86 Isozaki, "ターニングポイント、空間から環境へ [Turning Point: From Space to Environment]," 115.

87 Isozaki, "Recalling the Days of Expo Art (?) (2001)," 74–75.

88 Isozaki, "Architecture of Quotation and Metaphor 1977," 214.

89 Isozaki, "ターニングポイント、空間から環境へ [Turning Point: From Space to Environment]," 115–116.

90 Ibid., 116.

91 Isozaki, "Recalling the Days of Expo Art (?) (2001)," 77.

92  Isozaki briefly explains the technical details of performance equipment as "Lighting, divided into ordinary night illumination and special performance lights. For ordinary illumination there are 789 400 Watt metal-halleid [sic] lamps attached to the roof frame and directed upward plus 215 1-Kilowatt halogen lamps directed downward. When all of them are turned on the plaza area is illuminated to an intensity of 150 lux. The main features of the performance lighting system are 112 strobe lights, attached in an upward position to the roof frame, and 3 lighting booths suspended on moving trolleys from the roof. This latter is capable of illumination effects of 2,500 lux. In addition, the plaza is outfitted with such other standard stage lighting devices as pin-arc spotlights, long-focus spotlights, and Brenkart [sic] effect machines. Sound systems are divided into input and output equipment. In the main control station there are four six-channel tape recorders, four two-channel tape recorders, two stereophonic record players, electronic musical instruments for live performances, and more than seventy microphones. In addition, in the sub-control station there are two-channel tape recorders and four-channel wireless microphone systems. An eleven-channel switch panel in the main control room has final say in the activation and distribution of sound effects. Amplification is effected by 288 systems consisting of 700 speakers placed throughout the plaza: 96-channel ceiling speakers (30W), 130-channel floor speakers (10 and 20W), 12-channel speakers placed in the bases of the columns (30W), and 2-channel ceremony speakers (400W). There are 15 sound-power outlets in the floor into which 6 movable 240W speakers may be plugged for special purposes. The 11 input and the 288 output systems can be freely interchanged by means of a master speaker matrix panel." Isozaki, "Festival Plaza," 54.
93  Ibid.
94  Ibid.
95  Isozaki, "Festival Plaza, Expo '70 Osaka Suita, Osaka 1967–70," 86.

## Bibliography

Isozaki, Arata. "1966: Invisible City." In *Architecture Culture: 1943–1968, A Documentary Anthology*, edited by Joan Ockman with the collaboration of Edward Eigen, 403–407. New York: Rizzoli International Publications, Inc., 1993.

Isozaki, Arata. "Arai House (Responsive House) 1968–69." In *GA Architect 6: Arata Isozaki Vol. 1 1959–1978*, edited by Yukio Futagawa, 96–97. Tokyo: A.D.A. EDITA, 1991.

Isozaki, Arata. "Architecture of Quotation and Metaphor 1977." In *GA Architect 6: Arata Isozaki Vol. 1 1959–1978*, edited by Yukio Futagawa, 214–217. Tokyo: A.D.A. EDITA, 1991.

Isozaki, Arata. "City in the Air 1960–63." In *GA Architect 6: Arata Isozaki Vol. 1 1959–1978*, edited by Yukio Futagawa, 24–29. Tokyo: A.D.A. EDITA, 1991.

Isozaki, Arata. "Computer Aided City 1970–72." In *GA Architect 6: Arata Isozaki Vol. 1 1959–1978*, edited by Yukio Futagawa, 98–101. Tokyo: A.D.A. EDITA, 1991.

Isozaki, Arata. "Electric Labyrinth: 14th Triennale Di Milano, Milan, Italy 1968." In *GA Architect 6: Arata Isozaki Vol. 1 1959–1978*, edited by Yukio Futagawa, 92–95. Tokyo: A.D.A. EDITA, 1991.

Isozaki, Arata. "Festival Plaza." *The Japan Architect: Reprint Edition Expo '70* 113 (Spring 2019): 53–54.

Isozaki, Arata. "Festival Plaza, Expo '70 Osaka Suita, Osaka 1967–70." In *GA Architect 6: Arata Isozaki Vol. 1 1959–1978*, edited by Yukio Futagawa, 86–91. Tokyo: A.D.A. EDITA, 1991.

Isozaki, Arata. "From Manner to Rhetoric, and Now . . . 1976." In *GA Architect 6: Arata Isozaki Vol. 1 1959–1978*, edited by Yukio Futagawa, 180–184. Tokyo: A.D.A. EDITA, 1991.

Isozaki, Arata. *GA Architect 6: Arata Isozaki Vol. 1 1959–1978*, edited by Yukio Futagawa, 4. Tokyo: A.D.A. EDITA, 1991.

Isozaki, Arata. "Library at Oita." *Architectural Design* 34, no. 12 (December 1964): 612. Accessed January 30, 2023. http://designtheory.fiu.edu/readings/kurokawa_architecture_of_action.pdf.

Isozaki, Arata. "Recalling the Days of Expo Art (?) (2001)." Translated by Machida Gen. *Review of Japanese Culture and Society* XXIII (December 2011): 72–80.

Isozaki, Arata. "Responsive House 1968–69." In *Arata Isozaki: Architecture 1960–1990*, 142–143. New York: Rizzoli International Publications, Inc., 1991.

Isozaki, Arata. "Selected Buildings and Projects: The Festival Plaza, Expo '70." In *Arata Isozaki: Architecture 1960–1990*, 286. New York: Rizzoli International Publications, Inc., 1991.

Isozaki, Arata. "The Theory of Process Planning 1963." In *GA Architect 6: Arata Isozaki Vol. 1 1959–1978*, edited by Yukio Futagawa, 30–31. Tokyo: A.D.A. EDITA, 1991.

Isozaki, Arata. "『空間へ』《お祭り広場》『日本の都市空間』 一九六〇年代における都市論の方法をめぐって." [To Space, Festival Plaza, and Urban Space in Japan: Towards the urban theory of the 1960s] Interview by Naohiko Hino. In 磯崎新インタヴューズ [*Isozaki Arata Interviews*], 40–58. Tokyo: LIXIL出版 [Publications], 2014.

Isozaki, Arata. "ターニングポイント、空間から環境へ." [Turning Point: From Space to Environment] Interview by Naohiko Hino. In 磯崎新インタヴューズ [*Isozaki Arata Interviews*], 102–121. Tokyo: LIXIL出版 [Publications], 2014.

Kenzo Tange Team. "A Plan for Tokyo, 1960." Translated by Charles S. Terry. *Ekistics* 12, no. 69 (1961): 9–19. Accessed October 10, 2020. www.jstor.org/stable/43613534.

McLuhan, Marshall. *Understanding Media: The Extensions of Man*. New York: McGraw Hill, 1964.

Tange, Kenzo. "EXPO '70: The EXPO '70 Master Plan and Master Design." In *Kenzo Tange 1946–1969: Architecture and Urban Design*, edited by Udo Kultermann, 282–299. London: Pall Mall Press, 1970.

Tange, Kenzo. "Function, Structure and Symbol, 1966." In *Kenzo Tange 1946–1969: Architecture and Urban Design*, edited by Udo Kultermann, 240–245. London: Pall Mall Press, 1970.

Tange, Kenzo. "Kenzo Tange 1987 Laureate: Ceremony Acceptance Speech." Speech, Pritzker Architecture Prize Ceremony, Kimbell Art Museum, Fort Worth. May 2, 1987. Accessed October 14, 2020. www.pritzkerprize.com/sites/default/files/inline-files/Kenzo_Tange_Acceptance_Speech_1987.pdf.

Tange, Kenzo. "A Plan for Tokyo, 1960: Toward a Structural Reorganization." In *Kenzo Tange 1946–1969: Architecture and Urban Design*, edited by Udo Kultermann, 114–149. London: Pall Mall Press, 1970.

Tange, Kenzo. "Tokaido-Megalopolis: The Japanese Archipelago in the Future." In *Kenzo Tange 1946–1969: Architecture and Urban Design*, edited by Udo Kultermann, 150–167. London: Pall Mall Press, 1970.

Tange, Kenzo and Noboru Kawazoe. "Some Thoughts about EXPO '70: Dialogue between Kenzo Tange and Noboru Kawazoe." *The Japan Architect: Reprint Edition Expo '70* 113 (Spring 2019): 8–20.

Unknown Author. "World: Toward the Japanese Century." *Time*, March 2, 1970. Accessed February 9, 2023. https://content.time.com/time/magazine/article/0,9171,904215,00.html.

# 4    Richard Rogers and Renzo Piano

## Change as the only constant

The construction of the Center Pompidou right from its inception to completion spans from 1970–77. In order to understand Richard Rogers's narrative regarding the artificially intelligent architecture, this chapter case studies the projects that he conceived and executed since 1961 when he was a master's student in the United States of America. During his stay in the States, he was immensely inspired by the Case Study House Program (1945–62) and the School Construction Systems Development (1961–67) projects. Similarly, projects and aspirations of his partner in the Pompidou project, Renzo Piano, have also been case studied from 1966–77. Consequently, the spatial and phenomenological characteristics that its architects attempted to physicalise in the Pompidou have been approached through their technologically advanced projects that they either conceived or designed during the span of 1961–77.

### Section I: Pre-history of the Center Pompidou, Paris

#### The Case Study House Program: war-born technological advances carried over into the construction techniques, materials and gadgets

The *Case Study House Program* was sponsored and executed by *Arts and Architecture* magazine from 1945–62 with the aim of designing and realising an ideal, inexpensive and efficient post-war house initially in the Southern California, the United States of America. The objective was to present "a practical point of view based on available facts that can lead to a measurement of the average man's living standards in terms of the house he will be able to build when restrictions are lifted" and one of the several considerations for the house was "of duplication and in no sense be an individual 'performance.'"[1] John Entenza – editor of the magazine – invited a number of architects for participation in the Case Study House Program. The criteria of selection were their realistic evaluation of the needs for housing. Participating architects included Alfred Newman Beadle (1927–98), A. Quincy Jones (1913–79), Calvin C. Straub (1920–98), Charles Eames (1907–78), Conrad Buff III (1926–89), Craig Ellwood (1922–92), David Thorne (1924–2017), Donald C. Hensman (1924–2002), Donn Emmons FAIA (1910–97), Don R. Knorr (1922–2003), Edward A. Killingsworth (1917–2004), Eero Saarinen (1910–61), Frederick

DOI: 10.4324/9781003401858-4

E. Emmons (1907–99), John Carden Campbell (1914–96), John Rex (1909–2003), J. R. Davidson (1889–1977), Jules Brady (1908–96), Kemper Nomland Jr. (1919–2009), Kemper Nomland Sr. (1892–1976), Pierre Koenig (1925–2004), Ralph Rapson (1914–2008), Raphael S. Soriano (1904–88), Richard J. Neutra (1892–1970), Rodney Walker (1910–86), Sumner Spaulding (1892–1952), Theodore C. Bernardi (1903–90), Thornton M. Abell (1906–84), Waugh Smith (1917–2010), Whitney R. Smith FAIA (1911–2002), William Wilson Wurster (1895–1973) and Worley K. Wong (1912–85).[2]

New materials and new techniques were to be adopted from the war-born innovations as the magazine announcement stated that "the house . . . will be conceived within the spirit of our time, using as far as is practicable, many war-born techniques and materials best suited to the expression of man's life in the modern world."[3] Announcement of the program elaborately stated the very nature of being contemporary and thus granted the architects a free hand of modifying their designs even during construction. The magazine attempted to seek answers to questions being posed by living problems in Southern California immediately after the war. It stated that in this uncontrollable environment, they intended to immediately begin the study, planning, design and construction of eight sample houses. The magazine announced:

> Eight nationally known architects, chosen not only for their obvious talents, but for their ability to evaluate realistically housing in terms of need, have been commissioned to take a plot of God's green earth and create "good" living conditions for eight American families[4] [emphasis in original].

The architects were given free hand to choose or reject among a variety of products being produced by national manufacturers offering old or new materials feasible for contemporary dwelling units. The meaning of *contemporary* was believed to change every minute, consequently affecting the ideas of architects, as they would have been changed when the time of implementation arrived. In this case also, architects were not to be put to blame but were completely encouraged to go with their decisions, condition being if those were based on satisfactory justifications. The reason behind the selection of eight from a group of almost thirty-one architects was the fact that these eight were "chosen for, among other things, reasonableness, which they have consistently maintained at a very high level."[5]

Architects were responsible to the magazine, who was the client. New materials and techniques were highly encouraged for the construction of this pilot project. These materials and construction techniques were to be selected purely on a merit basis by the architects. Manufacturers of products and appliances assured the magazine their complete cooperation regarding sharing the results of their research on the products that they intended to sell to the public. The magazine made it explicit:

> [n]o attempt will be made to use a material merely because it is new or tricky. On the other hand, neither will there be any hesitation in discarding old materials and techniques if their only value is that they have been generally regarded as "safe"[6] [emphasis in original].

In March 1956, after having been sponsored and constructed a number of these Case Study Houses, Entenza reaffirms the aim of this program in the view of the feedback he received. He confirmed that the reason behind inviting first-rate architects and designers for the thinking and execution of these Case Study Houses is to produce a provocative body of work having a considerable value servicing not only users of these houses and the profession but informed public at large. These houses have served as an explanation and have inculcated clarity in the minds of the public, resulting in purification and replacement of rusted ideas with the emerging and innovative trends in domestic architecture. Not every Case Study House was a perfection nor did it deliver complete satisfaction to its owners, Entenza argued, but these have been suggestive of the two highly significant reforms – introduction of new innovative, industrialised materials and reuse of old ones and presentation of contemporary living patterns. While utilising all the available resources and facilities that were available to the team at the time of construction of these houses, he aimed at making further valid contributions to the contemporary discourse on domestic architecture either for the profession or public at large.[7]

This chapter presents the works of Charles Eames (1907–78), Raphael S. Soriano (1907–88) and Craig Ellwood (1922–92) from the Case Study project, as the work of these architects acted as an inspiration for Richard Rogers as he mentions the work of these architects frequently. The Eames House – called as the *Case Study House for 1949* in the *Arts and Architecture* magazine – was designed by Charles Eames in 1949 (Figure 4.1–4.2). The editor of the magazine – John Entenza – skilfully introduced this house as an amalgamation of intelligent ideas brought together from a number of disciplines. Entenza presented this house with considerable pride for a number of reasons. Considering it as a beautiful, sensible and intelligently conceived project that happily solved a number of interesting problems, he said that "[t]his house represents an attempt to state an idea rather than a fixed architectural pattern, and it is as an attitude toward living that we wish to present it." When this house approaches the final stages, it starts becoming an assemblage of a lot of elements that may exist around, outside or even apart from it. He summarises the crust behind this ephemeralness and said that "we feel that the house must be judged on the basis of its appropriateness to the idea, and that its contributions are things to be derived from it rather than thing existing precisely within it." The project was composed of overlapping and juxtaposed solid, opaque and translucent planes. These planes were responsible for not only the breaking and opening up of greater spaces but for containing, enclosing and releasing of space – a process that ultimately led to an environment most feasible for a modern man. Within the preconceived notions of a traditional house, this project welcomes and generates a feeling of release and invites the user to an extension of one's personal acceptances. With a sense of pleasant surprise and playfulness, this house respects the essential qualities of the materials, skills and methodologies that brought them together. As this house acted as a generator of ideas with its sheer inherited ephemeralness, Entenza stated that it is "a kind of experience that once come upon is very likely to at least rearrange a

*Figure 4.1* The Eames House (1949).

*Source*: John Entenza and Charles Eames, "Case Study House for 1949: Designed by Charles Eames," *Arts and Architecture*, December 1949, 28, accessed March 17, 2023. www.artsandarchitecture.com/ issues/pdf01/1949_12.pdf. Photograph by Jay Connor. Copyright © Travers Family Trust. All rights reserved. Used with permission.

*Figure 4.2* The caption of the photograph reads, "This section of the east elevation is characteristic of the buildings. Of the three stucco panels shown here, one is pure white, one is brilliant blue, and one is black behind white crossed tension rods. The small rectangular panels and the sash are the natural warm grey of the Cemesto board; the two panels above the door are covered with gold leaf. The drapes are a natural coloured rayon and linen fabric."

*Source*: John Entenza and Charles Eames, "Case Study House for 1949: Designed by Charles Eames," *Arts and Architecture*, December 1949, 26, accessed March 17, 2023. www.artsandarchitecture.com/issues/pdf01/1949_12.pdf. Photograph by Jay Connor. Copyright © Travers Family Trust. All rights reserved. Used with permission.

number of the spectator's ideas." The *Arts and Architecture* magazine welcomed any reactions that either the professionals or the greater public held on this pilot project, and the magazine further solidified their commitment to the service to domestic architecture by announcing that they intended to "leave the reader with at least one comforting thought: that in this case the architect will live in what he has done."[8]

Most of the materials and techniques implemented in this Case Study House were frequently used in the building industry but were absolutely new for the residential architecture. The structural system proved to be extremely flexible such that it permitted the most optimum conditions for living and working as Eames stated that "[c]ase study wise, it is interesting to consider how the rigidity of the

*Figure 4.3* Truscon open webbed joists and Ferro-board decking formed the exposed ceiling
throughout the house and the studio except for the bathrooms.

*Source*: John Entenza and Charles Eames, "Case Study House for 1949: Designed by Charles Eames,"
*Arts and Architecture*, December 1949, 34, accessed March 17, 2023. www.artsandarchitecture.com/
issues/pdf01/1949_12.pdf. Photograph by Jay Connor. Copyright © Travers Family Trust. All rights
reserved. Used with permission.

system was responsible for the free use of space and to see how the most matter-
of-fact structure resulted in pattern and texture."[9] Truscon open webbed joists and
Ferro-board decking formed the exposed ceiling for the entire house and studio
unit with the only exception of the bathrooms (Figure 4.3). The steel structure
was further coated with a paint in order to protect it from the corrosive effects
resulting from the nearby sea. In this case also, a paint that is primarily designed
for industrial plants was used. Protection of the surface of the steel structure that
happens to be close to the sea takes priority, and for this case, a covering that was
designed for the industrial plants was used being capable of withstanding attacks
of corrosive fumes. Specifications stated it as a rubber-based #5 coating from the
AC Horn Company. The colour of the paint was a mixture of dark, neutral and
satisfying grey. The inherent qualities of materials used for this house not only

provided structural support but psychological as well. "The texture of the ceiling, the metal joists, the repetition of the standard sash, the change of glazing from transparent to translucent – the surprise of seeing the plane in space by the wire glass in the studio" were the joys provided by the materials and techniques used, Eames explains.[10] The use of colour was strictly structural with structural steel and metal sash painted as dark, warm grey and stucco panels were of white, blue, red, black and earth colours.

The Eames House can said to be artificially intelligent architecture, as it incorporated many of the technological advances that were absolutely new at the time of its construction. Most of these technological appliances were highly self-decision-making artefacts.[11] For example, automatic kitchen appliances manufactured by *Sunbeam* were introduced, including Wafflemaster, Coffeemaster, Mixmaster, Ironmaster, Shavemaster, Toaster, etc. (Figure 4.4). They were publicised on the basis of the word *automatic*. It is interesting to note how the manufacturers emphasised the word *automatic* and portrayed it as an artificially intelligent system in order to sell their product to its best.

Sunbeam Coeffeemaster [sic]
    Women to whom coffee-making poses an impossible problem will be delighted with the Sunbeam Coffeemaster. This appliance guarantees perfect coffee every time – because everything is *automatic*. In Sunbeam Coffeemaster the water is always at the same high heat – *automatically*. The brewing time is always the same – *automatically*. What's more there's absolutely no dilution, whether you make one cup or eight. All these factors are your guarantee of the most scrumptious cup of coffee this side of the pearly gates[12] [emphasis added].

Another advertisement from the same manufacturer advertises their *automatic* toaster:

Sunbeam *Automatic* Toaster
    Pop-up toasters have become more or less common during the last several years. But the new Sunbeam Radiant Control Toaster introduces a completely different principle into the toaster field – Radiant Control. All one does, is drop in the bread. The bread lowers itself *automatically*, which turns on the current. When perfectly toasted, the current turns off *automatically*. Then the toast raises itself silently, without popping or banging. There are no levers to push. This radically different toaster is so simple, even a child can operate it. And no matter what kind of bread is used, moist or dry, thick slices or thin, perfect toast is the result[13] [emphasis added].

These appliances were highly artificially intelligent, such as the Coffeemaster automatically stopped when the coffee was done or it automatically kept it warm, etc. Although it seems a less significant move towards artificial intelligence at present,

*Figure 4.4* Technologically advanced self-decision-making kitchen appliances were used
in the Eames House, including automatic kitchen appliances manufactured by
Sunbeam, for example, Wafflemaster, Coffeemaster, Mixmaster, Ironmaster,
Shavemaster, Toaster, etc.

*Source*: John Entenza and Charles Eames, "Case Study House for 1949: Designed by Charles Eames,"
*Arts and Architecture*, December 1949, 35, accessed March 17, 2023. www.artsandarchitecture.com/
issues/pdf01/1949_12.pdf. John Entenza, "Preview of some products merit specified for the 1950 Case
Study House," *Arts and Architecture*, December 1949, 42, accessed March 17, 2023. www.artsandarchi-
tecture.com/issues/pdf01/1949_12.pdf. Photograph by Jay Connor. Copyright © Travers Family Trust.
All rights reserved. Used with permission.

but back in 1949, this approach proved to be a great leap towards home automation, such as the way the Kelvinator Electric Range promoted itself:

> Kelvinator's "Automatic Cook" Electric Range . . . offers all of the many advantages of electric cooking, toped off by its three-way automatic control-oven, Scotch Kettle, or appliance outlet. This range has finger-tip control of all cooking operations, seven-heat surface units which tilt up for easy cleaning, "upside down" unit for Scotch Kettle or surface use, a two-unit oven which will hold a 25-pound turkey, and good design. All controls are grouped on an easy-to-read, easy-to-reach control panel. Recessed light illuminates the panel and work surface. The range is equipped to cook an entire meal automatically by proper setting of dials[14] [emphasis in original].

Similarly, home music system manufactured by Altec Lansing was introduced that incorporated a speaker, amplifier, AM-FM radio receiver and an approved record changer. With this system, a television was also to be coupled at will. Furthermore, the manufacturers of this system also promoted its durability by publicising that "[t]his system can never become obsolete; it can be modernized unit by unit, in the event that advances in broadcast and recording science are made."[15] This system acted much like today's highly advanced artificially intelligent home maintenance or security systems that include many self-decision-making gadgets and appliances.

The *Case Study House 1950* was designed by Raphael S. Soriano in 1950. The structure exhibited great simplicity and straightforwardness and fundamentally followed the same principles as those of the Eames House by utilising modular steel frame structural system as a whole. 3 1/2 inch steel pipe columns were arranged on a 10 × 20 feet grid. 6 inch wide flange beams were utilised for covering 20 feet intervals with steel roof decking covering the remaining 10 feet spaces between the beams. 4 inch concrete slab was used as a floor. Furthermore, a number of technologically advanced products were short-listed to be used in this project, such as the Kelvinator Electric Range, Incinor Disposal Unit, etc. (Figure 4.5).[16]

The *New Case Study House* was designed by Craig Ellwood in 1953. As have been the case with the Eames House and Case Study House 1950, this project also utilised the steel structural system. 8 feet modular steel structural system was designed with 2 1/2 inch square pipe columns and 6 inch I beams. All of the structural steel frame was painted with red lead oxide paint of terracotta colour. Further exterior materials included glass, masonry, plaster and siding. The covered area was approximately 3,200 square feet with the functional house reduced to further 1,750 square feet. The sizes of the bedrooms and baths were minimised with an entrance of 8 × 12 feet, living area of 16 × 28 feet and a dinning area of 12 × 12 feet. Technologically advanced systems were used for controlling the indoor environment, such as the Payne perimeter forced-air heating system to warm the exterior walls and to control the heat loss through the glass.

**PREVIEW OF SOME PRODUCTS MERIT SPECIFIED FOR THE 1950 CASE STUDY HOUSE**

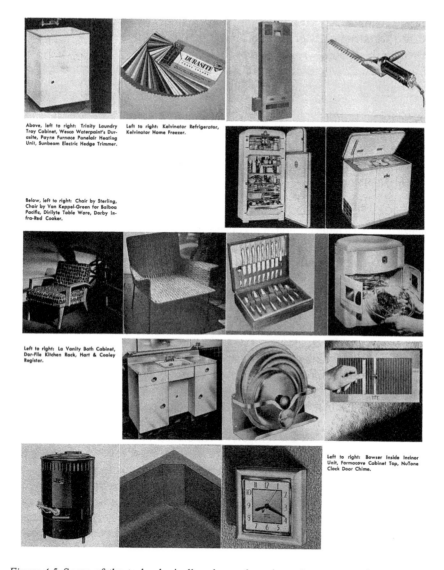

*Figure 4.5* Some of the technologically advanced products that were merit specified by Soriano to be used in the Case Study House 1950.

A Thermodulor furnace control was used for modulating the flame and fan opera-tion. One of the interesting architectural elements was separation of the walls from the continuous planes of the roof and the floor resulting in a floating roof slab and freestanding wall partitions. The proportion of automatic appliances utilised for this project was comparatively less as compared to the previous Case Study Houses. Ellwood merit specified some technologically advanced appli-ances for this house, including the following:

> Automatic Built-in-Gas Cooking Units by Western-Holly Appliance Company, Gas-Fired Automatic Incinor by Bowser Inc., Water Heater by General Water Heater Corporation, Automatic Washer and Automatic Dryer by Bend Home Appliances, Refrigerator by Servel Inc., and Electric Barbecue Spit by Rotor Company (Figure 4.6).[17]

The *Case Study House #17* was also designed by Craig Ellwood in 1956. Entenza devoted a large portion of his magazine's March 1956 issue for the public-ity of this technologically advanced magnificent house. He classified this house as a handsome object. Modular steel frame structure was used as a whole because of the advantages of stability, minimum maintenance and moisture and termite-free nature. All the interior and exterior walls were non-load bearing. The exposed steel beams and columns have been painted black in order to form a contrast with the natural terracotta colour of the masonry panels constructed with 6 inch clay blocks. The floor slab is of Portland Cement concrete construction carrying the advantages of noiseless walking, easy maintenance, low cost and being vermin and termite proof. As have been the case with previous Case Study Houses, this house also fea-tured a number of technological advancements, such as built-in appliances for the kitchen area. "Westinghouse refrigerator, freezer, dishwasher and garbage disposer, Thermador range, twin ovens and warming drawer" were merit specified for the kitchen. The selection of these refrigerator and freezer units was based on the fact that their construction and design features presented a number of advantages, such as vapor, sealed wrap construction that resulted in greater strength and rigidity, bet-ter insulation of Lamlnar Fiberglas, double self-sealing door gaskets, plastic sliding crisper doors, easy adjustable shelving and Thermocycle defrosting. Westinghouse dishwasher was also suggested, as it perfectly matched the cabinet finish by harmo-nising itself with the surroundings, a concept that was completely new at that point in time. This unit featured automatic water heating and sanitising qualities, greater capacity, flexible control for rinsing, easy loading through accommodating rack design and an indicator dial that showed the progress of each cycle.[18] Appliances that were short-listed for this project included built-in ovens, refrigerator-freezer, upright freezer, warming drawer and cooking tops, dryer units, dishwasher, food waste disposer, water heaters and electric barbecue unit.[19] Furthermore, HI-FI equipment was manufactured and supplied by the Kierulff Sound Corporation and included "Conrac Television Set, Concertone Tape Recorder, Mc Intosh Amplifier, James B. Lansing Speaker, Thorens Record Changer, and National Radio Tuner" (Figure 4.7).[20] As is the case with the smart homes of today, this house also featured

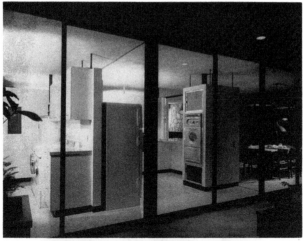

*Figure 4.6* Automatic built-in gas cooking unit by Western-Holly Appliance Company.

*Source*: John Entenza and Craig Ellwood, "The New Case Study House," *Arts and Architecture*, June 1953, 30, 39, accessed March 18, 2023. www.artsandarchitecture.com/issues/pdf01/1953_06.pdf. Photograph by Marvin Rand. Copyright © Travers Family Trust. All rights reserved. Used with permission.

*Figure 4.7* Kierulff Sound Corporation's HI-FI Home Music System advertisement.

a home security kind of a system called as the inter-communication system. It is stated regarding this system:

> Dalmotron Talkmaster electronic inter-communication system is used throughout the house. This system allows the entry and service doors to be answered from several stations within the house. Also children's bedrooms may be monitored in several areas, including the master bedroom, kitchen, living-room, nurse's room and the hobby shop.[21]

Ellwood, in his short essay titled *The Machine and Architecture* that was published in the *Art and Architecture*'s June 1958 issue, explicits the influence of the technological advancements on architecture that was brought by mechanisation and the need of adapting machine products and machine techniques as the essence of our buildings. This belief can easily be experienced in all of the Case Study Houses he designed. He states in this essay that the Barcelona Pavilion, by Ludwig Mies van Der Rohe, a great variety of the houses on the Wisconsin Prairie and Villa Savoye, Poissy, by Le Corbusier have been sources of inspiration in the past. Each of these possessed an intrinsic crystal clarity and precisely and poetically expressed the qualification of a space in the specific point in time and purpose it was intended for. The need of the hour tends to be an architecture that needs no rationalisation. He stressed that we need "[a]n architecture that spiritually transcends the prosaic limitations the machine has seemingly begun to impose. An architecture that gives us esthetic *and economic* pleasures" [emphasis in original]. The trends and demands of this new age are absolutely not achievable through the applications of Navajo Pueblo and hand-tooled Arabesque stone tracery or the hand-formed Ferro concrete, he said. The only way forward was to re-examine the motivations of the machine so that it may yield a "properly qualified and truly meaningful architecture."[22]

The *Case Study House #18* was also designed by Craig Ellwood in 1958. This house, while being treated as a system, was composed of a number of elements that were separated by their representative colours. Ceiling and panels were coloured off-white and steel framework blue. The modular steel structural frame was load bearing, and panels acted as mere partitions, while both were prefabricated. 2 inch square tube columns and $2 \times 5\ 1/2$ inch rectangular tube beams were used as a steel structural system. This system was selected because of its connection simplification and standardisation (Figure 4.8). Steel has been the characteristic of all of the Case Study Houses for the construction of frames, and this project states the basis of selecting it because of its many advantages over wood. Entenza and Ellwood appreciated steel due to "[i]ts relative newness, its latent potential in residential construction, its strength/weight, strength/size ratios, its permanence, [and] its crisp fine line." They further stated that moment-resisting structural connections in steel were simple. While a steel column can easily be fixed to resist rotation, a wood post serving in the same situation would have to be nine to twelve times larger in section because of its nature and connections being expansive and complex. Smaller wood members were insufficient for the design details they were supposed

CASE STUDY HOUSE NO. 18

DESIGNED BY CRAIG ELLWOOD ASSOCIATES

These photographs show the ease of installation of the pre-fabricated wall panels in Case Study House #18. The panels are 9/32" thick "Harborite" plywood, glued and nailed to both faces of 2" (net) Douglas fir framing. "Harborite" is a marine grade Douglas fir plywood, plastic-faced with resin-impregnated overlays to prevent common plywood failures such as grain-raise, checking and delamination. The plastic face also allows a smooth application of paint, free from grain transfer.

All interior and exterior wall panels in the house were erected after pre-fabrication as shown here. Panels to receive wiring and plumbing were built with one open face to allow access. All panels are thermal acoustic insulated with "Celotex" insulating blankets, a highly efficient, fireproof mineral wool.

Also shown here are typical wall plan sections of actual components. One connection method applies to all "in-line" exterior wall conditions. Pre-fab wall panels, "Steelbilt" sliding glass wall units, "Cal-State" louvre sash and fixed glass attach directly to the 2" square structural steel tube or are held in place with a 2" wide, 3/16" thick, continuous steel batt attached to

*(Continued on Page 32)*

1  ACTUAL 1" LONG EXTERIOR WALL SECTION. THIS SECTION SHOWS PRE-FAB INTERIOR WALL PANEL CONDITION AT EXTERIOR WALL. THE 1"x1"x1/8" CONTINUOUS STEEL ANGLES AT INTERIOR PANEL EDGE ALLOW THE PANELS TO BE UNDERSIZED FOR TOLERANCE AND "TRIM" THE JOINTS.

2  EXTERIOR WALL SECTION, CONDITION AT PRE-FAB PANEL AND FIXED GLASS. GLASS AND PANEL ARE HELD IN PLACE WITH THE CONTINUOUS 2" WIDE, 3/16" THICK STEEL BAR.

3  EXTERIOR WALL SECTION, CONDITION AT FIXED GLASS AND "STEELBILT" SLIDING GLASS WALL JAMB. HERE AGAIN THE CONTINUOUS 2" STEEL BAR "FIXES" GLASS AND THE "STEELBILT" UNIT. THE CONTINUOUS WHITE MASTIC BEAD IS WEATHERPROOFING.

4  EXTERIOR WALL SECTION, CONDITION AT "STEELBILT" JAMB AND JALOUSIE SASH. THE JALOUSIE FRAME ATTACHES TO A CONTINUOUS LIGHTWEIGHT FORMED STEEL CHANNEL WHICH IS ATTACHED TO THE 2" SQUARE TUBE. THE JALOUSIE SCREEN FRAME ATTACHES TO THE OUTER FACE OF THIS LIGHTWEIGHT CHANNEL.

5  EXTERIOR WALL SECTION, CONDITION AT CORNER. THIS IS TYPICAL CORNER OF JALOUSIE SASH AND PRE-FAB PANEL. ALL OTHER CORNER CONDITIONS, ANY COMBINATION OF PANELS, SASH, FIXED GLASS AND "STEELBILT" UNITS, ATTACH IN A SIMILAR MANNER.

6  ACTUAL SECTIONS OF 2"x3-1/2" RECTANGULAR STEEL BEAM AND 2" SQUARE STEEL COLUMN. BOTH SECTIONS HAVE 1/4" THICK WALLS. THE BEAM WEIGHS 11.5# A LINEAR FOOT. THE COLUMN 5.6# A LINEAR FOOT.

P. E. PHILBRICK COMPANY, GENERAL CONTRACTORS

*Figure 4.8* Prefabricated wall panels of the Case Study House #18. Details regarding their standardised components, connection simplification and ease of installation.

*Source*: John Entenza and Craig Ellwood, "Case Study House No. 18," *Arts and Architecture*, March 1958, 26, accessed March 18, 2023. www.artsandarchitecture.com/issues/pdf01/1958_03.pdf. Photographs by Marvin Rand. Copyright © Travers Family Trust. All rights reserved. Used with permission.

to perform, and shear walls that were supposed to withstand lateral forces were to be introduced, thus further complicating the system.[23] Appliances included built-in three two-burner cooking tops, two refrigerators and freezers, two ovens, washing machine, dryer, dishwasher and a garbage disposer by Westinghouse Electric Supply Company. Built-in food centre comprising of a mixer, juicer, blender, meat grinder and knife sharpener was installed and manufactured by NuTone. Furthermore, built-in vacuum cleaner by Central Vacuum Corporation was also fitted in. This project was also equipped with a number of built-in appliances and HI-FI systems. These accessories included components by Altec Lansing Corporation and Intercom-Radio System by G and M Equipment Company.[24] Security system somehow with far less advanced technological gadgets replicating today's smart home system was also introduced with the following features:

> The built-in radio-intercom system from G and M Equipment Company provides instant communication between the master control station in the kitchen and the remote speakers in all bedrooms. Additionally, this system provides radio reception at any or all stations, two-way auto-electronic sound "squelch" which interrupts and transmits a baby's cry or unusual noise, a fire warning device and alarm which operates from any and all stations, and the protective, walk-saving entry door substations which allow identification without opening the door[25] [emphasis in original].

### The School Construction Systems Development Project: more variety, greater flexibility, higher quality and lower costs in a decade in which change had been the only constant

The *School Construction Systems Development* (SCSD) project – that originated in order to answer the "demands of a decade [of 1960s] . . . in which change would be the only constant," – was started in 1961 by Educational Facilities Laboratories, Inc. (EFL).[26] EFL was a nonprofit corporation that was established by the Ford Foundation in 1958 in order to facilitate American schools and colleges through research and experimentation for innovation in school architecture and for assistance in educational facilities related problems. SCSD aimed at industrialisation of the building processes, resulting in better quality and reduced construction costs on a condition that the client was able to present his clear-cut needs and a market. In this case, where secondary education was a priority, behavioural process analysis was suggested in order to determine the design of major and minor building components – a process facilitating the aforementioned. As the building systems that were already in use during the time of this proposal limited the Architectural expression and design freedom to a certain extent, with the introduction of these highly industrialised school systems, a greater variety of design tools and freedom for better organisation and control of components was to be provided to the architect responsible for the design of these systems.[27] SCSD schools were to be completed till 1966–67. The industrialisation of school projects by the British due to the critical shortages of building materials, site labor and schools due to World

War II acted as an inspiration for this project as they introduced the *erector sets* of prefabricated components. This component or kit-of-parts approach was utilised by some 20% of the British schools and resulted in reduced construction costs and time and a higher proportion of teaching area per school. An interim report by EFL added in this regard:

> [i]t seemed sensible to suppose that the same principles – standardised but versatile component and a large, guaranteed market for them – would work here [in the USA], and that the English systems might even be improved on. So when the Board of the East Side Union High School District (San Jose, California) agreed to build three proposed high schools with a component system developed to meet its needs, EFL set up SCSD to give the building system approach a full-scale trial.[28]

In order to achieve shortened construction spans and reduced costs, following goals were to be followed:

1. Developing new products designed specifically for schools.
2. Encouraging manufacturers to work together so that their products would constitute a system.
3. Guaranteeing a sufficiently large market for the products.
4. Finding a satisfactory way to bring products, producers, and purchasers together.[29]

SCSD aimed at filling the gap that was being created by the increasingly complex and constantly changing demands of schools and insufficiency of the traditional spaces, practices and products to meet them. With the advent of new and innovative instructional spaces, new teaching methods and equipment were pressing the authorities for up-gradation of existing old-format school arrangements. With the arrival of revised curriculum, innovative teaching methodologies, new organisational and group formulations of students and faculty members demanded considerable modifications in the architectural system as well. Educators were the first ones to feel and recognise this change and arrival of new trends and techniques in the educational scene. With this up-gradation in the educational standards, up-gradation in the architecture also pointed towards enhanced lighting, effective sound control, better air conditioning and durable carpeting. All of this has to cater the fluctuations being posed by the student population that grew and shifted while the budget remained constrained and extremely tight. To summarise, an interim report by EFL requested for "more variety, greater flexibility, higher quality, and lower costs – a combination the schoolhouse can seldom provide."[30] This flexibility and higher quality while keeping in view all the other factors was to be achieved by developing a group of standardised building components in order to " build better schools; to build them more economically; and to build them more rapidly."[31] SCSD project was administered by the Stanford University School Planning Laboratory, University of California and EFL's Western Regional Center under a national advisory committee that comprised of architects and educators. It included Ezra D. Ehrenkrantz as Project Architect, John R. Boice as Project Coordinator, Charles M. Herd as Consulting Engineer, Christopher W. Arnold, Visscher Boyd, Vernon C. Bryant and Bert E. Ray as Architects and Peter Kastl as Architectural Assistant. This project involved thirteen California School Districts, ten architectural firms, twenty-two separate building projects and in gross 2,000,000 square feet of school space that costed an estimated amount of 30,000,000 US dollars at that time.[32]

A mock-up was erected at the Stanford University campus in order to test the qualities of SCSD project. In just a night with a labor of only 59 man-hours – 48 for moving partitions, 6 for ceiling-lighting work, 2 for air-conditioning adjustments and 3 for cleanup – a complete layout of the interior was renovated that was presented as a supreme example of flexibility or the ability to re-arrange space by the project architect, Ezra D. Ehrenkrantz. He expressed his remarks regarding the versatility of the project that, as in all schools, a need of re-arrangement of space arises at least every year in order to accommodate their ever-changing requirements. This project contributes a system of *demountable partitions* designed specifically for schools. He considered this development as a significant leap towards technological advancement for a school system. It was a system in which all of the components, structure, services, partitions and other elements were designed as to be completely movable as per the need and requirements in a short span of time – whether it be a summer or a weekend, during the ongoing term, in-between classes or even overnight. "The result is near-total flexibility in arranging and rearranging interior space, without compromising the quality of the physical environment," he added.[33]

All the participating school districts and their architects placed an overwhelming demand on the flexibility of the overall system. Qualities for any acceptable component system were proposed unanimously and included freedom, economical arrangement and ease of re-arrangement of spaces. Freedom in overall planning was requested, ranging from the large loft building to multi-unit, campus-style school system. Simple and economical arrangement for a variety of spaces and purposes was to be accommodated, as the traditional demand for a thirty-student classroom was no longer the fundamental yardstick for the designing of an instructional space. Furthermore, alterations and re-arrangements were to be given a free hand, as the design criteria assumed that on average, around 10% of the interior partitions would be changed on a yearly basis. Components to be used in the SCSD projects were analysed on their function rather than their nature and involved the clients as active participants in the decisive processes. The education program apart from pointing towards the requirement of flexibility also stated need of the components of structural, ceiling-lighting, air-conditioning systems and movable and operable partitions.[34] These components along with lockers, casework and fixed lab equipment accounted for almost 58% of the total cost of a typical California secondary school.

In order to maintain the interior flexibility at minimum cost, clear spans of 30 to 110 feet with an average of 60 feet were achieved through orthotropic structural design. The structure was designed by Architect Robertson Ward from Inland in collaboration with The Engineers Collaborative. This structural system that was commonly used for bridge construction was put to use for the first time in a school building. This roof structural system thus permitted the flow of roof-mounted mechanical equipment via the space available between the roof and the ceiling. The ceiling-lighting system comprising of wall-to-wall lighting, ceiling and acoustical members were also designed to accommodate utmost "ability to rearrange lighting-ceiling components within the structural module." The lighting-ceiling system requirements were quite stringent, as a high seventy candles illumination level was to be achieved in combination with low fixture brightness in order to minimize the glare. As a result, half the ceiling was supposed to be a light source as per this requirement. The lighting and ceiling components had to be equally effective during the changes in the room sizes. They had to be flexible and to re-adjust themselves within the structural module. In addition, this system had to incorporate all those functions that were leftovers from the structural or mechanical systems.[35]

The ceiling-lighting system was also designed by Robertson Ward and The Engineers Collaborative for Inland. Being the most versatile component, this system presented the features of sound absorption and attenuation, fire protection for the structure, air-distribution devices for the mechanical system and lateral support for demountable partitions, in addition to the lighting and finished ceiling. This system was made-up of a 5 × 5 feet metal grid and filled with a flat ceiling panel or a lighting coffer that was suspended from the structure. Semi-indirect, direct and luminous ceiling lighting was incorporated. The air conditioning – heating, cooling and ventilation system – was designed by Lennox Industries for serving a flexibility for a space of 450 square feet or more regardless of the shape or arrangement. 9 inch flexible fiberglass ducts and movable diffusers were designed for carrying air. The airconditioning unit with dimensions of 8 × 21 × 4 feet on the roof of the mock-up constructed at Stanford University Campus was placed through a helicopter instead of a traditional crane. Three types of partitions were specified for achieving the required flexibility – fixed, demountable and operable. The movable and operable partitions were designed by E. F. Hauserman Company. 60% of the partitions were movable, and all the panel's faces were independently changeable. Thirty-five different colour variations and flexibility for unforeseen conditions were the prime considerations. 3 inch thick partitions were used, comprising of steel studs clipped on both sides with gypsum panels sandwiched between prefinished steel sheets.

On the basis of these components, the SCSD project was advertised specifically as a *system* instead of a traditional school building such that it was based on the principles of a machine, as an interim presentation stated:

[s]pecifications call for a high degree of integration of the basic subsistence. The manufacturers bidding in each category were required to recognise the limitations of the others. For example, the structural system might also perform as the light reflector and the mechanical air duct system. The desired degree of integration approaches that necessary to build a modern jet airliner in which all components must fit in a restricted space and function compatibly.[36]

The interim report also explains this fact:

the most important contribution to the quality of the schools which will use the new components is the fact that SCSD is a system. The flexibility built into movable partitions will not be undercut by the air conditioning or sabotaged by the structure. Manufacturers were forced by the nature of the project to work together in teams to integrate their products for the benefit of the client.[37]

## Section II: Rogers, Piano and the Center Pompidou, Paris

### *Richard Rogers: kit-of-parts systems utilising monocoque and do-it-yourself construction techniques*

*Reliance Controls Electronics Factory*, Swindon, Wiltshire (1967), was designed by Richard Rogers, Susan Rogers, Norman Foster, Wendy Foster, Frank Peacock and Mark Sutcliffe, all being members of a team called *Team 4* with Anthony Hunt acting as their structural engineer. Reliance Controls was a perfect example of a flexible space incorporating the functions of a factory, an office building and a research station, acting as a business park. The client, Sir Peter Parker, presented strict cost guidelines and requested that construction should be finished within ten months that the architects strictly followed and even finished the work earlier and on budget of around £3.50 per square feet. Comprising of lightweight, standardised components, this kit-of-parts structure was inspired by architectural experience that Rogers gained while visiting the West Coast during his studies in the United States of America, the Case Study Houses and the School Construction Systems Development (SCSD) projects. In alignment with Roger's political views of democracy and anti-hierarchy, the Reliance Controls project exhibited both social and architectural radicalism by forcing both managers and workers to co-exist in one uniform space. The structure consisted of a major component that is of an I-section steel beam that was used both in place of the columns and also acted as a continuous beam in order to form one large roof structure. Roof and wall cladding was of 12 feet high panels of corrugated steel, plastic coated and insulated. Steel cross bracing was designed at all the perimeter bays in order to protect the roof and, particularly, the structure against strong winds. Hunt mentions that only two elevations have this cross bracing that was functionally necessary while the rest of it is fake. Internal partitions were of aluminum, glass and, in some cases, of block-work. These movable partitions allowed the interchangeability of spaces into production, research or managerial or into any desired functions. Open courts were designed to allow light to penetrate into the structure. All the services were confined in a centralised duct with secondary distribution in the floor plate for the functions of heating, electricity, gas and telephones. The double-skin perimeter walls also incorporated the ducting. The troughs of the roof deck incorporated lighting and ventilation facilities. Flexibility and extendibility were the most important considerations. Although the structure was extended during its lifetime, in 1991, due to the sharp rise in the land prices of the area, the whole complex was demolished. Rogers also refused to stand for the preservation of this project as a monument, as he believed that it has served its purpose by functioning flexibly for a quarter of a century, and its preservation would negate the philosophy on which it was designed.

*Rogers House*, Wimbledon, London (1968–69), was designed by Rogers and his then-wife, Susan Rogers, along with Pierre Botschi, John Doggart, Ingrid Morris, Richard Russell and John Young for his parents on a garden site located opposite to Wimbledon Common in Southwest London. Anthony Hunt acted as the structural engineer. Rogers House is a direct implementation of the ideas and inspirations that Rogers developed and carried over from the Reliance Controls Electronics Factory and Californian Case Study Houses projects, specifically those from Charles and Ray Eames, Raphael S. Soriano and Craig Ellwood. The brief called for a retirement, easy-to-manage home as a replacement to a conventional suburban villa in which Rogers's parents lived since the early 1950s'. Flexibility of space was the most important consideration presented by the clients to Rogers as his father, Dr. Rogers, wanted to pursue his medical practice and was interested in having a consulting room. Furthermore, the needs of the expanding family and their frequent visits were also to be accommodated. Construction, maintenance and running costs were to be highly economical, as they were going to be managed by Rogers's, who were in their 60s'. Rogers answered this brief with the help of an industrialised production – a house that was to be assembled on-site instead of being built. A steel frame of welded rigid portals was introduced. Five of these portals were proposed for the house and three for the studio or lodge located across a paved courtyard. 2 inch thick Alcoa plastic-coated aluminum panels were used as walls that were insulated and jointed with a neoprene zip jointing system. Custom-made sliding units were used for glazing east and west elevations. Reinforced wood wool slabs were used for roof with a suspended plaster ceiling that incorporated a radiant heating system. Except for bathroom walls and the low wall for the kitchen, all the internal partitions were movable. The bathrooms were enclosed by glazed, neoprene-zipped and solar-reflecting roofs. All of the components used were of standardised dimensions, except the custom-made windows and plaster ceiling. Rogers explains that the idea behind this standardisation was to make it extremely easy for the client to replace any component that needs repairing without the help of an expert. The presence of strong and vibrant colours for the steel frame and internal elements was the result of Rogers's and those of his mother's tastes.

Rogers explains that the Wimbledon House acted as a precursor and inspiration for the Pompidou Center, Paris. This house was designed for his parents most probably in 1967, and it has been through a variety of clients and uses up till now. At present, this house is being utilised by Harvard University for housing its visiting scholars and graduate students in London. He frequently stated Raphael Soriano, Craig Ellwood, Jean Prouvé and Charles and Ray Eames as his inspiration for the design of this house. This project comprises of a prefabricated system, in short, a processed construction. The construction was intended to be as fast as possible and so it was supposed to be all built up in a factory and only assembled on-site in order to avoid as many on-site construction problems as possible. The idea behind these industrialised standard components was to make this prefabricated product available for sale on a local shop so that anyone could purchase it and assemble on their lot without any technical expertise being called for. The plan of the house was simple – a rectangular plan was divided into two parts through a courtyard in the middle and the house on the North. The other side contained the lodge. A simple steel frame was used, depicting the shape of an upside-down alphabet *C*, and these frames were placed in a line being in as many in number as would have been required. This enabled the house to be as long as desired with open endings on both ends of this long tube. Rogers states that he particularly bought bus doors and windows and incorporated these on the sides, and on the tube ends, just glass was placed in order to maintain the visual continuity from within the house to the gardens. He negates the similarity of this project with any of his previous architectural endeavors. If this project would have received the attention it deserved, it could have solved the problems of the British housing through standardisation of the components, but it was not able to do so, Rogers argues, "but it did certainly lead to most of the work which I still do some fifty years later and more." Furthermore, while calling this house as an inspiration towards the Center Pompidou, Paris, he said:

in a sense [Wimbledon House] is a prototype also towards the Pompidou Center. Now the Renzo Piano had obliged [?? – 1:48/2:26] his technological knowledge which was absolutely brilliant so if you put the Wimbledon House and you put Renzo's work; you sort of get the Pompidou Center. Now it's a much bigger thing, it has escalated across the facade, the actual open spaces and the floors are the size of two football fields, you can't say that about Wimbledon and so on but the concepts were there and the bright colors were there.[38]

The intention, he mentions, behind both the Wimbledon and Pompidou projects was to produce somewhere that could be fun, enjoyable, in which everyone could be invited and can joyfully participate. Rogers House was a total negation of the traditional concept of a brick house with rectangular windows cut into it, he said.

*Zip-Up Enclosures No 1 and No 2* (1968 and 1971) – the prototype housing units were designed by Richard Rogers, Susan Rogers, Sally Appleby, John Doggart, Marco Goldschmied and John Young. The structural engineer for the project was Anthony Hunt. The Rogers were of the view that housing must also be conceived in a mass-production manner. Houses must be treated as portable, expandable resources instead of as traditional fixed masses. The Zip-Up Enclosures No 1 project utilised monocoque construction technique adopted from the manufacturing of cars and aeroplanes, etc., in which the skin of the vehicle also acts as its structural support, as is the case with the eggshells. Due to this monocoque structure, the interior became free from any structural supports and thus provided maximum flexibility. All of the internal partitions were adjustable in daytime, and bathrooms were designed to be repositionable at will. Also, the house was lifted on a series of steel jacks that acted as its foundations and resulted in enhancing its portableness. Insulated aluminum-skinned sandwich panels similar to the Rogers House, Wimbledon were used but enhanced with high-performance cellular polyvinyl chloride core that was also adopted from the aircraft industry. This technique resulted in a load-bearing panel that was capable of spanning up to 10 meters. With no segregation between the wall, floor or roof, these elements acted as system components and formed a one uniform ring which can be jointed as much as required to form infinite length of the house. The house was conceived as a low-cost, low-maintenance and high-performance environmental control system. As have been the case with his Wimbledon project, Rogers also presented this house as a do-it-yourself (DIY) approach such that either the assembling or disassembling of the house required the minimum most external assistance, and the household was able to perform these tasks as and when desired. He wanted this house or its components to be available at a local home store from where the household members could buy as many units or its parts as and when needed. The Zip-Up Enclosures No 2 utilised the same design and technique to a 2 storey house that was supposed to be placed in a tight urban site, and its structure was also enhanced and reinforced with a light steel frame for structural stability.

Although the Zip-Up Enclosures No 1 and No 2 projects were not built, their ideas were applied to another project called *Extension to Design Research Unit, London* (1969–71). An interesting fact regarding the team of this project is that Renzo Piano also collaborated with Richard and Susan Rogers. The team also included Sally Appleby, Pierre Botschi, John Doggart, Marco Goldschmied, Andrew Holmes, Jan Kaplicky and John Young. Also, Anthony Hunt served as the structural engineer. The Design Research Unit company moved to the new premises of an industrial building in Aybrook Street in London in 1969 and commissioned the Rogers first for the conversion and then in 1971 for a rooftop extension. The Zip-Up system was applied, as it was lightweight and could be built on the top of the same existing building, permitted fast-track construction and provided uninterrupted span, thus maximising the floor space flexibility. In order to satisfy the local planning commission, the sides of the extension were proposed as sloping so to render it as a roof space instead of an additional floor. Glass Reinforced Plastic was proposed first but then it was replaced with the aluminum panels. These panels were coated with bright-yellow paint, were 3 meters wide and carried lightweight arched steel portals. Aluminum-framed windows were fixed into these aluminum panels. Rogers also designed an advanced furniture system for the entire office.

*Association for Rural Aid in Medicine (ARAM) Module* (1971) was proposed by Richard Rogers, Susan Rogers and Renzo Piano along with Marco Goldschmied, Peter Ullathorne and John Young with Anthony Hunt as the structural engineer. The client was ARAM Inc., USA. Piano and Rogers were approached by an American doctor, Lalla Iveson, requesting a design for a hospital project for developing countries. The hospital was to be a demountable, portable, extendable and highly adaptable and flexible system that can be carried over to places as and when needed during famine, war, epidemics, natural disasters, etc. The imagery of the space and UK's then-emerging North Sea oil industry, for example, structures planted in the middle of the oceans depicting cranes, etc., are said to be the inspirations behind the designs for ARAM Module and the Pompidou Center. Piano and Rogers proposed a freestanding structure with hanging services. The hospital module comprised of a hard core that consisted of the technical equipment and services for the diagnosis and treatment of patients. A highly flexible space of 2,500 square meters for almost 200 beds was proposed that could be adjusted as needed. The entire structure was made-up of a crane for assembling small, standardised parts that can be transported anywhere and assembled by non-specialists and operable with little or no prior technical knowledge. Latticed steel columns along with lightweight trusses supported the space decks that were in turn suspended from high tensile steel cables. Space was designed above and below this floor deck for mounting of the services. In case of power shortages, a standby generating equipment was also provisioned within the module. Although the project was a perfect example of technologically advanced mobile architectural unit, it was never realised. Rogers implemented the ideas he proposed for this mobile module in his later projects, such as the Fleetguard Factory, Quimper (1979) and the Inmos Microprocessor Factory, Newport, Wales (1982).

The *Universal Oil Products Factory*, Tadworth, Surrey (1973–74), was designed by a team of Richard Rogers, Renzo Piano, Sally Appleby, Rita Bormioli, Peter Flack, Marco Goldschmied, Eric Holt, Peter Ullathorne, Niki van Oosten, Neil Winder and John Young. As have been the case with all the previous projects, the structural engineer was Anthony Hunt. This project seems to be a mixture of ideas from the Rogers House (1968–69) and Zip-Up Enclosures No 1 and No 2 (1968 and 1971) projects. This project was initially proposed in 1969 when Richard and Susan Rogers were working on the Zip-Up principles but was finally constructed by Rogers and Piano in 1973–74. An extremely flexible and high-performance structure was requested by the client with a potential for continuous growth and change. Internal partitions erected between the interchangeable offices, laboratories and manufacturing areas were of full-height demountable glazed walls. Only the stores area was enclosed in a 2 hour fire wall. The basic structure consisted of a steel frame covered with 6 inch thick large prefabricated full-height glass-reinforced cement sandwich wall panels that were sealed with neoprene. Being highly economical, extremely flexible in terms of space and highly colourful, this building extended Rogers's ideas that he applied on much smaller scales in Wimbledon and Zip-Up projects to a much larger industrial vision.

The *PA Technology Laboratory*, Melbourn, Cambridgeshire (1975–85), was designed in three phases. Phase 1 comprised of a team of Richard Rogers, Renzo Piano, Sally Appleby, Michael Burckhardt, Peter Flack, Marco Goldschmied, Don Gray, Alphons Oberhofer, Richard Soundy, David Thom, Peter Ullathorne, Neil Winder and John Young. Phase 2 included Richard Rogers, Pierre Botschi, Mike Davies, Sally Eaton, Marco Goldschmied, John McAslan and John Young. Phase 3 consisted of Richard Rogers, Pierre Botschi, Mike Davies, Marco Goldschmied, Nathalie Moore, Brendan O'Neill, Mark Roche and John Young. The structural engineers for this project were Felix J. Samuely and partners. This project seems to be a direct implementation of the principles of the Case Study Houses and SCSD projects that Rogers visited while he was a student in the USA. This project is also the implementation of repetitive bay construction and sophisticated kit-of-parts approach – truly representative of Roger's architectural design. The client – PA organisation, a significant international research, management and development consultancy – requested a highly-serviced laboratories building complimented with support areas and offices. First phase consisted of approximately 2,500 square meters of space. The structure that was submerged in the landscape consists of a steel frame infilled with stressed skin plywood roof panels supported on precast cruciform columns. A solid, insulated concrete slab acts as the foundational support. The cladding consists of glass and insulated sandwich panels. As have been the case with almost all of the Rogers projects, the interior partitions of this project are also highly flexible and can be positioned anywhere as and when required. Offices are aligned along the perimeter of the design, while laboratories are concentrated in the centre. As all of the services are suspended below the main slab at undercroft level along with the parking, maintenance, upgrading and even replacements are extremely convenient. Phase 1 was completed in 1975, while Phases 2 and 3 were completed in 1982 and 1984 respectively.

### Renzo Piano: experimentations with flexibility, transparency and lightness of a space

Piano had some architectural projects to his name before he participated with Rogers and others in the Pompidou competition in 1971. After his graduation, he worked in the offices of Louis Kahn (1901–74) in Philadelphia and the Polish engineer Zygmunt Stanislaw Makowski (1922–2005) in London. Makowski has been a prominent figure in the development of space frames such as the 747 Hangar at Heathrow Airport, London. Piano also expresses his admiration for engineers such as Pier Luigi Nervi (1891–1979), Jean Prouvé (1901–84) and Buckminster Fuller (1895–1983). Impressed with the technological optimism of the 1960s', he also cites Peter Cook and Cedric Price from Archigram as sources of inspiration. Piano states that he was only 7 years old when the era of post-war reconstruction began. He believes that in the name of progress and modernity, a lot of unreasonable things were said and implemented. He says:

> But for my generation, the word "progress" really meant something. Every year that went by took us further from the horror of war and our life seemed to improve day by day. Growing up in that period meant having an obstinate belief in the future[39] [emphasis in original].

He also admired Peter Rice (1935–92), who worked on the Sydney Opera House and with whom he worked on the Pompidou project. His early works concentrated on experimentation with new and nontraditional materials and construction methods exploring the flexibility, transparency and lightness of a space. This research, such as on polyester and its derived fiberglass, yielded in experimentation with the qualities of lightness, strength, flexibility, ease of fabrication and assembly. Furthermore, his workshop states regarding his initial endeavor as of focusing on the concept of an *open plan* space. This concept presented a free space, a space that existed without any kind of partition walls. It was to be modulated to suit a great variety of ever-changing needs and concerns. This concept of an open plan extraordinarily equipped Piano with a range of possibilities. For example, he applied this concept of free space in his light and modular structures, such as the Italian Industry Pavilion for the Japan World Exposition Osaka 1970, in the office spaces he designed, such as for B&B Italia, Novedrate (1971), and in residential projects, for example, the experimental free-plan houses he designed in Garrone and Cusago (Figure 4.9). All of this experimentation with the free, open plan space was eventually continued to the Center Pompidou, Paris, in which the equipment rooms and public services were all fitted on the exteriors and the interior was kept totally modular. Another of his project that was directly linked to this discussion has been the Sulphur Extraction Plant in Pomezia that consisted of a lightweight modular structure capable of walking around the excavation site.[40]

Piano's early projects comprising majorly of technical and theoretical experimentation included *Prestressed Steel and Reinforced-Polyester Structure*, Genoa (1966), *Mobile Structure for Sulphur Extraction*, Pomezia, Rome (1966), *Shell Structural System for the 14th Milan Triennale*, Milan (1967), *Italian Industry Pavilion at the Japan World Exposition Osaka 1970*, Osaka (1969), and *Free-Plan Houses*, Cusago, Milan, completed in collaboration with Rogers, (1970–74). This approach of considering architecture as a whole, unified process from conception to construction and even till its destruction has been with Piano all of his professional career. He stated in his acceptance speech for the Pritzker Prize 1998 that architects have to live on the frontier, and most often, they have to cross it in order to observe what is on the other side. They also use telescopes in order to read what they do not find in the sacred manuscripts. He stated:

> Brunelleschi did not just design buildings, but also the machines to build them. Antonio Manetti recounts how he studied the mechanism of the clock in order to apply it to a system of large counterweights: this was how the structure of the cupola was raised. This is a lovely example of how architecture is also research.

He also said that these classics to whom we look up to as reference materials or things of the past were in fact great, cutting-edge innovators of their time. They only found their paths and directions by experimentation and taking extreme risks.[41] Lightness tends to be a significant approach for architecture, states Piano. Lightness is not particularly referenced as the physical mass of objects only but as a phenomenological concept as well. He explains that at the time of his early architectural projects, it tended to be a game that manifested itself as in the shapeless

*Figure 4.9* Open plans or free space achieved with the light and modular structures in the Italian Industry Pavilion for the Japan World Exposition Osaka (1970) and the office spaces for B&B Italia, Novedrate (1971).

spaces and weightless structures. Gradually, it became his signature as an architect. "In my architecture, I try to use immaterial elements like transparency, lightness, the vibration of the light. I believe that they are as much a part of the composition as the shapes and volumes" says Piano.[42]

Piano explains that Center Pompidou was intended to be a *funny machine*, and *curiosity* was the element he along with Rogers attempted to incorporate into it. In an interview, he proclaimed that a building must be executed intelligently, but it must also sing and tell a story to its observers. In his Center Pompidou project, he states that he and his partner for this project, Richard Rogers, were both young at the time of this project, as he was 33 and Rogers was 36 and carried with themselves the inherent qualities of provocation and impoliteness. Referring to himself and his partner as *bad boys*, he says that their idea of transferring all the internal circulation to the facades was absolutely perfect, as it added a new dimension to the project. Their approach was to eliminate that feeling of being frightened or threatened by a great or cultural institution – a characteristic that these kinds of institutions inherent with themselves. Without understanding what the meaning of the word *culture* has been or understanding it, he says that they tried to replace that intimidating feeling with that of curiosity. He states and reaffirms that even the Gothic cathedrals were like these spaceships landing in between our cities at their time of construction [emphasis in original]:

> Curiosity's the first sparkle of a cultural attitude. So the idea to make that funny machine or that kind of – people was talking about refinery. But for us, "factory," "refinery" were a great compliment. . . . It is a kind of spaceship.

Without thinking of this approach as misleading or having something wrong with it, he thinks of architecture as a continuous process of balances. In cases, architecture acts as an addition, and in other stances, it is absolutely not just adding something. With this approach of cleaning and clearing a very big space and landing a spaceship in it was similar to the creation of a sense of community. This sense of belonging that he claims to achieve was through the introduction of a piazza that covers half the site of the Center Pompidou, and it was probably the first piazza in Paris that was particularly designed for the public after a long period of time, he states.

Recalling President Georges Pompidou, he states:

> [President] . . . said to us, "You have to make a building that will last five centuries," you know? And we watched each other, and we said, "My God, five centuries," for culture? We didn't know what culture was at that time and we thought, "Whatever culture will be in five centuries?"

As an answer to this question of the President, what he and his partner designed was a building comprising of five floors that acted as script-boards and were completely flexible. Connections were developed among these floors as of crossings

and going up and down, and this notion was to be continued forever. While referring to the opening of the Center Pompidou, he recalls:

> [t]he funny thing that's true, that when on the 31st of January, '77, we opened
> the building, half of the people there – big politicians, kings, princes, half of
> them understood only at that moment that the building was finished like that.
> They thought that was the scaffolding of the building, something – finally,
> "Ah, that's finished like that?" "Yes. Yes." [laughs].

And the very reason he believes that they were able to achieve this kind of
structure was the fact that nobody was able to perceive exactly what these architects were doing or intended. For this very reason, the Pompidou became a turning
point in the history of museum designing, and it was not because this centre revised
and modified the design of such function but because circumstances were about to
change at that very point in time regarding the museum design, Piano states. "That
was the turning moment when museum became more and more popular," he mentions.[43] On another account, Piano explains this element of *curiosity* that he portrayed in the Pompidou as "[a]rchitecture is thus the mirror of life. This is why the
first thing I see in it is curiosity, social tension, the desire for adventure. These are
things that have always kept me outside the temple."[44] He skilfully summarises the
design approach he took while designing the Pompidou in his Pritzker Prize 1998
Acceptance Speech by stating that he belongs to that generation of people who
maintained an experimental approach throughout their life and have been exploring different fields and transdisciplinarities, reshuffling cards, making mistakes and
taking risks. He explored a number of different cultural fields, such as theater,
painting, cinema, literature and music, without even giving consideration to what
the word *culture* was about. He states:

> Culture is a fragile term which can disappear like a will-o'-the-wisp just
> when you call it up. This all makes you grow up instinctively optimistic and
> makes you believe in the future. It is inevitable. But at the same time, you
> love your past (as an Italian, or, rather, European, you have no choice). And
> so you live in a limbo between gratitude towards the past and a great passion
> for experimentation, for exploration of the future.[45]

### The Center Pompidou, Paris: an information-disseminating machine

In 1969, President Georges Jean Raymond Pompidou presents the idea of the creation of a polyvalent cultural centre and a public reading room, and on his orders, the
French State purchases the Plateau Beaubourg area from the City of Paris. Because
of its location, this project was initially known as the Center Beaubourg, and only
after the death of President Pompidou in 1974 was it renamed (Figure 4.10). In
1970, an international competition was announced for the conception of this centre. The members of the jury included Architects Émile Aillaud (1902–88), Jean
Prouvé (1901–84), Philip Johnson (1906–2005), Oscar Niemeyer (1907–2012),

*Figure 4.10* The Center Pompidou, Paris: An information-disseminating machine acknowledged as a convergence of the plastic arts, architecture, music, cinema, industrial creation, etc.

*Source*: The Center Pompidou, Paris: Northwest and Southwest facades, August 2019, photograph. Courtesy of the author.

Jørn Utzon (1918–2008) and people from other walks of life, including Sir Frank Francis (1901–88) (an academic librarian and curator), Michel Laclotte (1929–2021) (an art historian and museum director), Gaëtan Picon (1915–76) (an author, art and literature critic and historian) and Willem Sandberg (1897–1984) (a typographer and museum curator).[46] The program of the competition not only summarises the reason behind the conception of this centre but also classifies it as a mixture of different forms of art or to say in other words, merely as an information-dissemination machine. The program of the competition stated that the President of the Republic of France announced on December 11, 1969, to build a centre dedicated specifically to the contemporary arts and design incorporating a grand public library covering all aspects of knowledge right in the heart of Paris, near to Les Halles on the plateau Beaubourg. This announcement came at the very point in time when the traditional notion of art and culture was being questioned in France. The aim was not to regenerate and depict the past no matter how grand or prestigious it might had seemed and neither to project future but only to reassure through the richness of the past and all the contradictions that the future may hold that "creation in all of its sensitive forms has rendered itself the most immediate and significantly all encompassing need of our epoch." Culture was to be acknowledged as a convergence of the plastic arts, architecture, music, cinema, industrial creation, and any other forms of art as well. In short, this centre was to be established for art as a whole. This centre was supposed to be an eye-opening event to the public so that they may interpret and analyse the current situation and to express it as physicalised in their creation, autonomy and hierarchy of expressions of art. They must also be able to evaluate the fictitiousness being represented in the productions of art in the society and to better express the freedom and free will these art physicalisations hold in themselves. This centre was intended to be an architectural and urban ensemble which was to represent the time and economy in which it was constructed.[47]

The program requested a grand library, a museum, space for contemporary activities, such as exhibitions, documentation, research, etc., space for the Center for Industrial Creation (Centre de création industrielle), multi-purpose spaces for theater, music, cinema, conferences, seminars, etc., and space for contemporary musical research. The program particularly stated that all of these activities must not be considered in isolation but as a unified whole. Through this statement, the program automatically rendered all of these activities as a form of information, and only the public was responsible for extracting the meaning out of it. The program stated:

> [a]ll of these activities are meaningful only to the extent as they contribute to a common spirit, allowing a mixing of ideas and men. None is sufficient, but all are necessary. It is up to the public to reveal their unity[48] [author's translation].

The program requested a centre for audiences from all nationalities, all origins and all ages, without any discrimination – a hallmark of information. It was intended to be a global centre representing contemporary civilisation. Furthermore, this information was to be the most significant, useful or entertaining and was not considered as static but was to be updated continuously in order to attract the audience. Information was supposed to be as exciting as possible in order to attract audiences for the dedicated purposes as this passage states regarding the selection of books for the library that "[t]here will be a 'pocket sized' collection and a frequently updated library made up of books chosen from among the most significant, the most useful or the most entertaining in all fields"[49] [emphasis in original; author's translation]. The program stated in this regard that the centre was conceived from an equally original perspective with the aim of constantly updating news, artistic creation in its most diverse manifestations, topicality of industrial creation and the memories that were presented as ideas and forms through the library and the museum.[50]

This global vision of the Pompidou was to be further extended beyond the geographical boundaries of France through the dissemination of information, as the program elaborated:

[t]his Center should therefore not be a closed world: its action will necessarily extend beyond the limits of the building, crossing the district, extending in France and abroad, through circulating exhibitions, television programs, publications . . . In addition, the possibility of remotely consulting files stored in the Library's computer will be a means of dissemination and a service, the effects of which will be greatly appreciated[51] [author's translation].

An information network was also envisaged operating and originating from the Center Pompidou. Its focal point was to be the library, but in general, all of the disciplines were to be covered within its scope. The program stated that the library will "provide general information broadly covering all of the fields and will create an information network with specialised documentation bodies through the exchange of services."[52] In addition, a computer system was also suggested in the program the purpose of which was to process and disseminate general information, as the program suggests that an IBM 360/50 or Iris 50 type computer was to be used in this centre for processing of information. This information was to be from all the libraries and documentation centres not only in Paris but also all over France and furthermore extended internationally. It included all the catalogs, management, documentary research, etc. For the computer technologies of the time, a computer room was proposed containing perforation room, storage rooms for disks, magnetic tapes and offices for programmers covering a space of almost 500 square meters in total.[53]

Another significant criterion that was outlined in the program for the Center was of *flexibility*. In this regard, the program mentioned that an essential and original characteristic of the Center Pompidou was to be transdisciplinarity and exchangeability of spaces. Whether the space was of a library, Museum of Modern and Contemporary Art, National Center for Contemporary Art or the Center for Industrial Creation, the areas were kept to be interchanging. Unless and until the collections were periodically renewed, extensions were not deemed necessary. In order to accommodate these spatial requirements, the element of flexibility was assigned supreme significance. It was stated:

> [i]n a living and complex organism where it will be necessary to take the greatest account of changing needs, all of the sectors whether considered as a whole or in the individualistic sense will be articulated in such a way that these can be utilisable at each and every level, such that the flexibility and adaptation are deemed extremely essential[54] [author's translation].

The program of the Center considered the rooms, galleries, etc., not in their strictest interpretations, but these terms only represented the categorisations of spaces that were reserved for certain functions. Consequently, this flexibility of spaces was intended to be a means of communication between them, as the program elaborated that an architect was responsible for designing of the 4,000 square meters of interior surfaces that were intended to be a unified whole and can be fragmented on demand. This fragmentation was to be achieved through removable partitions and consequently granting the space with utmost flexibility. The temporary exhibition area was to be designed in such a way so as to allow its users to communicate and interact with museums and multi-purpose rooms. A pleasant atmosphere was intended, where the public can relax, and in order to achieve this, multi-rest areas were proposed being open to the outside, thus enabling communication with the gardens.[55]

From the 681 entries, Project No. 493 was declared as a winner by the jury and was designed by Richard Rogers, Renzo Piano, Gianfranco Franchini and John Young, while Ove Arup and partners acted as the structural engineers. The team operated simultaneously from Milan, Italy, where Piano was based and London, UK, where Rogers was practicing. While elaborating the architectural concept with reference to the guiding principles of the Center, the team emphasised on the dissemination of information through advanced technological means by stating that "[t]he basic idea is of an information centre which presents information on the outside, as well as on the inside, of the building, relays it and is linked up to other centres throughout the world."[56] A report, *Analyse Du Projet Lauréat*, translated in English as *Analysis of the Winning Project*, further elaborated that the winning team presented the Pompidou as a *live centre of information* spanning across not only Paris, France, but also internationally. For locals, it acted as a pleasant meeting space. This report further added that "[t]his centre of constantly changing information is a cross between an information orientated, computerised Times Square and the British Museum, with the stress on two-way participation between people and activities/exhibits." The Plateau Beaubourg was to act as an information centre that was supposed to be linked up through information-dissemination and collection centres throughout France and internationally. Some of the examples quoted in this regard were of university centres and town halls, etc. This information was to be displayed in the following three areas:

a. Within the building, which offers a number of large, flexible, uninterrupted floor areas (varying between 5,500–7,500 square meters), housing books, fine arts, architecture, cinema, industrial design, etc.

b. On two long facades, one facing west across a sunken square and the other facing Rue du Renard. A three-dimensional, load-bearing wall carries constantly
changing information, news, what's on in Paris, artworks, traffic situation, maps,
weather and financial reports, cinema, television, robots, temporary structures,
electronic two-way games, information, etc.

c. The facade facing Rue du Renard will have visual displays related to moving
traffic, whilst the facade facing the sunken square will relate to pedestrians.[57]

The competition statement accompanying the design sheets repeatedly mentioned
the designing and detailing of the information areas. Furthermore, the type of information that was supposed to be displayed was also specified, as the competition
statement indicated that the display of information on the Rue du Renard was proposed to be of mobile vehicles and passing pedestrians. On the side of the square,
more static viewing points were proposed. As the whole structure was proposed as
lifted well above the ground level on pilotis, it was possible to see while standing
on the Rue du Renard the facades of the houses located on the Rue Saint-Martin.
For those entering from the Les Halles direction, they were presented with the
*information grill*. The specifications of this information grill were such that it was
designed to carry an ever-changing clip-on system of information. Cranes were
also proposed on the roof in order to lift and maintain the different clip-on parts,
wall panels or electronic components of the building. As the piazza or square in
front of the Pompidou Center was proposed as an open space intended for congre-
gation of people and exhibitions of all sorts of events, the structure while standing on the pilotis also presented a square underneath. This space was protected
from the weather and could have been used for erection of temporary structures.
Information that was to be of significance to the locals and at the national level was
to be displayed within these squares, for example, information-dissemination relating to the latest world catastrophes and the consequent collection of aid.[58]

The flexibility of space particularly achieved through demountable partitions
has been a specific quality of almost all of Rogers projects, and it was this quality
that highly impressed the jury. Jury members stated that it was due to the desire of
functional, flexible and polyvalent construction that renders this project as widely
as possible extremely adaptable to the changing needs and unpredictable means
and tastes. The Center Pompidou's competition entry statement clearly stated this
aspect by emphasising the maximum flexibility of use. The exterior of the building was equipped with all the vertical services and movements, thus resulting in
uninterrupted floor space in the interior (Figure 4.11). All of the three-dimensional
walls, floors and partitions were completely mobile and detachable and were to
be clipped/unclipped or extendable as and when needed. Any functions, such
as offices, were to be positioned anywhere, and those spaces that needed more
services were to be placed near the exterior so that connections with the vertical
service runs could be established. As all the services were to be clipped on the
exteriors, those areas that needed more views towards the exteriors, uninterrupted
daylight or open spaces, such as rooftop restaurants, experimental and temporary
exhibitions, outdoor museums, children's reception areas, etc., were proposed to
be placed on the roof on the South or in the open square below the structure. Only

*Figure 4.11* Facades facing Rue Saint-Martin and Rue du Renard.

*Source*: The Center Pompidou, Paris: Northwest and Southeast facades, August 2019, photograph. Courtesy of the author.

these areas were free from the vertical grill. The roof of the Center was kept clear of all the services in order to utilise it for display and community uses, and the restaurant was suspended over it. Three types of partition panels were proposed to be used in different situations: a Glass Reinforced Plastic (GRP) cored solid sandwich panel that was highly opaque, insulated, lightweight and cladded with GRP. An Okalux laminate – hermetically sealed, insulated slab of colourless, translucent capillary tube – panel that was highly insulated and translucent. The third option that was proposed to be used was a simple *glass panel*.[59]

The structure was truly a kit-of-parts, as Rogers and Piano's competition statement elaborated that whole of the structure was assembled from different elements. Permanent elements included the columns and cross members that were responsible for providing basic stability. The columns were fabricated on-site from steel tubes of the similar external diameter. In order to retain a true flexibility for futuristic uses, floors and their supporting beams were kept movable which were capable of being dismantled and repositioned as needed. This flexibility was achieved with the help of introduction of a special friction collar that was specifically designed and produced for this purpose. Steel was used as the fundamental material for construction, and in order to make it fire and corrosion proof, all the tubular spaces were filled with treated water. Further structural specifications confirmed:

deflection of the floor elements is controlled by ensuring that the precast concrete topping acts monolithically with the steel supporting beams. Transverse stability is provided by the fire wall needed to separate the temporary from the permanent exhibition space and by infill panels at the end of the buildings. These infill elements are also used to reduce the spans in the heavily loaded library areas.[60]

The structural engineer for the Center Pompidou project was Peter Rice from Ove Arup and Associates. He states that right after winning the competition, he made a visit to Japan and visited the Japan World Exposition Osaka 1970, where he observed the giant space frame designed by Kenzo Tange and his team, including Prof. Tsuboi. There, Rice witnessed the cast-steel nodes and got the idea of constructing the Pompidou Center using cast steel as its core material. Instead of using the factory-produced standardised steel elements, he preferred cast-steel as a way of incorporating emotions, feeling of contact between the maker and the observer, thus granting humanistic scale to the Center, qualities that both Rogers and Piano wanted to have in their structures. Rice further mentions that Piano and Rogers derived the idea for Pompidou from Archigram, Cedric Price and Joan Littlewood and the technological optimism of the 1960s', such as the belief that culture must be similar to any other form of information that is distributed and accessible to all without any discrimination (Figure 4.12). Piano states regarding his collaboration with Rice that when the two started to work on the Pompidou project, they immediately started understanding each other's language, and the communication was without any barriers, as it was like different pieces started coming together without any effort. Piano further states:

> [when they] sketched something, but it was immediately basically a machine, an urban machine. . . . To make a building for culture that looked like a machine was exactly the opposite of the monumental, intimidating, you know, marble building. We wanted to create a sense of curiosity or enjoyment.[61]

Rogers recalls the inspiration that came from Japan for the Pompidou project:

> [w]e had seen some pretty big castings in Japan so we knew it was possible to do a cast-iron gerberette. And of course, it gives you a feel. One of the beauties about this material is that it's you can mould it to any shape.[62]

## Conclusion

The Case Study House Program (1945–62) was sponsored and built by *Arts and Architecture* magazine edited by John Entenza to design and realise an ideal, inexpensive and efficient post-war house in the Southern California, United States of America. War-born techniques, technologically advanced materials and innovation were supreme conditions. The Eames House (1949) boosted a number of technological advances in construction techniques, materials and gadgets. Kitchen appliances by *Sunbeam* and *Kelvinator* were self-decision-making objects. *Alter Lansing's* home music system precedented today's smart home maintenance or security systems. The Case Study House (1950) also featured a number of technologically

*Figure 4.12* Flexible and free spaces of the Center Pompidou, Paris.

*Source*: The Center Pompidou, Paris: Main entrance hall and hanging walkway, August 2019, photograph. Courtesy of the author.

advanced products, such as the *Kelvinator* Electric Range, *Incinor* Disposal Unit, etc. The Case Study Houses for 1953, 1956 and 1958 also featured technologically advanced systems for different purposes, such as *Payne* perimeter forced-air heating system, *Dalmotron* Taskmaster electronic inter-communication system, *G and M Equipment Company's* built-in radio-intercom system, etc. Furthermore, standardised components and modules were used for construction.

The SCSD Project (1961–67) introduced erector sets of prefabricated components that resulted in structural (roof), ceiling-lighting and air-conditioning systems and movable and operable partitions. The structural system that was used for this project was commonly used for bridge construction previously and was put to use for the first time in a school building. Flexibility was greatly emphasised, resulting in freedom in overall planning from single to multiple units, presenting variety of spaces, alternatives and arrangements. Consequently, re-arrangement of spaces became utmost easy and convenient.

Regarding Rogers's projects, both Reliance Controls (1967) and its extension, Rogers House (1968–69), were comprised of lightweight, standardised components, kit-of-parts structures that were inspired by Rogers's visit to the Case Study Houses (1945–62) and SCSD (1961–67) projects. Flexibility and extendability were prime considerations. Zip-Up Enclosures No 1 and 2 (1968–71), Extension to Design Research Unit (1969–71) and Universal Oil Products Factory (1973–74) all treated construction as a mass-production entity, portable, expandable and utilised monocoque construction technique adopted from the manufacturing of cars and airplanes. Rogers presented a do-it-yourself (DIY) approach for assembling or dis-assembling of this system. Association for Rural Aid in Medicine Module (1971) was a proposal representing a demountable, portable, extendable, adaptable and flexible hospital workable during natural or man-made disasters. Imagery of the space and structures planted in the middle of the oceans depicting cranes are said to be inspirations behind this project and the Center Pompidou, Paris. The entire structure was to be assembled with a crane by non-specialists. The PA Technology Laboratory (1975–85) was an extension of the Case Study Houses (1945–62) and SCSD (1961–67) projects. This project featured repetitive bay construction and sophisticated kit-of-parts approach. Piano's Italian Industry Pavilion at the Osaka Expo '70 was among his early works in which he experimented with innovative materials and construction methods exploring the concepts of flexibility (open plan, modular structures), transparency and lightness of a space. Impressed with the technological optimism of the 1960s', he also cites Peter Cook and Cedric Price from Archigram as sources of inspiration.

The Center Pompidou, Paris (1970–77), was initially conceived as a poly-valent cultural centre and a public reading room, as the program publicised it as an information-disseminating machine. The program demanded a number of activities as a unified whole, as a form of information, and public was to extract meaning out of it. Constant renewal and update of information were prime considerations, and an information network was envisaged operating and originating from it with library being its focal point. Rogers and Piano's competition entry presented a live centre of information with information on the outside, inside, and linking the building with other centres throughout the world. It was conceived as a cross between information-oriented, computerised Times Square and the British Museum, with stress on two-way participation between people and its activities. As have been the case with Rogers's previous projects, it was considered as a living and complex organism emphasising flexibility and adaptability. Rooms or galleries were not interpreted strictly, and space was reserved for multiple uses. Piano states that Pompidou was intended to be a funny machine. Curiosity, social tension and desire for adventure were intended. Archigram, Cedric Price and Joan Littlewood along with the technological optimism of the 1960s' acted as inspirations for Pompidou.

## Notes

1 John Entenza, "Announcement: The Case Study House Program," *Arts and Architecture*, January 1945, 38, 39, accessed February 13, 2023, www.artsandarchitecture.com/issues/pdf01/1945_01.pdf.
2 Contradictory sources exist regarding biographies of the Case Study program's participating architects. Following websites have been consulted for the information:
"Case Study House Program: Architects," *Arts and Architecture*, Travers Family Trust, accessed January 28, 2021, www.artsandarchitecture.com/case.houses/architects.html.
"Persons: Architects, Designers, Landscape Architects, and Other," Pacific Coast Architecture Database, Alan Michelson, Built Environments Library, University of Washington, Seattle, accessed January 28, 2021, http://pcad.lib.washington.edu/persons/.
3 Entenza, "Announcement: The Case Study House Program," 39.
4 Ibid., 37.
5 Ibid.
6 Ibid., 38.
7 John Entenza and Craig Ellwood, "Case Study House #17 by Craig Ellwood," *Arts and Architecture*, March 1956, 20, accessed February 15, 2023, www.artsandarchitecture.com/issues/pdf01/1956_03.pdf.
8 John Entenza and Charles Eames, "Case Study House for 1949: Designed by Charles Eames," *Arts and Architecture*, December 1949, 27, accessed February 15, 2023, www.artsandarchitecture.com/issues/pdf01/1949_12.pdf.
9 Ibid., 29.
10 Ibid., 30.
11 The technologically advanced artefacts incorporated in the *Eames House* included "Truscon Steel Products, Sunmaster Automatic Clotheslines, Case Plumbing Fixtures, Howard Miller Wall-Hung Chronopaks, Flush Wall Radios, Lumite Plastic Screening, Blackstone Automatic Clothes Dryer, Hornrock, Horn-O-Tone, Florcrex, Galvanide, Rocklite Lightweight Aggregate Structural Blocks, Calchrome Built-In Seating, Century Contemporary Lighting Fixtures, Gotham Architectural Lighting, Warcraft Plumbing Fixtures, Blackstone Automatic Washer, Payne Forced Air Units, Modernfold (Accordion) Doors, Herculese Closet Vault, Tackless Carpet Gripper, Gulfspray Shower Enclosures, Celotex Products, Sunbeam Automatic Kitchen Appliances, Wall-Tex Fabric Wall Covering, Altec Lansing Home Music System, Milliken Drapery Fabrics, Alexander Smith Crystal Point Carpet, Laverne Squared Circle, Kohler Bath Fixtures, Shopsmith Woodworking Tool, Blo-Fan Ceiling Ventilator, Void Rubber Tile, No-shok Electrical Outlets, Kirsch Drapery Hardware, Plywood and Decorative Micarta, Mississippi Obscure Glass, Kelvinator Electric Range, Kelvinator Home Freezer,

Kelvinator Moist-Master Refrigerator, Berger All-Steel Kitchen Cabinets, and Pylon Wall Covering Material."
"Merit Specifications for 1949 Case Study Houses," *Arts and Architecture*, December 1949, 8–14, accessed February 15, 2023, www.artsandarchitecture.com/issues/pdf01/1949_12.pdf.

12 "Preview of Some Products Merit Specified for the 1950 Case Study House," *Arts and Architecture*, December 1949, 46, accessed February 15, 2023, www.artsandarchitecture.com/issues/pdf01/1949_12.pdf.

13 Ibid.

14 "Merit Specifications for 1949 Case Study Houses," 13.

15 Ibid., 12.

16 Products specified for the Case Study House 1950 included the following: "Kelvinator Electric Range, Home Freezer, Moist-Master Refrigerator, Built-In Mail Box with Flexible Chute, B-Safe Wide Angle Door Lookout, Rotir Electric Barbecue Spit, Modernfold (Accordion) Doors, The Lam Lamp, Wilcox Indoor Planting, Grant Sliding Door Hardware, Incinor Disposal Unit, Aluma-Life Light Weight Roofing Material, Dodge Vinyl-Cork Tile, Allen Rubber-Loc Rubberized Waffled Rug Cushion, Johnson-Carper Prize-Winning Furniture, Leco-Latch Cabinet Door Catch, L & S Portland Cement Paint, Sash and Trim Colors, Payne Forced Air Units, Nutone Door, Clock Chime, Sterling Contemporary Furniture, Paine Rezo Hollow Core Flush Doors, Nutone Kitchen Ventilating Fans, Inner-Seal Weatherstripping, and Mississippi Obscure Glass." "Product Merit Specified for 1950 Case Study House," *Arts and Architecture*, December 1950, 45–48, accessed February 15, 2023, www.artsandarchitecture.com/issues/pdf01/1950_12.pdf.

17 Craig Ellwood, "Products: The New Case Study House," *Arts and Architecture*, June 1953, 46, accessed February 15, 2023, www.artsandarchitecture.com/issues/pdf01/1953_06.pdf.

18 Entenza and Ellwood, "Case Study House #17 by Craig Ellwood," 23–26.

19 Appliances for this house included "Built-in Ovens, Warming Drawer and Cooking Top by Thermador Electric Manufacturing Company, Built-in Refrigerator-Freezer, Upright Freezer, Laundromat-Dryer Twin Units, Dishwasher, Food Waste Disposer by Westinghouse Electric Corporation, Water Heaters by Rheem Manufacturing Company, and Electric Barbecue Spit by Rotir Company." Craig Ellwood, "Products: Case Study House #17," *Arts and Architecture*, March 1956, 38, accessed February 15, 2023, www.artsandarchitecture.com/issues/pdf01/1956_03.pdf.

20 Ibid.

21 Entenza and Ellwood, "Case Study House #17 by Craig Ellwood," 28–30.

22 Craig Ellwood, "The Machine and Architecture," *Arts and Architecture*, June 1958, 19, accessed February 15, 2023, www.artsandarchitecture.com/issues/pdf01/1958_06.pdf.

23 John Entenza and Craig Ellwood, "Study House 18 by Craig Ellwood," *Arts and Architecture*, June 24, 1958, accessed February 15, 2023, www.artsandarchitecture.com/issues/pdf01/1958_06.pdf.

24 Craig Ellwood, "Products: Case Study House Number 18," *Arts and Architecture*, June 1958, 30, accessed February 16, 2023, www.artsandarchitecture.com/issues/pdf01/1958_06.pdf.

25 Entenza and Ellwood, "Study House 18 by Craig Ellwood," 25.

26 Educational Facilities Laboratories, Inc., *SCSD: An Interim Report* (New York: Educational Facilities Laboratories, Inc., November 1965), 6, accessed February 18, 2023, https://files.eric.ed.gov/fulltext/ED031035.pdf.

27 Ibid., 14.

28 Ibid., 7.

29 Ibid., 8.

30 Ibid., 5.

31  Ibid., 2.
32  Ibid.
33  Ibid., 4.
34  Ibid., 11.
35  Ibid., 26.
36  Educational Facilities Laboratories, Inc., *School Construction Systems Development (Promotional Movie)*, redubbed June 6, 1995, original July 1965, no inventory number allocated, School Construction Systems Development Project, Video Home System, 16mm color/sound, 28 minutes, Ezra Ehrenkrantz's Archives, Littman Architecture Library, New Jersey Institute of Technology, Newark, accessed March 21, 2021, www.youtube.com/watch?v=6B_QETj5hsg.
37  Educational Facilities Laboratories, Inc., *SCSD: An Interim Report*, 13.
38  Richard Rogers, "Richard Rogers Interview: Wimbledon house, Architecture, Dezeen," interview by Benedict Hobson, YouTube video, 2:26, cited in "Wimbledon House Was Meant to Solve the British Housing Problem But Didn't, Say Richard Rogers," *Dezeen*, March 15, 2018, www.dezeen.com/2018/03/15/video-interview-richard-rogers-22-parkside-wimbledon-house-movie/.
39  Renzo Piano, "Renzo Piano 1998 Laureate: Acceptance Speech," speech, Pritzker Architecture Prize Ceremony, The White House, Washington, DC, June 17, 1998, 2, accessed February 11, 2021, www.pritzkerprize.com/sites/default/files/inline-files/1998_Acceptance_Speech.pdf.
40  "Early Works 1964–1974, Genoa, Italy," Renzo Piano Building Workshop Architects All Projects, Renzo Piano Building Workshop Architects, accessed February 10, 2021, www.rpbw.com/project/early-works.
41  Piano, "Renzo Piano 1998 Laureate: Acceptance Speech," 1–2.
42  Ibid., 2.
43  Renzo Piano, interview by Charlie Rose, *Charlie Rose*, April 12, 2002, https://charlierose.com/videos/16116.
44  Piano, "Renzo Piano 1998 Laureate: Acceptance Speech," 2.
45  Ibid.
46  Delegation pour la réalisation du Centre du plateau Beaubourg, *Titre I: Programme du Concours* [*Title I: Program of the Competition*], 1969–71, 20100307 9, Construction du Centre National D'Art et de Culture Georges Pompidou 1971–77, Archives et documentation, The Centre Pompidou, Paris, 32, https://archivesetdocumentation.centrepompidou.fr/functions/ead2/attached/FRCNACGP00ARCHIVES_000000002/FRCNACGP00ARCHIVES_000000002_e0000153.pdf.
47  Author's translation has been presented in the main text of the passage as follows: "Le Président de la République a décidé le 11 décembre 1969 d'édifier au cœur de Paris, non loin des Halles, sur le plateau Beaubourg, un centre consacré à l'art contemporain ainsi qu'une grande bibliothèque publique touchant tous les domaines de la connaissance. Cette décision prend une singulière valeur au moment même où la notion traditionnelle de l'Art et même celle de la Culture semblent mises en question. Or, il ne s'agit pas de dresser un bilan, si prestigieux soit-il, ni de faire un pari sur l'avenir, mais d'affirmer à travers sa richesse et même ses contradictions que la création sous toutes ses formes sensibles est devenue le langage le plus immédiat, le plus total de notre époque. C'est, en effet, une grande originalité que la conjonction en un même lieu du livre, des arts plastiques, de l'architecture, de la musique, du cinéma, de la création industrielle – celle que la culture n'a pas encore annexée comme témoignage d'art. Cette conjonction doit permettre de faire saisir au plus grand public qu'en dépit des apparences de liberté qu'affecte la création, l'autonomie, la hiérarchie des expressions de l'art sont fictives et qu'il existe entre les formes actuelles et les rapports de production dans la société, un lien profond. La réalisation de ce dessein permettra en outre de doter Paris d'un

ensemble architectural et urbain qui marquera notre époque et dont l'économie répondra à celle du programme." Ibid., 3.

48  "Toutes ces activités n'ont de sens que dans la mesure où elles concourent à un esprit commun, permettent un brassage des idées et des hommes. Aucune ne se suffit mais toutes sont nécessaires. C'est au public qu'il appartiendra d'en révéler l'unité." Ibid.

49  "On y trouvera les collections « de poche » et une bibliothèque fréquemment renouvelée, composée de livres choisis parmi les plus significatifs, les plus utiles ou les plus récréatifs, dans tous les domaines." Ibid., 12.

50  "Le Centre est envisagé dans une perspective également originale, celle de l'actualité constamment renouvelée: actualité de la création artistique dans ses manifestations les plus diverses, actualité de la création industrielle, mais aussi mise à jour constante de ces mémoires des idées et des formes que sont la Bibliothèque et le Musée." Ibid., 4.

51  "Ce Centre ne doit donc pas être un monde clos: son action débordera nécessairement les limites de l'édifice, elle marquera le quartier, elle s'étendra en France et à l'étranger, par des expositions circulaires, des émissions télévisées, des publications . . . En outre, la possibilité de consulter à distance des fichiers mis en mémoire dans l'ordinateur de la Bibliothèque sera un moyen de diffusion et un service dont les effets seront très appréciés." Ibid.

52  "dispenser à l'extérieur une information générale d'actualité dans tous les domaines et créer un réseau d'information avec les organismes de documentation spécialisés, sur la base d'échanges de services." Ibid., 18.

53  "Un ordinateur du type IBM 360/50 ou Iris 50 sera utilisé dans le Centre pour le traitement de l'information intéressant l'ensemble des bibliothèques de France et les centres de documentation français et internationaux (catalogues, gestion, recherches documentaires, etc.). Outre la salle de l'ordinateur proprement dite, seront prévus des salles de perforation, des salles de stockage des disques, des bandes magnétiques, les bureaux des programmateurs, occupant une surface totale de 500 m2." Ibid., 21.

54  "On appelle l'attention sur une caractéristique essentielle et originale du Centre: qu'il s'agisse de la Bibliothèque, du Musée d'art moderne et contemporain, du Centre national d'art contemporain ou du Centre de création industrielle, etc. les surfaces indiquées ont été jugées suffisantes pour le plein exercice des activités actuellement envisagées. Aucune extension n'est à prévoir, puisque les collections seront périodiquement renouvelées. En revanche, la flexibilité intérieure du Centre doit être aussi grande que possible. Dans un organisme vivant et complexe où il faudra tenir le plus grand compte de l'évolution des besoins, tous les secteurs et chaque partie d'un secteur seront articulés de telle manière que l'on puisse jouer sur toutes les surfaces pour obtenir la souplesse d'adaptation indispensable. À noter enfin que dans le présent programme les termes de « salles », « galeries », etc. ne doivent pas être interprétés dans un sens strict; ils ne désignent que des espaces réservés à certaines fonctions" [emphasis in original]. Ibid., 10–11.

55  "Par conséquent, l'architecte ne prévoira dans les 4 000 m2 de surfaces intérieures traitées par lui comme un ensemble, que des séparations amovibles permettant de le fragmenter à la demande, avec la plus grande souplesse possible. La zone d'exposition temporaire devra permettre au public, en divers endroits, de communiquer avec les musées et les salles polyvalentes. On devra y sentir une atmosphère agréable de détente, grâce à l'aménagement de nombreuses zones de repos (vues sur l'extérieur, communication avec les jardins)." Ibid., 14.

56  Delegation pour la réalisation du Centre du plateau Beaubourg, "Notice du Projet Lauréat," in *Quatrième partie: Analyse du Projet Lauréat* [*Fourth Part: Analysis of the Winning Project*], 1971–72, 20100307 20, Construction du Centre National D'Art et de Culture Georges Pompidou 1971–77, Archives et documentation, The Centre Pompidou, Paris, 109, https://archivesetdocumentation.centrepompidou.fr/functions/ead2/attached/

FRCNACGP00ARCHIVES_000000002/FRCNACGP00ARCHIVES_000000002_
e0000274.pdf.

57  Ibid., 101–102.
58  Ibid., 103–106.
59  Ibid., 104–105, 111.
60  Ibid., 110–111.
61  Arup, "Traces of Peter Rice, an Arup Documentary," YouTube video, 32:29, December
    14, 2012, www.youtube.com/watch?v=v8ubOlkQCf4.
62  Ibid.

## Bibliography

This chapter has benefitted from Construction of the Georges Pompidou National Center
for Art and Culture 1971–77, Archives and Documentation, at the Centre Pompidou, Paris.
This bibliography only lists the name of the collection that has been consulted instead of the
specific items. It is in accordance with the guidelines of *The Chicago Manual of Style*, 17th
ed. (Chicago: University of Chicago Press, 2017) and for more details, section 14.222 can be
consulted. The details of specific items have been listed in the notes. Unless otherwise noted,
all translations are by the author.

Arup. "Traces of Peter Rice, an Arup Documentary." *YouTube Video*, 32:29, December 14,
    2012. www.youtube.com/watch?v=v8ubOlkQCf4.

"Case Study House Program: Architects." *Arts and Architecture*, Travers Family Trust.
    Accessed January 28, 2021. www.artsandarchitecture.com/case.houses/architects.html.

Delegation pour la réalisation du Centre du plateau Beaubourg. "Notice du Projet Lau-
    réat." In *Quatrième partie: Analyse du Projet Lauréat [Fourth Part: Analysis of the
    Winning Project]*, 1971–72, 20100307 20, Construction du Centre National D'Art et de
    Culture Georges Pompidou 1971–77, Archives et documentation, The Centre Pompi-
    dou, Paris. https://archivesetdocumentation.centrepompidou.fr/functions/ead2/attached/
    FRCNACGP00ARCHIVES_000000002/FRCNACGP00ARCHIVES_000000002_
    e0000274.pdf.

Delegation pour la réalisation du Centre du plateau Beaubourg. *Titre I: Programme
    du Concours [Title I: Program of the Competition]*, 1969–71, 20100307 9, Construc-
    tion du Centre National D'Art et de Culture Georges Pompidou 1971–77, Archives et
    documentation, The Centre Pompidou, Paris. https://archivesetdocumentation.centre-
    pompidou.fr/functions/ead2/attached/FRCNACGP00ARCHIVES_000000002/FRC-
    NACGP00ARCHIVES_000000002_e0000153.pdf.

"Early Works 1964–1974, Genoa, Italy," *Renzo Piano Building Workshop Architects All
    Projects, Renzo Piano Building Workshop Architects*. Accessed February 10, 2021. www.
    rpbw.com/project/early-works.

Educational Facilities Laboratories, Inc. "School Construction Systems Development (Pro-
    motional Movie)." *Redubbed*, June 6, 1995, original July 1965. No inventory number
    allocated. School Construction Systems Development Project. Video Home System,
    16mm color/sound, 28 minutes. Ezra Ehrenkrantz's Archives, Littman Architecture
    Library, New Jersey Institute of Technology, Newark. Accessed March 21, 2021. www.
    youtube.com/watch?v=6B_QETj5hsg.

Educational Facilities Laboratories, Inc. *SCSD: An Interim Report*. New York: Educational
    Facilities Laboratories, Inc., November 1965. Accessed February 18, 2023. https://files.
    eric.ed.gov/fulltext/ED031035.pdf.

Ellwood, Craig. "The Machine and Architecture." *Arts and Architecture*, June 1958. Accessed February 15, 2023. www.artsandarchitecture.com/issues/pdf01/1958_06.pdf.

Ellwood, Craig. "Products: Case Study House #17." *Arts and Architecture*, March 1956. Accessed February 15, 2023. www.artsandarchitecture.com/issues/pdf01/1956_03.pdf.

Ellwood, Craig. "Products: Case Study House Number 18." *Arts and Architecture*, June 1958. Accessed February 16, 2023. www.artsandarchitecture.com/issues/pdf01/1958_06.pdf.

Ellwood, Craig. "Products: The New Case Study House." *Arts and Architecture*, June 1953. Accessed February 15, 2023. www.artsandarchitecture.com/issues/pdf01/1953_06.pdf.

Entenza, John. "Announcement: The Case Study House Program." *Arts and Architecture*, January 1945. Accessed February 13, 2023. www.artsandarchitecture.com/issues/pdf01/1945_01.pdf.

Entenza, John and Charles Eames. "Case Study House for 1949: Designed by Charles Eames." *Arts and Architecture*, December 1949. Accessed February 15, 2023. www.artsandarchitecture.com/issues/pdf01/1949_12.pdf.

Entenza, John and Craig Ellwood. "Case Study House #17 by Craig Ellwood." *Arts and Architecture*, March 1956. Accessed February 15, 2023. www.artsandarchitecture.com/issues/pdf01/1956_03.pdf.

Entenza, John and Craig Ellwood. "Study House 18 by Craig Ellwood." *Arts and Architecture*, June 1958. Accessed February 15, 2023. www.artsandarchitecture.com/issues/pdf01/1958_06.pdf.

"Merit Specifications for 1949 Case Study Houses." *Arts and Architecture*, December 1949. Accessed February 15, 2023. www.artsandarchitecture.com/issues/pdf01/1949_12.pdf.

"Persons: Architects, Designers, Landscape Architects, and Other." *Pacific Coast Architecture Database, Alan Michelson, Built Environments Library*, University of Washington, Seattle. Accessed January 28, 2021. http://pcad.lib.washington.edu/persons/.

Piano, Renzo. Interview by Charlie Rose, *Charlie Rose*, April 12, 2002. https://charlierose.com/videos/16116.

Piano, Renzo. "Renzo Piano 1998 Laureate: Acceptance Speech." Speech, Pritzker Architecture Prize Ceremony, The White House, Washington, DC, June 17, 1998. Accessed February 11, 2021. www.pritzkerprize.com/sites/default/files/inline-files/1998_Acceptance_Speech.pdf.

"Preview of Some Products Merit Specified for the 1950 Case Study House." *Arts and Architecture*, December 1949. Accessed February 15, 2023. www.artsandarchitecture.com/issues/pdf01/1949_12.pdf.

"Product Merit Specified for 1950 Case Study House." *Arts and Architecture*, December 1950. Accessed February 15, 2023. www.artsandarchitecture.com/issues/pdf01/1950_12.pdf.

Rogers, Richard. "Richard Rogers Interview: Wimbledon House, Architecture, Dezeen." Interview by Benedict Hobson. YouTube video, 2:26. Cited in "Wimbledon House Was Meant to Solve the British Housing Problem But Didn't, Say Richard Rogers." *Dezeen*, March 15, 2018. www.dezeen.com/2018/03/15/video-interview-richard-rogers-22-parkside-wimbledon-house-movie/.

# 5   Gordon Pask
## Information, communication and feedback

English cybernetician Gordon Pask adopted an innovative approach for defining and practicing the cybernetic environments. In the pursuit of these cybernetic experiments, he participated in an *International Concept Design Competition for an Advanced Information City* that was launched by the city of Kawasaki in 1986 in order to regenerate it from a declining traditional industrial city to a twenty-first-century international information and communications hub. After discussing the characteristics of an information and communications city as projected by the competition brief, this chapter then studies Pask's theories regarding cybernetic architecture and the relevant exhibition installations. Afterwards, Pask's competition entry proposal titled the *Japnet, Kawasaki* has been analysed in which he, as a major contributor along with Architect Cedric Price, outlines the intelligent systems for the city of Kawasaki.

### Kawasaki as an Advanced Information City: an international concept design competition

In 1986–87, an *International Concept Design Competition for an Advanced Information City*, also referred to as the *Campus City Competition*, was announced for the city of Kawasaki by the Japan Association for Planning Administration and *Mainichi* Newspapers in collaboration with the ministries and agencies of the government of Japan and a number of organisations. These organisations that extended their cooperation and support for the execution of this competition included ministries and agencies of the government of Japan, such as Management Coordination Agency, Ministry of Foreign Affairs, Finance, Education, Health and Welfare, Agriculture, Forestry and Fisheries, International Trade and Industry, Transportation, Posts and Telecommunications, Construction, Home Affairs, Economic Planning Agency, Environment Agency and National Land Agency. Special Cooperation was extended by the Prefecture of Kanagawa and City of Kawasaki. Cooperation was also provided by the Building Center of Japan, Engineering Consulting Firms Association, Japan, Foundation for Asian Management Development, Institute for Future Urban Development, Japan Center for Area Development Research, International Development Center of Japan, Japan Chamber of Commerce and Industry, Japan External Trade Organization,

DOI: 10.4324/9781003401858-5

Japan Foundation, Japan International Cooperation Agency, Kawasaki Chamber of Commerce and Industry, Mori Memorial Foundation, New Media Development Association, Tokyo Broadcasting System Corp. and United Nations Center for Regional Development.[1] Some of these organisations have ceased to exist at present. The cooperation and support that was extended from such a large number of Japanese ministries, agencies of the government and organisations along with the huge prize money of ¥42,000,000 that were approximately US$240,000 at that time, presents the significance of this conceptual competition. The aim of the competition was to develop conceptual plans and designs comprising of several themes for Kawasaki as an advanced twenty-first-century information-intensive and humanistic city. Kawasaki's transition from an industrialised, product-intensive city of the twentieth century to a high-technology, knowledge-based economy of the twenty-first century was intended, and consequently, innovation was assigned a critical significance for the achievement of this objective.

The concept of an advanced information city was newly introduced at that time, and an international perspective was urgently requested for collaboration between citizens and government, government and industry and community leadership and citizens. Kawasaki was selected for this competition because it shared certain qualities with the industrialised cities throughout the world and the ease of implementation of this conceptual competition to any other city in need of major revitalisation. Revitalisation was preferred by its citizens because of its negative image, first, as it was a crowded city with an obsolete heavy industry, and second, as it was facing a serious environmental pollution problem that was halted. Furthermore, the brief stated that Japan as a country itself is an information-intensive society based on rapid electronic development capabilities that consequently resulted in rapid economic development. Many observers at that time believed that Japan was one of the most feasible countries regarding information and communication systems knowledge-based development, and this was not only because of the potential of development of electronics it held but because it was an information-intensive society. The results of this experiment in Japan were supposed to be shared internationally specifically with other industrially advanced nations. Among these nations, those were particularly targeted whose information and telecommunications technological development coincided with the rapid economic achievements of Japan. Such an endeavor aimed at achieving a collaboration between businesses and even nations in order to enable them to swiftly climb up the developmental stages of industrialisation, a milestone that Japan achieved in some decades as compared to other countries that took several generations to accomplish the same. The speed at which the new and emerging communications technologies were being developed and the efficiency with which these were being adopted by businesses, government agencies and individuals was to influence the economic development of their nation, the program brief stated.[2] In addition, the competition brief made it clear that Japan was on its way of becoming an *advanced information and communication society*. Through the promotion of production and usage of information as a major industry, Japan intended to cater many of its social needs. While referring to the decades of 70s' and 80s', the brief stated that a rapid acceleration has been made in these decades by Japan towards the incorporation of microelectronic technology in all of its stages of collection, transmission, storage, processing and presentation of information.[3]

Innovations in traditional media in the 1980s' in Japan, for example, traditional items of television, radio, etc., resulted in a *New Media* after experimentations, for example, videotext, community antenna television (i.e. cable television, teletext, etc.). This new media was expected to reduce information discrimination between urban and regional areas through energy and resource-saving strategies. The brief states in this regard that Japan initiated to install an infrastructure that was capable of generating and carrying vast amounts of information. Whether it be fiber optics, satellites with high-power direct broadcasting capabilities or the development of super or fifth-generation computers, the Japanese regarded all of these infrastructure developments as of high national priority. Community antenna television (CATV) systems were made to operate in both regional and main city areas alike, and two-way communication, multi-channel CATV projects were initiated in urban areas. Videotext, a technology that was new at that time, was also commercially available throughout the country. In order to accelerate telecommunications growth in the nation, regulatory controls were lessened through relevant legislations.[4]

This experimental new media infrastructure was to be utilised in a number of ways, for example, in sectors like real estate, road traffic information, elderly care and chronically ill citizens caregiving, CATV advanced management training, consumer-oriented information systems in stores, transportation centres and public plazas, etc. Large-scale and long-term community communication programs were introduced by the Japanese government, such as *New Media Communities or Teletopia Cities*. Teleports and single or combined information systems were introduced for sectors like tourism, social education, agricultural management, library systems, health prevention, forestry management and business support systems. Japanese government also promoted public-private partnership in which the private sector was encouraged to invest in the public infrastructure in exchange of certain financial incentives, an initiative called as the *Third Sector*. Japanese government was particularly interested in projects that utilised advanced information technologies and telecommunications. Competition brief states that its intention was to go beyond this Third Sector approach in order to encourage wider public participation in this competition. Furthermore, it clarified the aim that it was the citizens who were responsible for shaping the use of technology and, to be precise, the technology itself to their particular needs. Up till this competition, technological developments towards an information society have focused majorly on the hardware of technology, and it was suggested that due to the rapid pace of technological developments, its creators and users have not been able to cope with understanding of the range of possibilities it could offer. It was the time when applications that were useful and not simply technically sound were to be researched and designed, the brief stated.[5]

A development strategy titled *2001 Kawasaki City Plan* was to act as a foundation for transition of the existing city into an advanced information city using high technology as a tool for this revitalisation. Highlights of this plan included development of a social welfare society possessing the characteristics of a human-friendly environment, identity of the city and development based on the linked-city concept. The goals of the 2001 Kawasaki City Plan included guidelines for development of an urban environment feasible for human interaction, such as lifetime guarantee of an independent, fulfilling life for all the citizens and providing them with a pleasant environment, and in order to achieve these elements, it was deemed necessary to revitalize the regional economy. A city with its unique identity was also suggested based on the creation of new self-governing systems. International exchange between cities, their people and beyond the geographical borders of Japan was also promoted. The aim was the creation of an independent culture free of any restrictions. Furthermore, the urban development of the city based on the concept of a *linked city* was also promoted in which Kawasaki was to be transformed into an entirely new type of industrial city possessing matured residential environments, redevelopment of the city centre and its adjoining sub-centres, spanning to an extensive redevelopment of the coastal and interior areas of the city as well.[6] Emphasis was placed on Kawasaki's development through advanced information and communication systems. In 1985, an International Symposium on Regional Information Systems (IRIS) conference was sponsored by the Japan Association for Planning Administration in collaboration with the city of Kawasaki. During this conference, a concept was put forth that suggested this city's revitalisation and development as an advanced information city which was outlined to be an international scientific and cultural city. The IRIS Plan called for its development in accordance with this framework of an advanced information and communication system that included several aspects critical to satisfying and fulfilling the needs of a city and its citizens, as was defined in the 2001 Kawasaki City Plan.[7]

The major theme that was decided during the IRIS conference and acts as the foundation for the concept of the competition was to revitalize the city as the *Campus City*. The idea was to develop Kawasaki as a university campus so that characteristics like city identity, unifying physical aspects of a campus, educational benefits promoting learning, growth, shared values and social participation, satisfaction of the intellectual needs of the citizens, etc., could be accommodated in the competition proposals. There were certain values that Kawasaki City was interested in promoting through the implementation of a Campus City, such as an information-intensive, multinational, scientific community where innovation was promoted through shared common interests and goals. An information-intensive community was proposed to be closely associated with frontiers in science and technology, where people from different geographies, cultures and specialisations were to engage in constructive interchange of ideas, and it was proposed to be a place where people can learn and create a unique culture and explore innovative scientific methodologies and technologies. The innovation was to be portrayed not only through the production of goods and services but also through the lifestyle, consequently encouraging its users towards shared common interests and goals and involvement in public activities.[8] Competition schedule stated March 15, 1986, as the opening of entry registration for the competition. After progressing through a number of stages, April 24 or 25, 1987, was announced as the final judging and awards presentation ceremony days. The jury comprised of a panel of twelve jurors, including three honorary, the details of which are as follows[9] (Table 5.1):

The competition brief also lists the names of five persons under the heading of Special Advisors. These advisors were appointed in order to support the Jury for carrying out its responsibilities, and further advisors were to be appointed if the nature of the submitted works required special expertise. The details of the Special Advisors are as follows[10] (Table 5.2):

*Table 5.1* Panel for the jury of the competition.

| | |
|---|---|
| *Chairman of the Jury* | |
| Saburo Okita | President of Japan Association for Planning Administration; President of International University of Japan |
| *Vice Chairman of the Jury* | |
| Atsushi Shimokobe | President of National Institute for Research Advancement; Director of Japan Association for Planning Administration |
| *Jurors* | |
| Arata Isozaki | Architect |
| Hanae Mori | Fashion Designer; President of Hanae Mori International |
| Joseph Belmont | Chief Architect of French Government |
| Kan Kato | Professor of Keio Gijuku University; Director of Japan Association for Planning Administration |
| Roger Kennedy | Director of National Museum of American History, Smithsonian Institution |
| Shunsuke Ishihara | Professor of Science at the University of Tokyo; Director of Japan Association for Planning Administration |
| Soedjatomoko [sic] | Rector of United Nations University |
| Takashi Asada | Chairman of Japan Urban Science Promote [sic] Association; Judge of First Mainichi International Industrial Design Competition |
| Takemochi Ishii | Professor of the University of Tokyo; Member of Japan Association for Planning Administration |
| Yujiro Hayashi | Vice Chairman of Institute of Future Technology; Honorary Member of Japan Association for Planning Administration |
| *Honorary Jurors* | |
| Daisuke Yamauchi | President of Mainichi Newspapers |
| Kazuji Nagasu | Governor of Kanagawa Prefecture |
| Saburo Ito | Mayor of Kawasaki City |

*Source*: Japan Association for Planning Administration and Mainichi Newspapers, International Concept Design Competition for an Advanced Information City, ca. 1985–86, DR2004:0470:001, Kawasaki Project, 30 × 22 cm, Cedric Price Fonds, Canadian Centre for Architecture, Montréal, 3–4.

*Table 5.2* Advisors appointed for the competition jury.

| | |
|---|---|
| George Lefcoe | Professor of University of Southern California |
| Kenji Ekuan | Director of GK Industrial Design Institute |
| Kenneth Kraemer | Director of Public Policy Research Organization, University of California |
| Michael Joroff | Director of Laboratory of Architecture and Planning, Massachusetts Institute of Technology |
| Michael Pittas | Urban Scholars Fellow, New School for Social Research |

*Source*: Japan Association for Planning Administration and Mainichi Newspapers, International Concept Design Competition for an Advanced Information City, ca. 1985–86, DR2004:0470:001, Kawasaki Project, 30 × 22 cm, Cedric Price Fonds, Canadian Centre for Architecture, Montréal, 4.

The listing of the Jury and Special Advisors points towards some interesting facts. Isozaki was also a member of the Jury, and he was involved in information- and communications-infused architectural projects since the decade of 1960s'. This competition was won by an American team from Massachusetts Institute of Technology (MIT) that was led by Architect Peter Droege that presented a proposal titled *Technology For People: A Campus City Guide*. Among the Special Advisors, Michael Joroff was also appointed, who was the director of Laboratory of Architecture and Planning at the MIT. Joroff and Droege were colleagues at MIT and were involved in the MIT East Asian Architecture and Planning Program. A passage from a report, *Massachusetts Institute of Technology: Reports to the President 1988–89*, states regarding activities of the Kawasaki Advanced Information City Workshop. This workshop explored different concepts, development strategies and city planning specifically for the twenty-first century. Students, practitioners and others interested in this workshop were invited from almost nine countries in Kawasaki and the rural town of Ogaki by the MIT East Asian Architecture and Planning program. Faculty members responsible for workshop arrangements included Droege and Joroff from the MIT in collaboration with their colleagues from the Tokyo Institute of Technology.[11]

The brief also discussed major economic and societal changes that Japan was going through when this competition was announced in 1986–87. Some of the major concerns it briefly touched included demographic changes, such as aging, nuclear family model and resulting social, health, housing and transportation systems, increasing presence of women in the workforce and changing child-rearing patterns, internationalisation of traditional Japanese societal values, reforms in educational system, such as introduction of flexible and innovative learning opportunities and research collaboration with international counterparts, improvements in the quality of the physical environment, transition of Japan's economy from resource-dependent industries to an economy dependent on advanced technologies, etc. Penetration of individualism among members of the society was also stated being forced by country's rapid rate of growth and post-war development.

### Elements of the Competition: Intelligent Plazas, Kawasaki Institute of Technology, Campus City Festival and Intelligent Network

Through the utilisation of advanced information systems, an urban design program for the major revitalisation of Kawasaki was to be carried out in order to transform it into a university campus, and four major themes were outlined as follows for this purpose:

1  Intelligent Plazas.
2  The Kawasaki Institute of Technology (KIT).
3  The Campus City Festival.
4  Intelligent Network.

### Intelligent Plazas

Intelligent Plazas acting as decentralised units of KIT were to be the existing or purpose-designed public or private buildings and spaces, undeveloped natural environment, or a combination of these, with the aim of serving as popular urban facilities. The aim was of exchanging information and meeting communication needs through online, real-time interaction, for example, as in the form of formal or informal education, festivals, ceremonies, research activities, etc. The events or themes to be hosted in these Plazas were based on the guidelines outlined in the Campus City Festival Plan. Proposals were requested to outline key features of these Intelligent Plazas, such as its basic concept, physical facilities, spatial arrangement, including required information and communication equipment, systems for running and usage, connectivity not only within but also linkages and communication with other plazas in the city and beyond. Contestants were requested to develop strategies and a justification for the methods they selected, for example, whether they were proposing entirely new construction or regeneration or extension of the existing infrastructure or a redevelopment plan combined with public or private facilities.[12] Furthermore, the brief also suggested some functions to be a characteristic of each of the Intelligent Plaza. The Plaza was supposed to act as a decentralised educational or research facility linked with the KIT, as a point for collection and dissemination of both text and visual information, for searches related to the information of all sorts, for information exchange and as an exhibition space for the Campus City Festival.[13]

### The Kawasaki Institute of Technology (KIT)

KIT was supposed to be a decentralised group of both existing and newly developed facilities that promoted learning and research. The educational program for the KIT was to be an open education system structured on informal and less rigid curriculum including degree, postgraduate, life-long learning and business entrepreneurship programs. Regarding the programs that were proposed to be taught at the KIT, the competition brief stated that these programs will focus on a specialisation in the *science of information*, as this institution will be exchanging and sharing ideas with similar nature of institutions around the world. It was supposed to retain its repute as equally accessible to locals in the city while maintaining linkages with the international community at large. The brief clarified:

> Science and technology, social science[s], humanities and the arts will be addressed by KIT and each area will be the focus of research and education. Marine biology, energy supply, civics, environmental enhancement, safety, art, health sciences, electronics and nutrition are examples of likely subjects of study.

Learning support systems were to be installed in the university in order to fully equip it with the advanced information systems consequently linking entities such as research centres, public facilities, homes, schools and offices to the KIT. The proximity of research and development laboratories and businesses were to be an important part of the KIT, resulting in collaborations between educational institutions, faculties, students, research laboratories, scientists and private enterprises. This open, decentralised campus was to be connected through advanced information and communication systems called as the Intelligent Network. The aim of this decentralised, informal university was to be an experimental model that serves the "high technology, information-oriented needs of the 21st century while encouraging richer lifestyle options for a population whose characteristics and personal expectations are changing."[14] Some of the fields of KIT as outlined in the competition brief focused particularly on the utilisation of information and communication technologies. These endeavors included introducing educational programs for under- and post-graduate degrees, life-long learning and business entrepreneurship, flexible degree programs, professional management courses and special education exchange programs for the transfer of technology between universities, businesses and nations, specific roles and engaging activities for faculties and students, arrangement of facilities and equipment required for managing information and communication systems, defining and enhancing the characteristics of the learning environments, establishment of linkages for information and communication with other cities within Japan and internationally and the constructive contribution that KIT's engagements and activities can make to Kawasaki and other international societies.[15]

## The Campus City Festival

The aim of the Campus City Festival was to involve stakeholders such as citizens, businesses and government leadership for improving the city identity of Kawasaki through multiple interactive mediums. Towards this goal, an *International Information Exposition* was also proposed to be held for a period of some years. The whole city of Kawasaki was to be used as a site for this exposition and preferably government-owned land was to be used initially. Sister cities, like Tokyo, Yokohama and Chiba, were to act as satellite festival sites linked through information and communication network, for example, conducting discussions through a video conference system, etc. The facilities designed for this exposition were supposed to be used permanently and believed to encourage further development. The brief states this exhibition as a specific event that was planned for 1995 with the aim of celebrating the spirit of the city. This exposition was also to be used as a medium of staging internationally the improvements that were brought to the quality of community life and education by the advent of advanced information city. The International Information Exposition was the first step towards physicalisation of the ideas and gains from the initial decade of Campus City Festival efforts and aimed at not only enhancing the city identity but also pushing efforts towards achieving the new media infrastructure. With reference to the Campus City Festival, participants were requested to incorporate features such as detailed implementation plans, required physical facilities and a site plan for arranging different activities and events, for example, the organisation of an International Information Exposition within the Campus City Festival. Furthermore, descriptions of the information and communication systems were also requested from the participants for linking decentralised sites or a mobile system for facilitating the easy arrangement of small-scale events.[16]

**Intelligent Network**

Intelligent Network was aimed at connecting all of the three elements of Intelligent Plazas, KIT and Campus City Festival in order to form an effective social network across Japan and abroad. Knowledge-based activities were to be networked through hardware system or Campus Area Network (CAN). CAN was comprised of acoustic, image and digital data transmission technologies, providing new information and communication means for Kawasaki. Stakeholders like government organisations, homes, private enterprises, service agencies, workers, etc., were to be connected in Japan, thus enhancing social and cultural activities and, as a result, providing employment opportunities. Six areas were suggested in the brief for the implementation of the Intelligent Network, such as maintaining the individuality of the work sites by allowing them to operate being decentralised but linking them through information and communication network, formation of physical environments and social networks for the elderly and the handicapped, technology transfer nationally and internationally, introduction of community security systems and channelising inter- and intra-city transportation systems both at personal and mass scales, and the purpose of all of these efforts was summarised to be as the achievement of a well-informed citizenry.

Decentralised but linked work sites were to utilize advanced information systems in order to promote satellite office complexes, where people from all walks of life, such as housewives, aged, handicapped, etc., could utilize their capabilities. Flexibility regarding commutation and work timings were major concerns. Specifically designed physical environments and social networks for advanced-age and handicapped persons were intended to boost their participation in the society through educational, social, cultural and economic opportunities. Increased accessibility to health, commercial and transportation services were considered. Technology transfer between Japan and other nations was supposed to be a mutual understanding regarding the social, cultural and industrial management between Japan and other nations for achieving financial benefits. Responsiveness of human, traffic and information networks of the city was considered vital for this transfer and communication of technologies. The aim of community security systems was to take into account the security of socio-economic, policy administration and technological issues. Consideration was given to the community concerns regarding the utilisation of information and the ethics of professionals handling this information. With this reference, concerns regarding the handling of information through information and communication networks were posed, as the brief stated that as the advancement of information and communication systems has taken place, socio-economic dependence on information networks has increased swiftly. It was projected that the available components or safety measures of an information and communication systems were insufficient, and any accidents were projected to occur due to overdependency or concentrated utilisation of these systems. It was also surveyed that the occurrence of such accidents was also on rise. However, it was also thought that arrangement of the network system or the establishment of any security plans would be able to solve such kind of overdependency or usage issues.[17]

Inter- and intra-city transportation systems at the personal and mass scales were proposed in order to improve the gates of the city, such as stations, ports and airports with the intervention of intelligent stations assisting travellers with information and communications. A well-informed citizenry initiation was to involve the citizens in day-to-day activities and to figure-out future possibilities. Points that were to be incorporated in the proposals regarding implementation of the Intelligent Plazas included the methods of citizen participation in the planning process and the types of information and communication systems that were to be used for this purpose, physical environments that were to be utilised for this purpose and the organisational and administrative procedures that were to be implemented for achievement of these goals.[18] Competition participants were supposed to develop the aforementioned four elements in greater detail while focusing on their purposes, functions, facilities and services critical for their implementation. Although it was a conceptual competition, but emphasis was placed on relating it to the city of Kawasaki and incorporating actual considerations as much as possible. Participants were supposed to focus on an element or theme of their choice and to relate it with two or more of the competition's concept elements. Interdisciplinary approach was encouraged, and participants from diversified disciplines and nationalities were welcomed.

## Gordon Pask: the architectural relevance of cybernetics

Andrew Gordon Speedie Pask – known as Gordon Pask (1928–96) – was an English author, inventor, educational theorist, cybernetician and psychologist credited of making significant contributions to the fields of cybernetics, instructional psychology, experimental epistemology and educational technology. In an article titled *The Architectural Relevance of Cybernetics* published in *Architectural Design* magazine's September 1969 issue, he attempts to sketch a relationship between the disciplines of architecture and cybernetics. Instead of focusing on superficial linkages between architecture and cybernetics, such as the utilisation of Program Evaluation and Review Technique (PERT) programming – a cybernetic technique – in the construction scheduling or the usage of cybernetics for calculations of architectural cost layouts with reference to modifications in the architecture, he believes that it is the responsibility of architects to sort out those methods and techniques from the discipline of cybernetics that benefit them the most. He argues that the discipline of architecture is shifting towards non-tangible system properties of development, communication and control. A theory derived from cybernetics can be used to fill the transitional gap between traditional architects and those acting as system designers.

He argues that cybernetics and architecture do enjoy a closer relationship such that they share a common philosophy. He quotes Stafford Beer and his relevance of cybernetics and operational research and argues that as Beer relates these two disciplines by elaborating their common characteristics, architecture and cybernetics can also be evaluated as having similarities on the similar grounds. Architects are fundamentally the system designers whose attentions have been diverted to organisational or non-tangible system properties of development, communication and control, most probably since the last hundred years. Problems of design and relevant concerns were taken care of as soon as they arose, but a foundational or unifying theory is urgent need of the time, he stated. Cybernetics, being an open-ended discipline that further explodes when probed closely, as Beer states, can also serve architecture, as the abstract concepts of cybernetics can also be interpreted in architectural terms and can be identified with architectural systems.[19] Pask suggested technical terminologies for this amalgamation of architecture and cybernetics, a new discipline that can be called as *architectural cybernetics* or the *cybernetic theory of architecture*.[20]

Pask states that in or before the 1800s', architecture was considered to be a building practice accomplished with engineering and historic or aesthetic sensibility, resulting in stable and stylish structures identifiable with a certain space, place and time. Architects in those times were also requested to accommodate human beings in their designs, a practice that he labels as *designing of systems*. Architects were provided with a brief, narrow-minded narrative and were supposed to follow rigid codes based on the conventions of a society, style manuals or of an individual practitioner. He states that a metalanguage was used for comparing, criticising and evaluating instructions, directives and ideas. Architects did not see themselves as system designers at that time, but they did design systems having the representations of a sophisticated house, college or theater. Exceptions also existed at that time, and there were some extraordinary architects who designed in a systemic and interdisciplinary fashion, Pask argues and mentions English architects such as Sir Christopher Wren (1632–1723), Sir John Soane (1753–1837) and John Nash (1752–1835) as examples. He suggests that under the tenets of the early 1800s', these architects were considered as organizers with a vision instead of traditional architects. The Victorian era presented architects with rapid developments that posed fresh questions to be answered, such as of designing a railway station or space for a great exhibition that could no longer be solved with traditional methods and techniques. Although there were structures that were up to the mark, such as Temple Meads, the Tropical House at Kew or the Crystal Palace, on average, general and critical discussion was prohibited. Pask also states regarding the Crystal Palace that even in its poor-quality regeneration, it remained a remarkable structure. As it was one of the first of prefabricated buildings, it can also be counted as a system design from an engineering point of view. He states exceptions such as English civil engineer Isambard Kingdom Brunel (1806–59), architect and urban designer Decimus Burton (1800–81) and gardener, architect, engineer and Member of Parliament Sir Joseph Paxton (1803–65), as prominent designers of glass and ironwork. Pask argues that significance of the work of these architects was not realised at that time, and consequently, their work did not get appreciation as a system design, although their work was in context of the architectural potentialities of that age. He states that innovation-discouraging metalanguage did exist for the early 1800s' architecture, but the emerging augmented architecture had yet to develop its new theory. He further elaborates in this regard that the lack and ignorance of an adequate metalanguage was not the only contributing factor. Sir Nikolaus Bernhard Leon Pevsner (1902–83) – a German-British art and architectural historian – points out that the engineers and artists of this period pursued in more or less similar trajectories. That was one of the major contributing reasons behind the architectural idiosyncrasy. However, Pask strongly believed that if there could had been a metalanguage in relevance to that point in time, then the synthesis of the present century could have been achieved much earlier.[21]

Pask argues that till the late 1800s', instead of a generalised theory, many sub-theories existed, such as relating to materials, symmetry, craftsmanship, etc. These sub-theories were responsible for instilling certain socio-architectural dogma in the society, such as futurism, etc. But the point that he wants to prove is the fact that many of these sub-theories were system-oriented and as he mentions that "in an embryonic sense, 'cybernetic' theories and the thinking behind them made a valuable contribution to the development of cybernetics as a formal science" [emphasis in original]. If the role of a structure is to provide its users with shelter or services (i.e. functionalism), then this functionalist approach can be directed and thus refined in a humanistic direction. He argues and states that a building is only meaningful if it is an inseparable component of a human environment and perpetually interacts with its inhabitants by serving them and controlling their behaviour. He presents the term *architectural mutualism* that promotes an interactive relationship between structures and their users on the whole, labelling buildings as perpetually interacting components instead of just being bricks and mortar masses. Architectural mutualism renders structures as dynamic entities that are in continuous conversation with their inhabitants. Furthering this idea of architectural mutualism, he presents an *architectural holism* approach that considers buildings controlling its inhabitants to a higher level of organisation, consequently resulting in improvised societal traditions. Pask outlined his approach to architectural holism by exemplifying it as a cycle that completes itself from functionally interpreted city to structure, a structure to its surroundings and again, the surroundings to its city. He elaborated that as a city is a dynamic entity, it or any of the structures it contains within it are all functionally interpreted in their respective contexts. This notion renders both this city and its structures as dynamic entities. These entities then can only be conceived in the context of their temporal dimensions, for example, through their growth and development patterns. A structure or a building in this dynamic city exists as its product, or in other words, a constituent of a whole. He then summarises this narrative through Frank Lloyd Wright's (1867–1959) statement that a person should be aware of his natural surroundings, and as a result, his buildings should also be embedded in or arise from these surroundings.[22]

Pask states that systems such as cities grow, develop and evolve. This concept depends on the functionalist or mutualist hypothesis that allows a system the possibility of growth, as the theories of architectural mutualism and architectural holism exhibit. He further adds that "architectural designs should have rules for evolution built into them if their growth is to be healthy rather than cancerous." An architect, who should be responsible enough, should focus on and be concerned with the evolutionary properties of architecture. He should be a part of it, not merely an outsider or observer who just stands back and observes evolution of his structures being progressed on their own. As the evolutionary approach is closely related with the architectural holism, Pask argues, the work of Japanese can be exemplified as being a specialised version of this approach.[23]

Pask highlights the significance of symbolic environments in architecture by elaborating that man communicates with his surroundings through visual, verbal and tactile symbols. Information systems such as the libraries, computers, works of art and buildings, or structures, can said to be the examples of symbolic environments. One of the key points that Pask makes in his article is the uplifting of human emotive responses, such as juxtaposition of releasers and supernormal stimuli through productive and pleasurable dialogue of humans with the structures of their choice. Surrealism can said to be the most notable example of this experiential process, that can be experienced in Catalan Architect Antoni Gaudi's (1852–1926) Parque Guell project. He states in this regard that this type of *vegetable surrealism* can be observed at an architectural level in some of the Art Nouveau, but it reaches considerable maturity in Gaudi's Parque Guell project in Barcelona. Pask states that this park is one of the most cybernetic structures that exist and further adds:

[a]s you explore the piece, statements are made in terms of releasers, your exploration is guided by specially contrived feedback, and variety (surprise value) is introduced at appropriate points to make you explore. It is interesting that Gaudi's work is often *contrasted* with functionalism. Systemically it *is* functionalism pure and simple, though it is aimed at satisfying *only* the symbolic and informational needs of man[24] [emphasis in original].

Pask states that as functionally interpreted buildings constitute a system, so do their construction techniques. Mechanisation of production techniques restricted implementation of forms, such as in the case of Bauhaus that further influenced certain sub-theories and consequently promoted limited forms associated with them. But he argues that in recent decades, a brief given to an architect has been widened essentially due to the cybernetic, sub-theoretical developments. This major shift in mind-sets has also been due to the fact that architects are being presented with problems that could not be solved through traditional mind-sets, as have been the case in the Victorian era – for example, designing of structures associated with aerospace developments, industry, research, entertainment, developments in the oceans, etc. While following the unconventional trends in the discipline of contemporary architectural designing, Pask argued that cities are being planned with a provision for their evolution. He presented this theory of architectural mutualism or holism in 1969 and further applied it two decades later in his proposal titled the *Japnet, Kawasaki* for the International Concept Design Competition for an Advanced Information City that was organised in 1986–87 by the city of Kawasaki in collaboration with the Japanese government authorities and other organisations. Back in 1969, he, while emphasising the intelligent nature of an educational facility, stated that it is not absolutely a requirement or a rule that a university has always to be a set of certain building blocks that are arranged around a central courtyard and incorporating accommodation and lecturing needs. He proposed that educational systems must be decentralised, or in other words, be distributed rather than being localised or concentrated in one place as have been the case traditionally with educational facilities. Architects were to be encouraged in order to equip themselves with the rapidly emerging trends in technological developments and in this case, the trends of educational technology and the impact these technological advancements are going to place upon the structures that would be to shelter them. Architects were only invited to play their role in the whole process of these educational developments only when a higher-level educational system was to be developed, such as universities, etc. Pask emphasised that architects should be involved in these kinds of projects in order to catch the essence of the emerging technologies and the influence they eventually render on the architecture. He further stated in this regard:

> [t]he Fun Palace project, by Joan Littlewood and Cedric Price, was an early entry project of this type in the field of entertainment and it is not difficult to find examples in areas ranging from exhibition design to factory building[25] [emphasis in original].

Pask, after discussing the segregated theories and sub-theories of architectural design from the nineteenth and early twentieth centuries till 1960s', concludes that system-oriented thinking has led to a generalisation that all of these sub-theories more or less have common constituents of control, communication and system. These characteristics point towards abstract cybernetics that can be interpreted as an architectural theory. He mentions Christopher Alexander, Nicholas Negroponte and his students and ex-students from the Architectural Association School of Architecture and from Newcastle as making prominent advances in cybernetic architectural theory. He believes that cybernetic architectural theory can provide a metalanguage for critical discussion. It can predict or explain self-organising systems, as he explained in his architectural mutualism and holism theories. Urban development can be treated as a self-organising system so that its growth trends of being chaotic or ordered can be measured or at least rational hypotheses can be tested. He mentions the significance of artificial intelligence computer programs that can be utilised by the discipline of architecture:

> The cybernetic theory can also claim some explanatory power insofar as it is possible to mimic certain aspects of architectural design by artificial intelligence computer programs (provided, incidentally, that the program is able to learn *about* and *from* architects and by experimenting in the language of architects, i.e. by exploring plans, material specifications, condensed versions of clients' comments, etc.). Such programs are clearly of value in their own right. They are potential aids to design; acting as intelligent extensions of the tool-like programs . . . Further, they offer a means for integrating the constructional system (the "machinery of production") with the ongoing design process since it is quite easy to embody the constraints of current technology in a special part of the simulation. However, I believe these programs are of far greater importance as evidencing out theoretical knowledge of what architecture is about. Insofar as the program can be written, the cybernetic theory is explanatory[26] [emphasis in original].

When Pask mentions the artificial intelligence computer programs, he states that he refers to Negroponte's Architecture Machine Group that he initiated with Leon B. Groisser at the MIT and functioned from 1967–85. But he stresses that other exemplars can also be referred. In a section of a paper titled *Speculations*, Pask outlines five areas in which rapid advances can be speculated guided by the cybernetic theory of architecture. These five areas tend to be computer-assisted design procedures, transdisciplinarity, architecture as a social control, liberation of intelligent housing to entire environments and Gaudi's architecture's dialogue between itself and its inhabitants. For computer-assisted design procedures, Pask states that these computer-directed design programs are going to be developed into extremely useful tools, helping humans tremendously in the future. Back at that time, he intended to show the applicability and usefulness of artificially intelligent architectural programs that aid architects and designers with the achievement of their ideas. He forecasted, being the transdisciplinary nature of cybernetics and artificially intelligent architecture, that different disciplines, such as social anthropology, psychology, sociology, ecology and economics, will be unified and incorporated within the discipline of architecture, consequently equipping architecture to cater entities, such as civilisation, city or educational system, in its broadest sense. Architecture was to act as a social control mechanism, and a proper and systematic formulation was forecasted. While presenting the concept of a house as a "machine for living in" as per functional-ist approach, he stated that in this case, the machine acted as a tool that served its inhabitant. He firmly believed that "[t]his notion will, I believe, be refined into the concept of an environment *with* which the inhabitant cooperates and *in* which he can externalize his mental processes, i.e. mutualism will be emphasised as compared with mere functionalism" [emphasis in original]. Pointing towards the smart homes of today, he projected back in the 60s' that as this machine for living in and its inhabitants are going to be in a state of symbiosis, this machine will be liberating its users from any needs to store large amounts of routine information in memory and will free its residents from the need of performing multiple calculations. Everyday chores, such as garbage disposal and washing of dishes, will be the tasks that this artificially intelligent machine for living in will be performing on behalf of its residents on its own. Furthermore, this intel-ligent machine will be able to attract or capture the attention of its users so that they are bound by interest to like and appreciate it, and any question-and-answer sessions will be taking place between the two, just as a conversation between two persons takes place. Pask presented the example of this artificially intelli-gent architecture in the work of Gaudi and stated that he, either intentionally or not, beautifully achieved a dialogue between the environments he designed and its inhabitants. He achieved this interaction while utilising the physically static structures, as has been the case in his Parque Guell, that the movements of its users or the shifts in their attentions while visiting this park keep on formulating dynamic processes with each other. He further expressed significant optimism regarding advancements in the modern technologies and said that this dialogue can further be refined and extended with the help of contemporary techniques that "allow us to weave the same pattern in terms of a reactive environment. If, in addition, the environment is malleable and adaptive the results can be very potent indeed." He experimented on these lines in his *Musicolor System* and *Colloquy of Mobiles* projects.[27]

Pask developed the *Musicolor System* in 1953–57 (Figure 5.1). Later, he also presented some of the revised versions of this system. The inspiration for the design of this system came from Prof. Lerner's *Color Music System* that was presented at the *Soviet Exhibition* in London, 1961. This work can also be related to Nicholas Schöffer and to a number of artefacts that were presented in the States.[28] Musicolor behaved as an assistant of a performer such that when an artist was performing, let's suppose, a piece of music or was composing one, then this system assisted him in order to enhance or improve his work by displaying instructions on its panel. The performer was then able to improvise his work of art by noticing and following the instructions being displayed by the Musicolor. Pask designed and inhabited the system with different learning mechanisms such that it was able to learn from its surroundings and consequently suggest improvements. For example, if a performer wanted to modify or revise a piece of music to a different interpretation, it was fully possible with the assistance of this intelligent machine. In another case, even if a musician was interested in improvising a piece of music in accordance with his intuition, he was welcomed by and fully trusted the Musicolor for assistance.

*Figure 5.1* The Musicolor System, its power boxes and reflector display.

*Source*: Gordon Pask, Musicolor System, power boxes, reflector display, ca. 1953–57, photographs. Heinz von Foerster, Gordon Pask & Cybernetics Archives, Department of Contemporary History, University of Vienna. Used with permission.

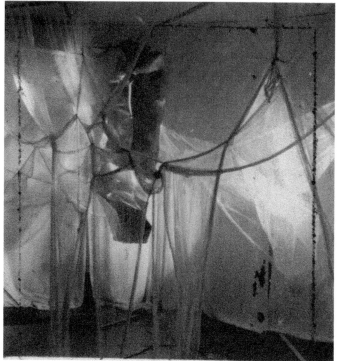

*Figure 5.1* (Continued)

The internal mechanism of this intelligent machine worked by interpretation of the information it received through a microphone and it was then amplified. The resulting electrical signal was then compared to and analysed with a bank of property or attribute filters, whose job was to listen to the sequence. The characteristics of these filters were then revised by an internal learning mechanism, in other words, technically, their parameters were adjusted. This machine was designed in such a manner that it listened to and interpreted the performer's activities. In other words, its mechanism was based on a machine learning process.[29] Pask discussed this project with John Clark – a psychiatrist – and in collaboration, they observed mesmerising consequences of a man-machine symbiosis, such as loss of time sense on the performer's part, the performer conceiving the machine as an extension of himself, etc. While utilising this system, the performer lost the sense of time. For example, one of the performers played his instrument from 10 pm till 5 am and seemed unaware that much time had passed. This effect was not particular to this performer but was rather ubiquitous. As this intelligent machine was equipped with learning capabilities, performers were able to fully train it according to their talents. It was case studied that usually, a performer just started with simple tricks that usually involved feeding descriptions, but gradually, when a performer felt that he was in full control of this system, the trick made the system behave in such a way that either the performer or an outsider was not able describe this behaviour at once. This man-machine interaction was said to be at a "higher level of abstraction." In this man-machine symbiosis:

> [f]rom the performer's point of view, training becomes a matter of persuading the machine to adopt a visual style which fits the mood of his performance. At this stage in the development of rapport, the performer conceived the machine as an extension of himself, rather than as a detached or disassociated entity.[30]

Cybernetic mechanisms within the Musicolor System were also responsible for linkage of motions of a dancer to the input of the machine. Pask stated that although this process was technically difficult, if achieved, its aesthetic possibilities were indisputable. A study was also conducted exploring the perceptual properties of the system. "Cogent visual symbols appear to act as 'releaser' stimuli and observations of Clark and myself suggested that the most effective 'releasers' are short sequences of visual events, rather than static configurations"[31] [emphasis in original]. Pask recalls the very first Musicolor machine that he designed:

> The Musicolour system was inspired by the concept of synaesthesia and the general proposition that the aesthetic value of a work can be enhanced if the work is simultaneously presented in more than one sensory modality. . . . The first Musicolour machine was built and demonstrated by McKinnon Wood and myself at Jordan's Yard, Cambridge in 1953. It was a transducer which accepted a musical input through a microphone (this input is conveniently formalized as the performer's section from an auditory vocabulary). The

output of the transducer consisted in a selection made from a predetermined vocabulary of visual symbols; coloured forms which were projected on to a large screen in front of the performer and an audience.[32]

Pask states that with the help of acquaintances, he was able to test his Musicolor System on a moderately sized group of people that consequently resulted in the system's improvement. The system was able to gradually develop as an intelligent device. He elaborates that one of the most interesting features of the machine was not its synesthesia but its learning capabilities. With the availability of a feasible design and sufficient visual vocabulary, the performer who was under the influence of the visual display was to become involved in an approximately never-ending interaction with the system. Pask adds that the performer:

> trained the machine and it played a game with him. In this sense, the system acted as an extension of the performer with which he could co-operate to achieve effects that he could not achieve on his own. Consequently, the learning mechanism was extended and the machine itself became reformulated as a game player capable of habituating at several levels, to the performer's gambits.

Pask believed and suggested that in this man-machine symbiosis, audience was also to be invited to become an active stakeholder in this very real interaction.[33] In the absence of an input, the system got bored, a characteristic of systems designed by Pask. The system was completely trainable, and a learning mechanism was incorporated in its mechanics. A strategy for this learning mechanism was selected in order to build up the transfer of information around a feedback loop comprising of visual display, performer, musical instrument and a learning machine. This was the aim of this intelligent machine:

> to entrain the performer and to couple him into the system. In these terms, the importance of "habituation" and "novelty seeking" are evident if we also accept the proposition that man (the converse participant) is impelled to seek, learn about and resolve novelty in his environment[34] (Figure 5.2) [emphasis in original].

The Musicolor System was fully workable but suffered from a number of defects. The maintenance of the system was costly, and the returns were modest that consequently led it to debt. Pask made every effort to sell it, even advertising it as a pure art form and as an attachment for the jukeboxes. In large-scale and commercially viable situations, the system was unusable. As almost every attempt failed, the Musicolor made its last appearance in 1957 and, afterwards, was formally shelved. Pask possessed a small portion of it but was not in a working condition and was of mainly sentimental value.

The *Colloquy of Mobiles* – an installation – was presented at the *Cybernetic Serendipity Exhibition of Cybernetic Art* at the Institute of Contemporary Arts,

*Figure 5.2* Electrochemical system attached with the Musicolor System.

*Source*: Gordon Pask, Electrochemical system, ca. 1953–57, photograph. Heinz von Foerster, Gordon Pask & Cybernetics Archives, Department of Contemporary History, University of Vienna. Used with permission.

London (Figure 5.3). This exhibition was curated by Jasia Reichardt and was at display from August 2 till October 20, 1968. In the Colloquy of Mobiles, the "[s]ystem and males were designed by Gordon Pask, females were designed by Yolanda Sonnabend, electronics were designed by Mark Dowson and Tony Watts, and patron of the project was Maurice Hyams in cooperation with System Research Ltd."[35] Exhibiting works from prominent techno artists, Reichardt defined the aim of the exhibition as to display and generate a discussion on computer-generated mediums of graphics, animated films, music, poems and texts, cybernetic devices as works of art, cybernetic environments, remote-control robots, painting machines, usage of computers as demonstrated by machines and the history of cybernetics as in an environment.[36] Pask's exhibit comprised of a set of mobiles – that he named as a *male* and a *female* – that communicated with each other even in the absence of a human being. These mobiles were system-designed and programmed and

*Figure 5.3* The Colloquy of Mobiles.

*Source*: Gordon Pask, Colloquy of Mobiles, ca. 1968, photograph. Heinz von Foerster, Gordon Pask & Cybernetics Archives, Department of Contemporary History, University of Vienna. Used with permission.

were made-up of electronic parts. When a human being entered this cybernetic environment, he became a part of it and resulted in enhancement of information and communication. Pask called this artificial cybernetic environment as a *socially orientated reactive and adaptive environment*. He explains that an aesthetically potent environment is the one that comprises of auditory, verbal, visual, tactile, etc., elements and forces participants to engage in it and thus enhances their feeling of well-being. Artists communicate messages through this environment. He further explains the characteristics of this artificial cybernetic environment as an aesthetically appealing environment that encourages the visitor to explore it further, to inquire about it, to learn about and experience it, to formulate a series of concepts referring to it, etc. This kind of an environment further guides an explorer's exploration and welcomes him to participate in it or become a part of it so that he may see his reflection in this environment. He classifies this environment as passive and the one that manifests itself physically and not necessarily psychologically and exemplifies it with those of music and paintings that are worth listening to and seeing repetitively. He further added that "[a]ctive and even reactive environments have been fabricated with this property. The *colloquy of mobiles* is an attempt to go one step further in the same direction"[37] [emphasis in original].

Pask explains the installation as composed of a male and female sculptures facing each other (Figure 5.4). This is the most simple arrangement, and further configurations are possible with the enlargement of this community of sculptures without any special effects on the set-up or design of the installation. The internal mechanism of the male mobile was composed of O and P drives. These drives were named based on the orange-and-puce-coloured intense light beams that they emitted. This male mobile was capable of projecting an intense beam of orange light from its central part which receptors in its upper part were able to receive. Similar was the case with the beam of puce light that was emitted and was received from the lower part of the male mobile. These receptors were closely bound to the main body of these sculptures, and in order to achieve their goals, these males were to request the cooperation of female mobiles. The female sculptures were equipped with vertically positionable reflectors that were capable of receiving the beams from the central parts of the male figures and reflected it back to their lower portion.[38] On another account, Pask outlines his exhibition proposal as a group of objects or programmed male and female mobiles that engage in discourse, compete, co-operate and learn about each other. Anyone can participate in their discourse and can very easily become a part of this set-up. He stated that a male and a female were supposed to cooperate with each other and to work in collaboration such that their achievements were more than what they were able to accomplish in isolation. He added:

> [i]ronically, this property is manifest in the fact that a male can project strong beams of light but it cannot satisfy an urge to have them play on its periphery, whereas a female (who cannot shine light) is able to reflect it back to a male (and, when she is competent, to reflect it upon the right position). . . . They [communicate] . . . in a simple but many-leveled language of light flashes and sounds.[39]

Pask mentions the work on reactive environments by Warren Brodey (born 1924) – a psychiatrist and psychoanalyst who became an MIT-affiliated cybernetician and led a group at the environmental ecology laboratory. He stated that Brodey and his environmental ecology group was working on an impressive scale. A computer was controlling the visual and tactile properties of environmental materials which were also available in greater variety to be used for architectural purposes. These materials contained tactile or visual sensors that returned layered messages to the computer. Due to certain pre-programmed invariants, the whole system was led to the state of stabilisation in the absence of a human inhabitant. A body of the material was supposed to maintain its mechanical stability and a prescribed value.

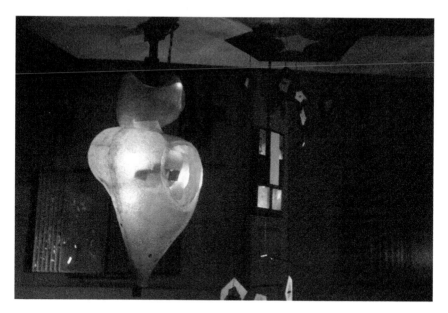

*Figure 5.4* The interaction of mobiles in the dark.

*Source*: Gordon Pask, Colloquy of Mobiles, ca. 1968, photographs. Heinz von Foerster, Gordon Pask & Cybernetics Archives, Department of Contemporary History, University of Vienna. Used with permission.

Furthermore, it was also responsible for maintaining a search process in which a material actively looked for any signs of human contact. A computer, material and any other stakeholders engaged a human in a dialogue if he was in their environment. In this way, the system was able to learn and adapt to his behaviour pattern and to upgrade itself. Pask concluded on this basis that "[t]here is thus one sense in which the reactive environment is a *controller* and another in which it is controlled *by* its inhabitants"[40] [emphasis in original].

A simple cybernetic architecture in the context of a reactive and adaptive environment comprises of interdependent stages, Pask states. With reference to the human inhabitants in a cybernetic architecture, the purpose or goal of the system must always be underspecified. It should be the duty of an architect to remain unaware of the goal of the system. This statement is a counter-thesis of the functionalist approach. For example, an architect designs a house by prioritising its functions, but in cybernetic architecture, he is responsible only for providing a set of constraints allowing for certain desirable modes of evolution. Fundamental environmental materials must be utilised for achieving these kinds of cybernetic systems. Certain invariants are programmed into the system, and the choice of these depends on the architect, as he determines the properties relevant to a man-environment dialogue in this cybernetic system. As this environment is capable of learning from its surroundings, the architect specifies which properties it will learn and how it will adapt. A feasible plan was to be selected for the adaptation and development of this system. As the aim of the system was kept underspecified, its plan was to be based on evolutionary principles.[41]

Pask further states that the aforementioned program is feasible for systems that operate for short time intervals of minutes or hours. In the Fun Palace project, this program was implemented for longer intervals of time, for example, spanning across eight hourly and weekly cycles. It is suggested that instead of manual operations, a computer can be utilised for the management of these time intervals, as its use will be economical and more efficient. For example, depending on the time constraints and the flexibility requirements, a computer program can easily handle the weekly cycle economically, as was proposed by John and Julia Frazer for Cedric Price's Generator project. Departing from architecture to the urban design, Pask suggests that the aforementioned cybernetic program can be successfully incorporated and utilised for long-term urban design evaluations. Keeping in view the span of urban design projects from years to decades, the plans that were being produced at that point in time were incapable of incorporating certain changing aspects of the urban design. Pask called this instatic, immobile plan as an *inflexible specification*. However, he suggested that it was fully possible to shape this dialogue of urban development and its users into an interactive session, in other words, as a reactive environment process. Through this method, physical contact between the inhabitants and their environment was achievable, and it was possible to survey their preferences and predilections. Pask argued that this was one of those numerous ways in which the *inflexible plan* was to be transformed into an *environmental computing machine*. Regarding the cases discussed, Pask stated that "[i]f so, the same design paradigm applies, since in all of the cases so far considered the primary decisions are systemic in character, i.e. they amount to the delineation or the modification of a control program." And this universality, he said, is typical of the cybernetic environments.[42]

Pask argues that when a designer uses a cybernetic program as his assistant, then he must have a higher level of organisational hierarchy in comparison to his assistant, but at the same time, the designer must be someone who acts as a catalyst, crutch or an arbiter so that the whole discourse must be somehow balanced. As is the case with cybernetic systems, the design goal is always kept underspecified, and consequently, the controller of the program is no longer in authority. In fact, a controller, Pask states, "is an odd mixture of catalyst, crutch, memory and arbiter." These are the roles that a designer must play when he takes the position, and he must also try to embed these very same qualities in the control systems that he designs.[43] In an article titled *A comment, a case history and a plan* (1971), Pask outlines and elaborates the characteristics of a reactive and adaptive environment:

a. It must offer sufficient variety to provide the potentially controllable novelty required by a man (however, it must not swamp him with variety – if it did, the environment would merely be unintelligible).
b. It must contain forms that a man can interpret or learn to interpret at various levels of abstraction.
c. It must provide cues or tacitly stated instructions to guide the learning and abstractive process.
d. It may, in addition, respond to a man, engage him in conversation and adapt its characteristics to the prevailing mode of discourse.[44]

## Competition Entry by Gordon Pask: the *Japnet, Kawasaki*

Pask participated in the *International Concept Design Competition for an Advanced Information City* with his proposal that he designed in collaboration with Cedric Price. Pask was credited as the major contributor of the competition entry, as he designed the first four presentation panels that were approximately of A1 size, and only the last one was designed by Price. So in total, five presentation panels were submitted to the competition administration for the judging process. Although Pask was a cybernetician, he was very interested in exploring the cybernetic discourse with reference to the discipline of architecture. He had worked on the Fun Palace project with Price previously, and the Japnet project once again provided him with the opportunity for extending his second-order cybernetics to the specialism of architecture, particularly through his involvement in teaching and visiting responsibilities at the Architectural Association (AA), London. Price's contribution to the Japnet project focused on the information exchange throughout the city of Kawasaki, as he proposed installation of appliances in order to formulate a network of information. Price outlines Pask's contributions to the AA in the 1960s' that "I . . . was delighted when Gordon agreed to sit on my architectural juries. . . . His presence and inventions within life of the Architectural Association school are both legendary and of day to day relevance."[45] With reference to the Japnet project,

Pask was the one who generated ideas for the competition proposal and acted as a major contributor, as Price explains that Pask possessed a modesty of mind and was always eager to learn innovative ideas and concepts. He was not only a superb teacher but also a magnificent cooperator, as Price experienced this while working in collaboration with him on the Japnet project. Price states and further adds:

> The design ranged from static units and their contained transportation and information network to the local outlet or terminal. Gordon took it further than I had dared to think of: the house became a component of the total plan but lost nothing of its serenity, warmth and domestic individuality in doing so. A splendid submission with Gordon's inspired doodles an added delight.[46]

The appearance of these panels suggests that rough sketches were photocopied and pasted hastily on the presentation boards. Sketches done on white paper were pasted on cream- or light-yellow-coloured presentation boards. Some sketches also have a layer of a tracing paper with yellow-coloured sticky notes having the descriptions of *50% Line Art and 100% Line Art* on them. Red ballpoint pen markings can also be observed. A comparative analysis of these presentation boards having tracing paper and yellow-coloured sticky notes with the ones presented by Hardingham in *Cedric Price Works 1952–2003: A Forward-Minded Retrospective* (2016) shows that these tracing papers and sticky notes are a latter addition and were not drawn by either Pask or Price during the assembly of these competition panels.[47]

Pask's sketches detail both the architectural and urban proposals for the Japnet competition entry. He was well aware with the scale of the site and probably would have been in consultation with Price, who could have used the length of a string for measuring the site's scale. Both of them studied the urban site in order to have the idea of scale of the site. Price normally used the length of a string for measuring the scale of the site and afterwards, comparing the site with a more familiar location. For example, as in the case of the *Sagamiwan Urban Resort Festival, Surf 90* (1990) competition, he used a length of string with the label of *5 miles mark* for having the idea of scale of the South Coast of England and of Kanagawa, Japan. He used similar methods for getting an idea of the scale of the site for the Japnet competition. Panel 5: 00–7B 5/5 was designed by Price, showing the understanding of the urban characteristics of the city of Kawasaki through geographical details and urban diagrams. As the competition participants were requested to select one or more of the elements from Intelligent Plazas, Kawasaki Institute of Technology (KIT), Campus City Festival and Intelligent Network of the competition and to formulate a relationship between two or more of them, Pask selected and designed the elements of Intelligent Plaza, KIT's Student Residences and the Intelligent Network. This chapter particularly focuses and analyses the first four competition panels numbered from Panel 1: 00–7B 1/5 till Panel 4: 00–7B 4/5 that were entirely designed by Pask. These panels, sketches, drawings and their captions have been studied in detail, and consequently, an attempt has been made to construct project's description, shedding light on Pask's approach to the competition.

The first panel comprises of five sketches and two handwritten notes composed on a cream-coloured presentation board. Sketches consists of an interior of a student dormitory that belongs to the KIT. Probably an entrance lobby has been sketched, depicting 6 storeys and a semi-circular full-height glass roof reminiscent of the crystal palace. Students can also be seen conversing in the sketch. Another sketch depicts possibly the exterior of the student dormitory with a courtyard in the middle having dense plantations. The 6 storey building can be observed right in the middle with a semi-circular glass roof, the interior of which is shown in another sketch. This sketch shows three blocks of 6 storey buildings in the centre and two wings of 4 storey buildings at left- and right-hand sides to the central block. A pagoda or a tower can also be observed at the back of this dormitory. Another high-rise building can also be observed at the back right-hand side of the dormitory that has not been drawn completely but just appears to be a glimpse. Further sketches depict the interior of a 4 storey building, the exterior of which can be observed in another sketch. This interior is similar to those depicted in the previous sketches with the difference being the width of the entrance lobby has been narrowed, and the number of storeys has been reduced to four from six. When the sketch is zoomed in, the floor seems to be designed in descending platforms towards the entrance of the building. The roof seems to be as a semi-circular full-height glass roof but far more narrower as compared to the one in a previous sketch. Three of the sketches on the presentation board seem to be interrelated, as all of them explain the concept of *Techno Trees* or *People Poles*. Sketches show these Techno or Technological Trees as hanging in different portions of the student dormitory. The passageways seem to cut through these Techno Trees, and they are depicted hanging from the roof and positioned right in the middle of the rooms. In a sketch, Pask points to one of these and mentions that these are the "Postboxes at the level of . . . the galaxy" and then continues that they can act as "A *Logo* For Our *Entry*"[48] [emphasis in original]. Another sketch depicts the information and communication processes in between these Techno Trees. A cube is sketched with its corners being occupied by these Techno Trees, and the black, abstract-looking shape inside the cube is the information and communication processes going-on between them. Pask mentions in this sketch the characteristics of these Techno Trees or People Poles as being of the "Ball and Stick Volume, Communications, Post Boxes and Market Barrows, [and] Shelter."[49]

A closer look at the sketch of the cube reveals that Pask attempted to present the whole city of Kawasaki within this cube. The details of this sketch can be broken down into a number of elements. For example, a cube is presented as a black-lined frame, with Techno Trees that have been presented as the black circles located at the corners of the cube. Coordinates have been written as *<1, 0, 1>* kinds of formats around the Techno Trees. An abstract shape coloured black has been placed inside the cube, depicting the process of information and communication between these Techno Trees, and black-coloured triangles have been introduced with numbers like (i), (ii), (iii), etc., indicating characteristics of people surrounded and using the Techno Trees. The legend of this cube incorporating information and communication technologies presents an interesting list of terminologies such as "Geographical

Proximity, Communication with others, Perception of others, Sensory Proximity, Hermit, Person with Headphones and Dark Spectacles, Sensory Deprivation of Solipsist, Gregarious Group, [etc.]." Another term, *too much togetherness*, has been taken by Pask from a paper titled *Limits of Togetherness* that he presented at the *International Federation of Information Processing Societies*, Tokyo (1980). Regarding the term *too much solitude*, he refers to the word *Point* and immediately cites Edwin Abbott's novella *Flatland: A Romance of Many Dimensions* (1884). Furthermore, he also cites his very own joint publication with Susan Curran titled *Micro Man: Computers and the Evolution of Consciousness* (Macmillan, 1982).[50] On the fourth panel, Pask knits these terminologies with the resultant architecture:

> It is interesting to place a hermit, a solipsist, a person with headphones and dark spectacles, a gregarious individual, a person in sensory deprivation within the coordinates of the cube. . . . This is *one* projection of the design. *Another* projection . . . represents a torus with perceptual and sensory flux around it in one direction and proximity flux in the other direction, the whole "torus" immersed in a "sea" of information flux. There are many other possible projections. But this one directly relates the network design of Drawings . . . to the plaza design of the Architecture of Knowledge[51] [emphasis in original].

The legend of these sketches states that these Techno Trees can be considered as information and communication devices that are supporting and enhancing the lives of the citizens of Kawasaki with reference to geographical, communicative and perceptual or sensory parameters. On one hand, these Techno Trees influence the citizens, and on the other, citizens help in reverting and improving the information and communication received from them. In other words, a continuous loop of information, communication and feedback is formulated between these Techno Trees and citizens, consequently enhancing everyday life experience through a cybernetic discourse. He refers to both the *Flatland* and *Micro Man* for clarification of concepts behind these sketches. He also refers to an invited paper, *The Limits of Togetherness*, that he presented at the *Eighth International Federation of Information Processing Societies Congress* held at Tokyo, Japan, on October 6–9, 1980, and Melbourne, Australia, on October 14–17, 1980.[52] In this paper, Pask argues that the current theories of communication and computation are not sufficient enough for engineering togetherness – that is, communication and conversation – and consequently proposes extra-theoretic props for distinguishing between communication and conversation. With reference to these terms, he then defines the information environment and states that conversation was disturbed in the past due to the lack of communication, but in the future, this will not be a problem, as geographical distances will be minimised, but conversation will be endangered by excessive togetherness. In elaborating the arrival of an information age, he states that these technological developments along with the social, national and industrial pressures are going to carry the technical breakthroughs into tangible structures or architecture. He states that technological developments have shortened human distances and have provided them with the ultimate ease of communication. By exemplifying technological advancements, such as the communication and fiber optic industry carrying infinite bandwidth channels, microwave and satellite communication, video and magnetic discs with storage capacities of greater than 80 megabytes (that were a huge development at that point in time), low-energy-consuming semiconductors and magnetic domain or bubble devices and, ultimately, computation advancements, such as microprocessors connecting storage media to channels and optical and array processors, have made the processes of information and communication processing far more easier and convenient in the urban districts. He further quoted Prof. Max H. Hines from Seattle University as "Others, amongst them Hines, have argued, cogently and convincingly, for these technologies and the social, national and industrial pressures that are, willy nilly, going to carry technical breakthroughs into tangible structures." Hines researched the role information and communication technologies play in the betterment of everyday lives, and his paper *Using the Telephone in Family Therapy* (1994) conducted case studies, examined some ethical issues and discussed the future impact of advanced telephone-related communication technology on the family therapy.[53] Pask further stated the burgeoning technological developments in the field of information handling and processing systems such as "Nelson's Hypertext[,] Winograd and Kaye's KRL." He also referred Nicholas Negroponte's work in this regard by stating:

[t]here is Negroponte's "data space," and the video disc store of Aspen, Colorado, so accessed that a user can drive through the streets, industries, history or everyday activity of that town. My own entailment meshes, perhaps, are candidates. There is a host of reactive animated graphics facilities, exemplified by De Fantis' work[54] [emphasis in original].

The Knowledge Representation Language was developed by Daniel G. Bobrow and Terry Winograd while they were working at Xerox PARC and Stanford University in 1976–77. They analysed and developed a high-level artificial intelligence programming language and a theory of knowledge representation. On the basis of these technological developments, Pask argued that communication or computation proximity has been released from the geographical constraints. These systems have rendered the natural environment as an information-infused environment. Pask expressed his concerns in the favor of any legislation against privacy or isolation, as he projected that these information and communication technologies were definitely going to invade the privacies of its users, *for our own good* – a term that he used in order to express his reservations. He said in this regard:

[f]orseeably, the industrial, social and national pressures which promote information technology will also give rise to legislation against privacy or isolation, all quite justifiable and "for our own good." Before long, the statute books will ordain that any partition, wall or enclosure is penetrated by a channel of so many megahertz capacity, and will include rules like "a fibre-optic-cable shall connect each *legal* house"[55] [emphasis in original].

He also argues in his paper that if there is no conflict to resolve, there is no conversation, that is information transfer between organisationally closed or autonomous systems. He states that conflicts give rise to the need of conversation, clarification and justifications. If all are satisfied with all that is happening, then there are only *doppelgangers* instead of thinking, living beings. An ant does not observe another of her companion as a mere *ant*, but an observer or an anthill may observe others as a group of living organisms that have shared goals, or robots that have a common programming for a common aim. "Something akin to this would be the fate of mankind if all concepts *really* had universally agreed definitions," he said[56] [emphasis in original].

In one of the sketches on his presentation boards, Pask presents a sketch of a *torus*, or what he calls as a *doughnut*, and states with reference to it terminologies such as "Communication Proximity and Flux" and mentions right next to it that these are *adaptable sensory partitions*. Another of the term that he introduces is "Geographical Proximity and Traffic Flux," and it follows the term *adaptable drawbridges*. He then explains the technical nature of these terminologies that it is a torus, or a doughnut, that floats in the sea of information having unlimited information bandwidth and storage capacities. For a single Techno Tree prototype, four fiber optic and coaxial channels, twelve phone lines, 60 gigabytes of random-access memory and compact disc read-only memory storages were suggested that were quite a challenge for that point in time regarding computation technologies. He also refers to detailed notes on the implementation of these technologies as "Observing Systems, Vow Foerster, Fig. 19, pp. 305" and states that Intersystem 1983 explains and explores the "general intelligent life process."[57] A sketch on the black-coloured torus, or doughnut, represents white lines moving in both inward and circular directions. Lines moving inward denote clockwise circulation, and lines moving in the circular direction denote an anti-clockwise movement. Pask explains the clockwise movement of the lines moving inwards as communication proximity and flux representing adaptable sensory partitions. Lines moving in the circular direction with anti-clockwise movement represent geographical proximity and traffic flux denoting adaptable drawbridges. This torus visualises the invisible flow of information between the Techno Trees. This invisible flow of information can be seen shaded black in another sketch with a number of toruses, or doughnuts, running in between. He mentions regarding these toruses that they represent information bandwidth and unlimited local storage. He idealises a torus, or a doughnut, as floating in the sea of information. After mentioning these technical specifications, Pask also refers to Foerster's *Observing Systems* (1984) and suggests that general intelligent life processes can be analysed and developed in detail.[58] Hardingham notes in this regard that Pask and Price's competition submission presented an innovative approach for a traditional urban typology of the plaza. They chose the element of an *Intelligent Plaza* for their entry and reimagined it as an intricate communication network that was distributed throughout the city, expanding its coverage to the remotest and disconnected most urban sites. An outcrop of *Techno Trees* was suggested to act as artificially intelligent post boxes to be utilised by the citizens of Kawasaki. Taking into consideration the technical specifications of these trees as have been mentioned earlier, she notes that "Pask specifies 60GB of RAM, at a time when personal computers, such as Apple's IIGS, had a maximum of 8MB of memory." Different versions of these technological trees were designed both by the architect and the cybernetician, Hardingham states and elaborates the one drawn by Pask:

[his] sketch of a techno-tree is a more distinctly mathematical model, denoting a continuous feedback loop of unlimited information storage floating in a "sea of information." The drawing is annotated as a ball-and-stick volume where the balls are communications post-boxes and the sticks are a market barrow, with shelter provided by an amorphous shaded area [emphasis in original].

However, she argues that these Techno Trees only represent the thoughts of the people of the city of Kawasaki through an invisible structure that can be visualised with the help of a computer-animated image of the built environment. She summarises the ideology of Pask behind this concept as "Pask suggests that this evolving image – of a city changing in real time in response to citizen input – could be made visible via 'computer graphics' across the plaza"[59] [emphasis in original].

The second panel consists of twenty sketches. This panel displays the concept of an Intelligent Plaza, or as Pask calls it, the *Architecture of Knowledge*, depicting the tensegrity structure, and the rest of the panel contains mathematical descriptions of toruses, or doughnuts, that are suggestive of the information and communication processes going-on within this tensegrity structure (Figure 5.5). Majority of the sketches on this presentation panel represent mathematical interpretations regarding information and communication processes. One of the key aspects of his design is the element of *flexibility* that he mentions at several instances. For example, under one of the sketches, he mentions "bifurcation that leads to pair of analogies, pair of distinct domains, or distinct meshes, and, in addition, to analogical universe or mesh." Analogies and design possibilities were infinite, highly flexible and objective so that the user can adjust or modify them according to his needs.[60] He states that these sketches have only been introduced as "the essential components of thought and may be regarded as the fundamental structural elements that are complementary to the kinetics of thought and conceptualisation, including the creative thought of analogy and of generalisation."[61] The second panel represents a tensegrity structure that Pask titles as *Kawasaki Suspension*. Although the purpose of this structure is not directly obvious, as no descriptions regarding its utilisation and incorporation in the city of Kawasaki have been identified on the competition panel, it can be supposed that this structure is a version of an Intelligent Plaza proposed by him. He also highlights viewing platforms at different levels of this structure.[62] The Kawasaki Suspension has been defined as the "integral composition space-frame for suspending structure, [representing] . . . the design and the existing habitation of Kawasaki. There is an auxiliary computer animation to show evolution and special occasions would, presumably, be celebrated by addition to the structure"[63] [emphasis in original].

As the aforementioned description of the Kawasaki Suspension by Pask elaborates, he sketched a version of an Intelligent Plaza for the competition that was quite different from the one that his collaborator Price proposed, but his explanation of the

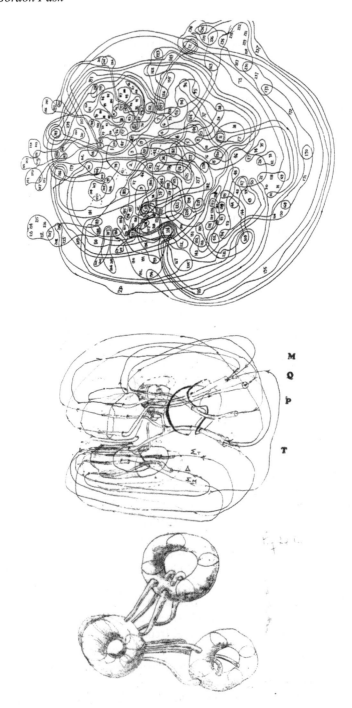

*Figure 5.5* Toruses, or doughnuts, as suggestive of information and communication processes going-on within the Intelligent Plaza or Architecture of Knowledge.

*Source*: Gordon Pask, Japnet/Kawasaki, ca. 1986, sketches. Heinz von Foerster, Gordon Pask & Cybernetics Archives, Department of Contemporary History, University of Vienna. Used with permission.

structure clearly denotes that he is not rigid in his design representation but rather, only suggestive. He is flexible enough in proposing just a tensegrity structure, and whatever form it may take will depend on factors that will be considered further in the design process. Pask elaborates that distinct sketches comprising of rough perspectives and sections were done in order to show the dynamic nature of the Architecture of Knowledge. This typology was tested to be theoretically valid, and only some basic forms were proposed for its physicalisation by Pask, and as he repeatedly mentions on the competition panels, any of these forms were merely suggestive of the structure. Aim was the representation of the thoughts of the people of the city of Kawasaki, and a computer-animated image was to be evolved based on these thoughts and observations. Reflecting Price's design approach for the Fun Palace project, Pask also suggested a minimalistic structure for this purpose and stated that "[t]he structure itself may, perhaps, be supported by a minimally built tensionally integral space frame to emphasise the global unity of thought and its local idiosyncracies." He stressed that the structure was to act as complimentary to the theoretically defensible but less developed kinetics. These were to be achieved through animation of the sculptural or physical structure, and the process was to be documented through the stages of its evolution. He also suggested the generation of proposals for the development of the city by a computer to be an example of this phenomenon.[64]

The third panel consists of eight sketches by Pask. It presents a layout of the Intelligent Network. The sketches depict a layout for the intelligently networked planning scheme of the Kawasaki Institute of Technology's (KIT) student residential units and blocks. Plans, elevations and sections of the plastic drawbridge have been shown. Pask emphasised the flow of information and communication both vertically and horizontally between the apartment units and blocks and proposed perceptual partitions and geographical movement through balconies and drawbridges. Communication bandwidth and information storage were proposed as unlimited, infinite entities, while only perceptual and geographical elements were considered as restrictive. Among other key features, 2,600 megabytes of information storage capacity were proposed for these residential units. Big partitions represented perceptual conception, balconies and bridges denoted geographical movement. Pask stated in this regard that "neither communication bandwidth nor information storage are limiting (only perceptual and geographical proximity restrict design)." As with the previous blocks, twelve phones, four coaxial and fiber optic lines were proposed for the information network. Static and rewritable storages were proposed with blocks being divided into large and small residential units. Regarding the sizes of these units, he stated:

[s]mall blocks 22 m × 24 m (or 26 m × 28 m with balconies) and large 40 m × 56 m (or 44 m × 60 m) blocks. . . . Atrium of small block is neglible [sic]; vertical access and servicing. But atrium in large block is a significant feature.[65]

The intelligently networked scheme of the KIT's student residential units and blocks was conceived as a habitation, *a monumental joke about the computer*, as Pask calls it. Pask further elaborated that this *computeroid carapace* was to be used for habitation and it serviced its users through the continuously changing and modifying geographical and perceptual neighbourhood conditions:

> It "looks like a computer" but lives rather than calculates, the "joke" is the idea of housing intellect in an old fashioned kind of machine that cannot have it because the old fashioned design disallows it. However, the structure can appear as a kind of computeroid carapace [emphasis in original].

Any dynamism was to be considered as a habitation. Pask clarified its further mechanisms:

> as the joke image must have some changeable, adaptable qualities (*these* are *not* its dynamics, its *use* as a habitation *is*) they are kept (as in the accompanying sketches) to a minimally complex mechanism of constraint upon, or play with, space. No mechanism more complicated than a hinge joint is used in the drawbridge and balcony design of the open labyrinth of sketches[66] [emphasis in original].

He emphasised the flow of information and communication through this Intelligent Network of KIT's student residential units and blocks. Cell-like forms were suggested that were connected in a variable manner. Spaces were segregated and isolated with the help of independently adjustable soundproofing and visual opacity systems. The flow of information was to be kept infinite with the help of fiber optic channels, microwave links, video disc and fast random-access memory storage capacities. The aim of this exercise, as Pask stated, was to maintain the "flow of meaning." This was to be conserved in the system, and the evolution of the network was to be maintained.[67]

The fourth panel consisted of details including seven sketches and a project description by Pask. Sketches presented plans and a section of the KIT's intelligently networked student residential units and blocks. Some of the sketches focused on the technical details, such as partitioning and servicing, communication ducts systems, etc. Legend of the sketches presented a project description and details of sketches from the first till fourth panels. In a sketch, Pask particularly mentions that "Sensory perpetual adaptible [sic] interior walling – used in only some room-to-room and module-to-atrium partitions."[68] The interior wall partitions were also proposed to be sensory perceptual and adaptable according to user's needs.

### Award-winning competition entries

Several selection stages were conducted, such as first preliminary selection by Subcommittee for Preliminary Selection of Japan Association for Planning Administration (JAPA), Pre-Judging Approval from the Jury, presentation and discussion at the IRIS '87, Second Preliminary Selection by JAPA, etc. The whole of this judging process led to a selection of seven total proposals for final judging from a pool of 213 proposals. This strict evaluation led to the selection of a winning proposal. Three proposals were selected as first runner-ups, six proposals were selected as second runner-ups and four proposals were selected as third runner-ups and, consequently, were awarded with trophies and prize money of ¥42,000,000 that was divided as ¥10,000,000, ¥5,000,000 (×3), ¥2,000,000 (×6) and ¥1,000,000 (×4) respectively.[69] Details of the winning entries can be found in Table 5.3. Criteria of final selection was based on the points that a proposal should have an inherent possibility for growth towards the final examination phase of the competition as compared to its perfection at the present stage, acceptability for unpredictable futuristic conditions was to be emphasised for the city of Kawasaki and the clarity and uniqueness of the design was prioritised as compared to perfection in terms of construction.[70]

On the basis of the aforementioned criteria, a total of fourteen proposals were short-listed for evaluation, but the jury recommended that none of the proposals still corresponded to the objectives and expected quality for the competition. Consequently, a document titled *What We Expect from the Finalists* was mailed to all of the short-listed candidates. Semifinalists were further informed that their proposals were to be based on discussions with the citizens of Kawasaki and relevant authorities at the International Symposium, IRIS '87 that was to be held in Kawasaki City from January 16 till 18, 1987. Discussions between competition participants, citizens and relevant stakeholders during this symposium concluded a number of points. As it was a conceptual planning competition, original and reality-based ideas were welcomed instead of detailed designing or working-level planning. All the designs were to be easy to understand and interpretable by the citizens of Kawasaki. A further set of selection criteria was introduced for the detailed judgement of the finalised fourteen competition proposals. Some of the key points of this selection criteria are as follows:

1 How much has the concept been developed in the reworked proposal using the standards applied in the preliminary selection?
2 Does this proposal further develop the concepts of the "Campus City"?
3 Does it have new points with which to handle its objective?
4 Is the concept clear, and does the entry contain many suggestions?
5 Does it contain many examples which can be applicable in a number of fields?
6 Does it contain any new proposal for the use of information and communication devices?
7 Is it easy to understand and interesting to the citizens of Kawasaki City?
8 Does it include any features which allow participation by the citizens?
9 Can the proposal's concepts be utilised in a real city?[71]

The final judging was conducted on April 24, 1987, at the Akasaka Prince Hotel, and the seven finalists were allocated a 20 minute's time frame for the presentation of their proposals, and afterwards, a 10 minute's question-and-answer session was conducted. The jury awarded the Grand Prix to Peter Droege, aged 34 at that time and was from MIT, USA. He along with his six team members presented a proposal

Table 5.3 Details of the winning entries.

| Award | Representative Name* | Age | Nation | Other Members | Title | [Format] | Prize | Special award from |
|---|---|---|---|---|---|---|---|---|
| Grand-Prix | Peter Droege | 34 | USA | 6 | Technology For People: A Compus [sic] City Guide | Reports | Trophy ¥10,000,000 | - |
| First Runner-up | Kikoh Mozuna | 46 | Japan | 3 | Eightfold discovery of Kawasaki | Drawings | Trophy ¥5,000,000 | Kanagawa Prefecture |
| | Susan P. Gill | 40 | USA | 4 | The International Intelligent Plaza: The Agora of the Future | Reports | | Kawasaki City |
| | Yoshio Okano | 52 | Japan | 21 | Matamorphosis [sic] into Advanced Information City & Infrastructure for Knowledge Exchange | Reports | | Mainichi Newspapers |
| Second Runner-up | Peter Cook | 49 | UK | 3 | Discovery Museum Amongst a Park in the Sky | Drawings | Trophy ¥2,000,000 | Building Center of Japan |
| | Yutaka Namiki | 38 | Japan | 11 | Building an Intelligent Life Environment for an Aging Society/ The Open Aging Society: Making the Kawasaki Family Reality | Reports + Drawings | | New Media Development Association |
| | Leo Jakobson | 67 | USA | 5 | A Concept Sketch for a Humanistic Advanced Information City Based on Integrated Knowledge | Reports | | Engineering Consulting Firms Association, Japan |
| | Frank Hotchkiss | 61 | USA | 7 | Campus City Kawasaki: Quest for a Shared Vision | Reports | | Institute for Future Urban Development |
| | Enrique Vila | 41 | Venezuela | - | MUKAI-Multi-University of Kawasaki for Advanced Information | Reports | | International Development Center of Japan |
| | Shin-ichi Okuyama | 25 | Japan | 2 | The Game on Environmental Image | Drawings + Reports | | Kawasaki Chamber of Commerce and Industry |

| | | | | | | | | |
|---|---|---|---|---|---|---|---|---|
| Third Runner-up | Hiroshi Shimizu | 39 | Japan | - | Strategies in the Construction Process to Insure the Success of KIT | Reports | Trophy ¥1,000,000 | Japan Association for Planning Administration |
| | Kei Iwasaki | 36 | Japan | 5 | The Citizen's School in the Community | Drawings | | Mori Memorial Foundation |
| | Koichi Mera | 53 | Japan | 9 | The KIT System: A Development Promotor of Kawasaki and the World | Reports | | Japan Association for Planning Administration |
| | *Kazutoshi Ito* | 35 | Japan | - | A tale of Seven Cities | Drawings | | Mainichi Newspapers |

* Refers to the italicised representatives' names denoting competition entries studied in this book.

*Source*: Japan Association for Planning Administration and Mainichi Newspapers, International Concept Design Competition for an Advanced Information City – Jury Report, ca. 1987, DR2004:0472, Kawasaki Project, 30 × 22 cm, Cedric Price Fonds, Canadian Centre for Architecture, Montréal, 1.

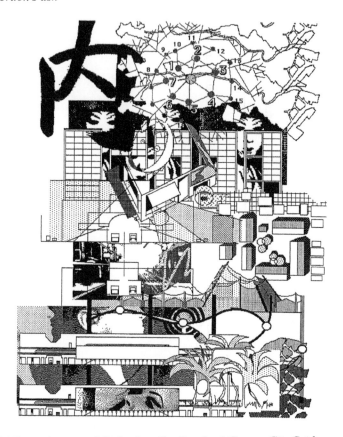

*Figure 5.6* Droege's proposal *Technology For People: A Campus City Guide*.

*Source*: Image courtesy of Peter Droege.

titled *Technology For People: A Campus City Guide* (Figure 5.6). His competition entry comprised of a report, and no drawings were submitted, as the Jury Report informs. He was awarded a trophy along with ¥10,000,000 prize money. The details of his team are[72] (Table 5.4):

Droege and his team's proposal presented ideas instead of rigid architectural, urban or working details. In his proposal, he focused on the concept of *Uchi* that is written in Japanese language as "内." He stated that Uchi represents the relationship between an individual and his surroundings, such as the *notion of my house, family, community, people*, or ultimately, as *my world*. He attempted to portray an idealised picture of a Japanese city with a top-down approach descending from Japan in the world, then comes its city, afterwards, communities, groups, individuals and ultimately ideas within those individuals. He stated that the symbol of Kawasaki City was a representation of this concept of Uchi. His proposal presented

*Table 5.4* Details of Droege team.

| | | |
|---|---|---|
| Julie Moir Messervy | Aged 36 | Environmental Designer (USA) |
| Leo Marx | 58 | Jr. Professor MIT (USA) |
| Lisa Peattie | 63 | Prof. Emer. of Urban Anthropology, Senior Lecturer MIT (USA) |
| Otto Piene | 59 | Director, Center for Advanced Visual Studies MIT (USA) |
| Peter Droege | 34 | Architect and City Designer (USA) |
| William Porter | 53 | Prof. of Architecture and Planning MIT (USA) |
| Winifred Richmond | 33 | Computer Graphics Consultant (USA) |

*Source*: Japan Association for Planning Administration and Mainichi Newspapers, International Concept Design Competition for an Advanced Information City – Jury Report, ca. 1987, DR2004:0472, Kawasaki Project, 30 × 22 cm, Cedric Price Fonds, Canadian Centre for Architecture, Montréal, 2.

the categories of KIT, Intelligent Places, City of Festivals and Managing Network Access and Participation. Droege and his team stated that their proposal was based on the concept of a *purposeful transparency* of city networks and facilities that were to be introduced. The aim of this transparency was to prepare the citizens of Kawasaki for a new city identity. In order to accommodate futuristic needs, a flexible process for physical and social community building was suggested. Traces of the past were to be studied in order to understand the opportunities and needs posed by the trends of that time. Citizens were considered as a significant stakeholder of this whole process, as Droege stated that "[t]he citizens of Kawasaki, rather than merely accepting technological innovations, are to collaborate in planning their evolution and introduction."[73] On another account, the team presented their proposal as the one that showed the technological innovations as being capable of building the communal identity, cultural continuity and a strong connection to the city's roots. KIT was proposed as a citizen-based university without any boundaries and any specific urban structure. A diverse network of Intelligent Plazas comprising of both private and public places and devices was introduced with the aim of open conversation and learning. The role of advanced technologies in these plazas was kept to a minimum, and it was suggested that people were supposed to utilise these with or even without the help of these technological innovations. A perennial web of personal and communal festivities was proposed in order to keep this city as ever-growing, evolving, and a way to keep in touch not only with itself but also with the world as well.[74]

This proposal was centred around the concept of a community and its different aspects that were linked with the help of technologies being operated by its users. The aim of all of the four components of KIT, Intelligent Places, City of Festivals and Network Access and Participation were to connect people with or without the relevant technologies available. It was said that "[i]nstead of merely accepting the introduction of technological innovations, the citizens of Kawasaki will collaborate in planning their introduction. The city thus will exemplify the idea of *Technology for People*" [emphasis in original]. It was further said regarding the utilisation of technology for the benefit of the people of Kawasaki:

> [i]nformation is indispensable, but in itself inert and static, useful only when combined with human intelligence, active imagination, and purpose. Similarly, the new technologies are instruments, and they may assist, reinforce and expedite the traditional activities of learning, but they do not in any sense supplant them.

Instead of taking communication systems, such as television or classrooms for granted, this proposal suggested selection, receiving and production of information based on one's individualistic needs. In this way, it was said, an optimistic outlook towards bright and exciting futuristic possibilities could be extended. Through the utilisation of these information and communication technologies, a number of goals were proposed to be achieved, such as cultural and group identity formation against internationalisation and technological upheavals in the society, formation of internationally networked but simultaneously internally unified city, decentralisation of learning facilities and making them more accessible, flexible specialisation resulting towards decentralised, custom-designed and swiftly responding industries instead of the mass-production schemes, etc. With the rapidly advancing information and communication technologies, this project rejected any fixed or rigid conclusion and rather adopted a highly flexible approach. Instead of predicting the future, they planned in a flexible manner, allowing for new interests, innovations and unanticipated possibilities. "We can plan for an unpredictable future, allowing for novelty, rather than for a future we attempt to control from today's vantage point," the proposal stated further that "[i]n preparing for an open tomorrow, we propose to focus on the substance of people's cultural needs, on the continuity of society and of knowledge. We can have our feet on the ground, yet our head in the stars."[75]

By considering the city of Kawasaki as a pool of infinite information, KIT was proposed as a multidimensional *Intelligent City Map* representing individual and institutional resources acting as first *KIT Catalog*. The aim of this exercise was to introduce a neighborhood involving people, companies and educational institutions possessing national and international links. New kind of technologies were to be utilised for this purpose, "such as satellites, microwave transmission, fiber optical links, small processors combined with large data repositories, spatial organisation of information," etc. The aim of Intelligent Places and devices were to provide structured learning for city-, nation- and worldwide students available at any place and time. KIT was supposed to suggest explorative directions in the intellectual, spiritual and sensory realms. Intelligent Places proposed a network of diverse components from the most public to the most personal as follows[76] (Table 5.5):

The City of Festivals further extended the idea of the KIT, Kawasaki's community structure and plazas. By proposing Kawasaki as the City of Festivals, events ranging across family to international scale were suggested acting as mental,

*Table 5.5* Components of the Intelligent Places.

| | |
|---|---|
| Information Fountains | enlightening street side whisperers |
| Intelligent Shoji | domestic central nervous systems, custom-designed and networked |
| Metro Plaza | integrating transformed train stations via an intelligent moving platform |
| Mobiles | the moving parts of Superplaza Kawasaki |
| Neighborhood Plazas | neighborhood-based and flexible infill spaces, highly equipped and multi-purpose |
| Smart Boxes | the intelligent version of the "Soba" shop |
| The River Project | the bridgehead of Kawasaki's intelligent infrastructure: 30 kilometers of advanced city gardens |

*Source*: Japan Association for Planning Administration and Mainichi Newspapers, International Concept Design Competition for an Advanced Information City – Jury Report, ca. 1987, DR2004:0472, Kawasaki Project, 30 × 22 cm, Cedric Price Fonds, Canadian Centre for Architecture, Montréal, 30–32.

physical and spiritual, or in other words, social glue of the community. Three themes for these festivals were suggested initially, including a *World Exposition, Language and Sky Festivals*. The aim of the World Exposition was to exhibit the city itself and its relevant learning network, the Language Festival was supposed to celebrate different varieties and forms of expression and communication and the Sky Festival aimed at "honoring the sky, the air and the heavens as the most vital, universal and supportive human environment, and as a high-technology medium." For the Managing Network Access and Participation category, the growth of Campus Area Network (CAN) was proposed in momentum with the KIT, plaza network and campus festival.

Personal, social, technical and legal aspects were considered regarding access and participation of the citizens. Different options regarding management and ownership of city's places were considered. Public Information Utility was introduced as a system for management of CAN, while managerial aspects were separated from the rights of programming it. The implementation of Droege's proposal was to be initiated with educating and inviting the people of Kawasaki for participation in it, pursuing the citizens to submit "an inventory of teachers, facilities, subjects of interests to others; a plan for future research, growth and development; [and] a list of specific technological and cultural needs, wants and projects."[77] To summarize the concept behind Droege's proposal, the people of Kawasaki were suggested not to accept technology as it is presented to them but to plan and utilize it according to their individualistic needs. The university, festivals and the city were proposed to be linked and integrated as in a network of information and communication. The ideas and concepts he presented were universal and presented general method of strengthening intelligence, identity and community. Only the concrete steps and devices were to be tailored to the particular culture and assets of any city where this proposal was to be implemented.

Three projects were awarded the first runner-up prizes. Mozuna's proposal, *Eightfold Discovery of Kawasaki*, suggested a twenty-first-century city can become a regional information brain that can help in solving the anticipated problems of environmental destruction, food shortage, the decline of heavy industries and increased unemployment. This project was based on the *Metabolism* architectural movement and was mythologically inspired by eight Buddhist wisdoms. Organic ideas resulted in application of brain hemispheric structures to the symmetrical city concepts, consequently resulting in genetically recognizable city form. Seven Intelligent Plazas replicated the seven hills of Heavenly Jerusalem in the Book of Revelations, while the city's famous Shinto-Buddhist shrine known as the *Kawasaki Daishi* is proposed as an eighth spiritual node. The concept was further based on the three themes of Urban Brain Hologram, Urban Recycling Technology and Urban Wind and Water Structure. Considering city as a collection of man's brain, memory and mind, the symbolic deities were assigned with the duty of regenerating the city through new and sustainable production forms and energy sources, and finally, this man-nature co-existence resulted in the introduction of biotechnological purification systems cleaning Kawasaki's water and atmosphere. These three themes then incorporated information services, transportation networks and civic fora.

Gill's project *The International Intelligent Plaza: The Agora of the Future* presented Kawasaki as a meeting place for national and international forums with the challenges of stimulating innovation and establishing mechanisms for the active participation of citizens and foreigners. Four core components were proposed as the Center for Innovation, the Globe Theater, the Shrine for World Harmony and the Intelligent Integrating System around which several other functions were grouped. It was suggested that "[t]hese four core functions will serve as symbols of Kawasaki's leadership in innovation, in globalization, in the search for harmony and inner peace, and in technological development 'beyond the fifth generation'"[78] [emphasis in original]. Okano's proposal was titled as *Metamorphosis into Advanced Information City & Infrastructure for Knowledge Exchange*. In this submission, he proposed that expansion of the human horizon must be performed via expansion of human activities, resulting in enhancement of human intelligence and sensibility. An infrastructure was suggested for exchanging knowledge and for supporting the creation, accumulation and exchange of information, for performing intelligent activities, promoting citizens' participation labelled as *Community Experiment* and, consequently, educating people for an advanced information society. The KIT was said to be such an infrastructure of knowledge. Furthermore, four KIT organisations were proposed as Campus City Foundation, Urban and Business Management College, Academic Plaza and Intelligent Plazas.

The second runner-up prizes were awarded to six projects. Project by Cook was titled as *Discovery Museum Amongst a Park in the Sky*. He along with his team presented the competition theme of the Intelligent Plaza through visionary detail. His museum was conceived as Kawasaki's landmark located on the waterfront. This Discovery Museum has been presented as a symbiotic super machine that is simultaneously filled and empty, composing of a museum, vertical park, watering place, resort and a voyage of discovery, or in other words, an experiential trail.

Cook proposes that the advent of new media has resulted in the death of traditional museum, and a symbiotic relationship between nature and advanced technology is taking shape with the help of the citizens, consequently tickling and enhancing their inspirations. He proposes that popular game parlors may serve the role of engaging people from different walks of life with electronic technologies, such as Pachinko parlors, etc., and thus can act as a source of inspiration for the Intelligent Plazas, where electronic data access can be made less threatening. Okuyama's project *The Environmental Image Game* attempted to work on the theme of the Campus City Festival. This proposal utilises non-hierarchical and instantaneous qualities of the new media to capture temporal dimension of the festivals of the city. City's under-used spaces, such as parking lots, highway rights-of-way, off-time school yards, etc., have been searched and transformed into enjoyable interactive media settings. Company- and city-sponsored trucks are proposed infilled with media gadgetry and public telephone booths have been turned into intelligence nodes. The negative approaches to the new media, such as excessive control and surveillance, have also been discussed, but political consensus and social attitudes are suggested as responsible for their development and usage.

Four projects were awarded the third runner-up prizes. In *A Tale of Seven Cities*, Ito attempted to answer the notion of Campus City Festival, where he utilised personal memories, media images and traditional mythologies of water, wind, tree, light, fire, dream and wood. Different elements were proposed responding to respective mythologies, such as the concept of an ocean theater introduced as a water-based element. The city of fire represented a thirty-year cycle of trees, eventually using them as the construction material for world exposition pavilions that are in turn incinerated and the site being used for growing another generation of trees. Ito also considered the life cycle of the media age, such as its images, events, etc., and the engagement of choreographer, stage designer and the art director in its production. He stated that place-making in any advanced information society is the cyclical and recycling process of physical entities being transformed into media images that in turn affects the built environment.

Pask's competition entry was not able to win any prize in this competition. In the Jury Report, the selection criteria have been outlined by the jurors that states that the proposal must be flexible so that it may accommodate the rapidly changing technologies of the present and the future. Any proposal that must be selected as a winner should have the scope for further development, its concept must be clear, a number of suggestions must be presented, it must present realistic examples relating to the themes of the competition, it must suggest new and innovative uses for the existing and forthcoming information and communication devices, it must be very easy to understand, it must appeal to the citizens of Kawasaki so that they must be able to participate in it, all of the ideas that a proposal presents must be applicable to a real city, etc. The entries selected by the jury as winners were all suggestions and contained no rigid urban and architectural working proposals. Almost all of the winning proposals utilised existing conditions first and then considered them as their base departed for further revisions within the surroundings of the Kawasaki City. All of these proposals utilised information and communication technologies in order to support their designs and to enhance the environment of the Kawasaki City. While on the other hand, Pask's proposal, although presented a remarkable utilisation of the technology of artificial intelligence in his entry for this competition, failed to show any realistic relationship both with the citizens and of the environment of the city of Kawasaki. Jurors wanted the winning proposal to be very easy to understand and implementable to the citizens and surroundings of Kawasaki City, but Pask's proposal was extremely difficult to understand for a lay person, and one needed to have a mathematical background for the complete interpretation of his design. It can also be noted that in international competitions, jurors mostly have a limited period of time for the selection and evaluation of competition entries, and not every person holds expertise for each and every design submitted. This factor could have acted against Pask's entry that failed to impress jurors during its preliminary selection, as his entry was highly technical. Also, he presented rigid architectural and urban design proposals in his entry that jurors negated, as they were interested in open, flexible and futuristic proposals, accommodating both present and futuristic technologies.

## Conclusion

The international concept design competition was launched by the city of Kawasaki in 1986 in order to transform it into an information-intensive community with people of different nationalities, cultures and specialisations engaging in creating a new culture and exploring new scientific methods and technologies. The competition jury also included Arata Isozaki among other prominent figures of that time. Participants were requested to present proposals for four different categories of Intelligent Plazas, the Kawasaki Institute of Technology (KIT), the Campus City Festival and the Intelligent Network. The international concept design competition entry by Gordon Pask – an English cybernetician – granted him with the opportunity of implementing his ideas and theories regarding the cybernetic architectural environments. By utilising cybernetics for filling the gap between traditional and innovative twenty-first-century architectural practices, he argued that the discipline of architecture can also benefit from cybernetics, such as considering cybernetic growth and development of a city, a structure or revisiting architectural designs as evolutionary systems. He argued that Antoni Gaudi's Parque Guell can said to be an excellent example of a cybernetic structure, as it pushed the visitor to "explore the piece, statements are made in terms of releasers, . . . exploration is guided by specially contrived feedback, and variety (surprise value) is introduced at appropriate points to make . . . [a visitor] explore." He argued that a dialogue must be achieved between a user or a visitor and his environment, and this interaction can be achieved through modern technologies, resulting in reactive and adaptive environments.

In order to experiment and demonstrate these reactive and adaptive cybernetic environments, he also designed a *Musicolor System* (1953–57) – a machine that transformed auditory signals into visual display – and presented the cybernetic *Colloquy of Mobiles* exhibition installation in 1968. The characteristics of a cybernetic environment that he strived for included potentially controllable, interpretable or learnable environments with cues or instructions guiding the learning and abstractive processes of the users and most importantly, captivating environments that must engage a visitor in conversation and adapt its characteristics. In his competition entry, the *Japnet, Kawasaki*, he attempted to achieve the aforementioned cybernetic discourse by designing and proposing the Intelligent Plaza, KIT and an Intelligent Network. He designed four out of the five competition panels along with Price. In the panels designed by Pask ranging from Panel 1: 00–7B 1/5 to Panel 4: 00–7B 4/5, he has been suggestive rather than being rigid in all of his sketches and legends regarding the intelligent environments. In Panel 1, he presented the concept of *Technological Trees* that were supposed to support the daily activities of the citizens of Kawasaki. In Panel 2, he introduced the concept of an Intelligent Plaza that he called as an *Architecture of Knowledge* and proposed a tensegrity structure as a suggestive approach. Panel 3 presented the Intelligent Network spanning across vertical and horizontal directions in both the units and blocks proposed for KIT student's residences. Lastly, Panel 4 demonstrated the "sensory perceptual adaptive interior wall partitions" that adjusted themselves in accordance with the user's needs. Although Pask's entry was not able to win any significant prize in the competition, it demonstrated a highly flexible cybernetic network spanning across architectural and urban paradigms that can be implemented successfully with present-day advancements of the emerging technologies of artificial intelligence, internet of things and big data.

## Notes

1 Japan Association for Planning Administration and Mainichi Newspapers, International Concept Design Competition for an Advanced Information City, ca. 1985–86, DR2004:0470:001, Kawasaki Project, 30 × 22 cm, Cedric Price Fonds, Canadian Centre for Architecture, Montréal, folio 1r.
2 Ibid., 6.
3 Ibid., 9.
4 Ibid., 10.
5 Ibid., 11.
6 Ibid., 4–5.
7 Ibid.
8 Ibid., 16–17.
9 Ibid., 3–4.
10 Ibid., 4.
11 MIT Corporation, *Massachusetts Institute of Technology: Reports to the President 1988–89* (Cambridge: MIT Corporation, 1988–89), 220, accessed February 21, 2023, https://libraries.mit.edu/archives/mithistory/presidents- reports/1989.pdf.
12 Japan Association for Planning Administration and Mainichi Newspapers, International Concept Design Competition, 23.
13 Ibid.
14 Ibid., 24.
15 Ibid., 25.
16 Ibid., 20, 27.
17 Ibid., 30.
18 Ibid., 31.

19  Stafford Beer, "What Has Cybernetics to do with Operational Research?," *Operational Research Quarterly* 10, no. 1 (March 1959): 1–21, accessed March 5, 2023, https://doi.org/10.2307/3007308.
20  Gordon Pask, "The Architectural Relevance of Cybernetics," *Architectural Design*, no. 9 (September 1969): 494, accessed May 21, 2021, https://arl.human.cornell.edu/879Readings/GordonPask_Architectural%20Relevance%20of%20Cybernetics.pdf.
21  Ibid.
22  Ibid.
23  Ibid., 495.
24  Ibid.
25  Ibid., 496.
26  Ibid.
27  Ibid.
28  Gordon Pask, "A Comment, a Case History and a Plan," in *Cybernetics, Art and Ideas*, ed. Jasia Reichardt (London: Studio Vista, 1971), 77, accessed May 27, 2021, https://pangaro.com/pask/Pask%20Cybernetic%20Serendipity%20Musicolour%20and%20Colloquy%20of%20Mobiles.pdf.
29  Ibid., 78–79.
30  Ibid., 85–86.
31  Ibid.
32  Ibid., 77–78.
33  Ibid.
34  Ibid., 80.
35  Gordon Pask, "The Colloquy of Mobiles," in *Cybernetic Serendipity – The Computer and the Arts*, ed. Jasia Reichardt (London: Studio International, 1968), 35, accessed May 27, 2021, https://monoskop.org/images/2/25/Reichardt_Jasia_ed_Cybernetic_Serendipidity_The_Computer_and_the_Arts.pdf.
36  Jasia Reichardt, "Introduction," in *Cybernetic Serendipity – The Computer and the Arts*, ed. Jasia Reichardt (London: Studio International, 1968), 5, accessed May 27, 2021, https://monoskop.org/images/2/25/Reichardt_Jasia_ed_Cybernetic_Serendipidity_The_Computer_and_the_Arts.pdf.
37  Pask, "The Colloquy of Mobiles," 34.
38  Pask, "A Comment, a Case History and a Plan," 89.
39  Pask, "The Colloquy of Mobiles," 35.
40  Ibid.
41  Ibid.
42  Ibid.
43  Ibid.
44  Pask, "A Comment, a Case History and a Plan," 76.
45  Cedric Price, "Gordon Pask," *Systems Research* 10, no. 3 (1993): 165–166, accessed March 7, 2023, https://doi.org/10.1002/sres.3850100320.
46  Ibid.
47  Cedric Price and Gordon Pask, "Japnet 1985–87," in *Cedric Price Works 1952–2003: A Forward-Minded Retrospective, Vol. 1, Projects*, ed. Samantha Hardingham (London: AA Publications, 2016), 658–663.
48  Gordon Pask, Competition Presentation Panel 1: 00–7B 1/5, 1986, DR2004:0449:001, Kawasaki Project, esquisse/sketches and drawings/collage on board, 64 × 85 cm, Cedric Price Fonds, Canadian Centre for Architecture, Montréal.
49  Ibid.
50  Ibid.
51  Gordon Pask, Competition Presentation Panel 4: 00–7B 4/5, 1986, DR2004:0449:004, Kawasaki Project, esquisse/sketches and drawings/collage on board, 64 × 85 cm, Cedric Price Fonds, Canadian Centre for Architecture, Montréal.

52 Gordon Pask, "The Limits of Togetherness," in *Information Processing 80, Proceedings of the 8th IFIP Congress 1980*, ed. Simon H. Lavington (Amsterdam: North-Holland Publishing Company, 1980), 999–1012, accessed May 18, 2021, www.pangaro.com/pask/pask%20limits%20of%20togetherness.pdf.

53 Max H. Hines, "Using the Telephone in Family Therapy," *Journal of Marital and Family Therapy* 20, no. 2 (April 1994): 175–184, accessed March 2, 2023, https://doi.org/10.1111/j.1752-0606.1994.tb01025.x.

54 Pask, "The Limits of Togetherness," 1000.

55 Ibid.

56 Ibid., 1006.

57 Pask, Competition Presentation Panel 1: 00–7B 1/5.

58 Heinz Von Foerster, *Observing Systems* (Seaside: Intersystems Publications, 1984).

59 Samantha Hardingham, ed., "Japnet 1985–87," in *Cedric Price Works 1952–2003: A Forward-Minded Retrospective, Vol. 1, Projects* (London: AA Publications, 2016), 659.

60 Pask, Competition Presentation Panel 4: 00–7B 4/5.

61 Ibid.

62 Gordon Pask, Competition Presentation Panel 2: 00–7B 2/5, 1986, DR2004:0449:002, Kawasaki Project, esquisse/sketches and drawings/collage on board, 64 × 85 cm, Cedric Price Fonds, Canadian Centre for Architecture, Montréal.

63 Pask, Competition Presentation Panel 4: 00–7B 4/5.

64 Ibid.

65 Gordon Pask, Competition Presentation Panel 3: 00–7B 3/5, 1986, DR2004:0449:003, Kawasaki Project, esquisse/sketches and drawings/collage on board, 64 × 85 cm, Cedric Price Fonds, Canadian Centre for Architecture, Montréal.

66 Pask, Competition Presentation Panel 4: 00–7B 4/5.

67 Ibid.

68 Ibid.

69 The Jury Report presents contradictory accounts of the prize money for the third run-ner-ups. It mentions both a prize money of ¥1,000,000 and ¥1,250,000 at different accounts.

70 Japan Association for Planning Administration and Mainichi Newspapers, International Concept Design Competition for an Advanced Information City – Jury Report, ca. 1987, DR2004:0472, Kawasaki Project, 30 × 22 cm, Cedric Price Fonds, Canadian Centre for Architecture, Montréal, 19.

71 Ibid., 21–22.

72 Ibid., 2.

73 Peter Droege, "Technology for People [International Concept Design Competition for an Advanced Information City – Five Proposals for Kawasaki, Japan]," *Places* 5, no. 3 (1989): 50, accessed June 13, 2021, https://escholarship.org/uc/item/9714p048.

74 Japan Association for Planning Administration and Mainichi Newspapers, International Concept Design Competition – Jury Report, 30–32.

75 Ibid.

76 Ibid.

77 Ibid., 33.

78 Ibid., 38.

## Bibliography

This chapter has benefitted from the archives of Cedric Price Fonds, Canadian Centre for Architecture, Montréal and Heinz von Foerster, Gordon Pask & Cybernetics Archives at the Department of Contemporary History at the University of Vienna. This bibliography only lists the names of the collections that have been consulted instead of the specific items. It is in accordance with the guidelines of *The Chicago Manual of Style*, 17th ed. (Chicago: University of Chicago Press, 2017) and for more details, section 14.222 can be consulted. The details of specific items have been listed in the notes. Unless otherwise noted, all translations are by the author.

Beer, Stafford. "What Has Cybernetics to Do with Operational Research?" *Operational Research Quarterly* 10, no. 1 (March 1959): 1–21. Accessed March 5, 2023. https://doi.org/10.2307/3007308.

Colloquy of Mobiles. *Heinz von Foerster, Gordon Pask & Cybernetics Archives*. Department of Contemporary History, University of Vienna.

Droege, Peter. "Technology for People [International Concept Design Competition for an Advanced Information City – Five Proposals for Kawasaki, Japan]." *Places* 5, no. 3 (1989): 50–51. Accessed June 13, 2021. https://escholarship.org/uc/item/9714p048.

Foerster, Heinz Von. *Observing Systems*. Seaside: Intersystems Publications, 1984.

Hardingham, Samantha, ed. "Japnet 1985–87." In *Cedric Price Works 1952–2003: A Forward-Minded Retrospective, Vol. 1, Projects*, 658–663. London: AA Publications, 2016.

Hines, Max H. "Using the Telephone in Family Therapy." *Journal of Marital and Family Therapy* 20, no. 2 (April 1994): 175–184. Accessed March 2, 2023. https://doi.org/10.1111/j.1752-0606.1994.tb01025.x.

Japnet/Kawasaki. Cedric Price Fonds. Canadian Centre for Architecture, Montréal.

Japnet/Kawasaki. *Heinz von Foerster, Gordon Pask & Cybernetics Archives*. Department of Contemporary History, University of Vienna.

MIT Corporation. *Massachusetts Institute of Technology: Reports to the President 1988–89*. Cambridge: MIT Corporation, 1988–89. Accessed February 21, 2023. https://libraries.mit.edu/archives/mithistory/presidents- reports/1989.pdf.

Musicolor. *Heinz von Foerster, Gordon Pask & Cybernetics Archives*. Department of Contemporary History, University of Vienna.

Pask, Gordon. "The Architectural Relevance of Cybernetics." *Architectural Design*, no. 9 (September 1969): 494–496. Accessed May 21, 2021. https://arl.human.cornell.edu/879Readings/GordonPask_Architectural%20Relevance%20of%20Cybernetics.pdf.

Pask, Gordon. "The Colloquy of Mobiles." In *Cybernetic Serendipity – The Computer and the Arts*, edited by Jasia Reichardt, 34–35. London: Studio International, 1968. Accessed May 27, 2021. https://monoskop.org/images/2/25/Reichardt_Jasia_ed_Cybernetic_Serendipidity_The_Computer_and_the_Arts.pdf.

Pask, Gordon. "A Comment, a Case History and a Plan." In *Cybernetics, Art and Ideas*, edited by Jasia Reichardt, 76–99. London: Studio Vista, 1971. Accessed May 27, 2021. https://pangaro.com/pask/Pask%20Cybernetic%20Serendipity%20Musicolour%20and%20Colloquy%20of%20Mobiles.pdf.

Pask, Gordon. "The Limits of Togetherness." In *Information Processing 80, Proceedings of the 8th IFIP Congress 1980*, edited by Simon H. Lavington, 999–1012. Amsterdam: North-Holland Publishing Company, 1980. Accessed May 18, 2021. www.pangaro.com/pask/pask%20limits%20of%20togetherness.pdf.

Price, Cedric. "Gordon Pask." *Systems Research* 10, no. 3 (1993): 165–166. Accessed March 7, 2023. https://doi.org/10.1002/sres.3850100320.

Price, Cedric and Gordon Pask. "Japnet 1985–87." In *Cedric Price Works 1952–2003: A Forward-Minded Retrospective, Vol. 1, Projects*, edited by Samantha Hardingham, 658–663. London: AA Publications, 2016.

Reichardt, Jasia. "Introduction." In *Cybernetic Serendipity – The Computer and the Arts*, edited by Jasia Reichardt, 5–7. London: Studio International, 1968. Accessed May 27, 2021. https://monoskop.org/images/2/25/Reichardt_Jasia_ed_Cybernetic_Serendipidity_The_Computer_and_the_Arts.pdf.

# 6  Artificially Intelligent Architecture

## Futuristic prospects

> When the Master went to Wei, Jan Yu drove for him. The Master said, "What a flourishing population!"
> Jan Yu said, "When the population is flourishing, what further benefit can one add?"
> "Make the people rich."
> "When the people have become rich, what further benefit can one add?"
> "Train them."
>
> — Confucius, The Analects, Book XIII

Climate change, technological disruptions threat of a nuclear war and migrations are inevitable at present and the times to come. Scientific estimates suggest that emission of greenhouse gases will be responsible for an increase of more than 2°C in average global temperatures. In addition to frequent weather extremes, such as hurricanes and typhoons, expanding desserts, melting ice caps, rising oceans and insufficient agricultural productions, these disruptions are going to result in uninhabitable and inundate cities forcing millions to search brand-new metropolises. Subsequent technological disruptions from artificial intelligence, big data and internet of things are going to yield biased algorithms leading to the abilities to hack humans and breakthroughs in life and social sciences, such as brain-computer interfaces, connectivity and updateability, media such as fake news, personal data ownership, free will, our minds, intelligence, consciousness, emotions, decision-making, meditation and, consequently, our individualities. These developments point towards well-planned strategic initiatives that are further strengthening digital dictatorship, localisation and solidified nationalism. While depriving millions of the luxuries they enjoy today and take for granted, these unpredictable events are going to encourage stark polarisation in the world heading towards brainwashing, cyberwar, racism, immigration on an extensive level, fascism, atheism and gay marriages or homosexuality. We cannot easily accept that an event or its consequence is not political because we are living in the times where any choice of being not political at all is in fact a political choice. Summarising these unpredictable times in geographical, urban and architectural vocabularies, this book chooses rather an antithesis approach. Instead of considering *architecture* in an *intelligent*

DOI: 10.4324/9781003401858-6

*environment*, it goes for *intelligence* as an *architecture*. It blurs the territories of intelligence and architecture, as Koolhaas in *The Generic City* states:

> the city no longer represents maximum development but borderline underde-velopment . . . the brutal means by which universal conditioning is achieved mimic inside the building the climatic conditions that once "happened" outside – sudden storms, mini-tornadoes, freezing spells in the cafeteria, heat waves, even mist; a provincialism of the mechanical, deserted by gray mat-ter in pursuit of the electronic. Incompetence or imagination?[1] [emphasis in original].

This book then questions the beginnings, development, apotheosis and culmination of the concept of artificially intelligent architecture in the endeavors of the archi-tects and cyberneticians presented in this book and case studies its applicability as per geographical, urban and architectural contexts.

This book presents a contemporary history of artificially intelligent architecture from 1949–87. While all of the architectural projects case studied in this book share a number of mutual aspects, one of the prominent characteristic is of process-ing of information, communication and feedback, in other words, formation of a cybernetic discourse. As this book discusses, architects since 1949 up till present have attempted to visualize this artificially intelligent architecture through a num-ber of ways – one of the most prominent being the kit-of-parts approach. Also, they tried their best to introduce some notion of intelligence in their architectural projects through some artificial means. Price and Negroponte attempted to intro-duce intelligence in their architecture through information or computer programs supporting cybernetic environments, resulting in intelligent architecture that exhib-ited the characteristics of organic and developing character. Site and its elements suggested a life and intelligence of their own through self-improving and self-replicating information system that utilised machine intelligence. Consequently, the information gathered and processed via participants have been available on demand and at any space, place and time. This system possessed excellent organic relationship with its external environment and thus was responsive, exhibited indi-viduality and excitement so that its users didn't get bored. Man-machine symbiosis was achieved at its best. Likewise, Tange and Isozaki attempted to depict their ideals of cybernetic environments through the realisation of the Festival Plaza. Some of the characteristics of this architectural cybernetic environment included a central civic axis of information and communication, introduction of human, emotional and sensual (i.e. tactual, auditory, visual, informational, etc.) elements and technologically advanced aspects, such as uniform functions without segrega-tions where only information and communication were supreme, interchangeabil-ity, moveable equipments, man-machine symbiosis and a self-instructing feedback loop. Similarly, Rogers and Piano also attempted to portray a live, organic pro-cessing and dissemination of information through their designs, especially the Center Pompidou, Paris, with mass-produced, prefabricated components, resulting in monocoque structures, freedom in overall planning and self-decision-making artefacts and gadgets. Pask attempted to incorporate his ideals of architectural cybernetic environments in his competition entry called the *Japnet, Kawasaki* and presented users with a reactive and adaptive environment that engaged its participants and enhanced their satisfaction. Another key factor mutual in all of these projects is the element of excitement – engaging humans in multiple activities through various techniques.

Since 1988, although technological advancements in the discipline of artificial intelligence came to a break, the reason due to which this period is known as the *AI Winter* in the history of technology of artificial intelligence, progress continued to be made in segregated attempts in the field of artificially intelligent architecture. In 1993, Zaha Hadid designed the Vitra Fire Station. In 1997, a collaboration between Frank Gehry, Jim Glymph and computer-aided three-dimensional interactive application (CATIA) software resulted in the design of the Guggenheim Bilbao. In 2000, Revit released its 1.0 version, and in 2001, Toyo Ito's Sendai Mediatheque opened in the city of Sendai, Japan. In 2002, Philip Bernstein advocates the purchase of Revit that propels the geometry-only CAD software to object-oriented, information-rich Building Information Modeling (BIM). Also in 2002, Bibliotheca Alexandrina opened in Alexandria, Egypt, with the aim of becoming a digital equivalent of the original Alexandria Library. In 2007, David Rotten creates Grasshopper. In 2008, Patrick Schumacher coins the term *Parametricism* as a successor to modern and postmodern architecture. In 2012, Prof. Geoffrey Hinton and other researchers at the University of Toronto developed deep learning technology that reignites broad interest in the discipline of artificial intelligence, and as a result, in 2015, the third AI boom centred on statistics and learning achieved by huge data-processing ability starts that is still going on. Also in 2015, the Minna No Mori Gifu Media Cosmos designed by Toyo Ito opens in the city of Gifu, Japan.

Since 2015 onwards, the prospects of the discipline of artificially intelligent architecture seem to be highly promising, as the interest and technological developments in the field of artificial intelligence are progressing at a rapid pace. Developments are being made in the area of reactive and adaptive artificially intelligent architectural environments. New experiments are being conducted, for example, in 2015, a collaboration between Kanno, Yamaguchi and Sakamoto resulted in a project called *Semi-Senseless Drawing Modules #2 – Letters*.[2] It is a machine learning program that learns the handwritten words, deconstructs them and, afterwards, produces innovative asemic formulations. In 2018, teamLab presents a project called *teamLab Borderless: Mori Building Digital Art Museum* that displays a group of digital interactive artworks covering complex, three-dimensional 10,000 square meters of space.[3] Furthermore, in 2020, Manabe and his team presents an expressive dance performance called the *Discrete Figures* that combines performing arts, mathematics, drones, real-time augmented reality, artificial intelligence and machine learning to explore the relationship between the human body, emotional expression and computer-generated movement (simulated bodies) on the basis of mathematical analysis.[4] These are only some of the examples. Architects in collaboration with media artists are experimenting with artificial intelligence in creating far more exciting and imaginative artificially intelligent architectural environments.[5] These examples seem to be segregated experiments, but attempts are also being made in order to combine them and exploit their potential for the user's benefit under the umbrella of artificially intelligent smart homes. For example, since 2000–15, internet has exponentially expanded, resulting in communication, trading, entertainment and educational developments. This phenomenon has led to the development of internet of things (IoT), resulting in global internet-based information smart homes, consequently facilitating the exchange of goods, services and integration of smart objects and real-world data. IoT and artificial intelligence in collaboration with smart homes are also being utilised for the elderly care in advanced economies. As said before, the utilisation of artificial intelligence in collaboration with IoT is just one facet, and experiments are being conducted of putting these technologies to greater human benefit these days.[6]

The history of artificially intelligent architecture is suggestive of an optimistic approach towards the implementation of the emerging technology of artificial intelligence and is suggestive of the projects in which reactive and adaptive artificially intelligent environments and their users interact as follows:

1 Modify each other through engaging and stimulating activities and computer programs.
2 Share environments that are organic (exhibiting growth and development), self-organising, full of information.
3 Learn, remember and respond to each other.
4 Share responsiveness, individuality and excitement.
5 Experience communication between man-man, man-function or function-function (IoT, etc.).
6 Experience emotional and sensual (tactual, auditory, visual, etc.), technologically intelligent and social-communicational elements.
7 Are the ones to extract meaning out of their interactions or collaborations.
8 Are under surveillance with or without their permissions (critical perspective).

Artificial intelligence could suggest some wonderful opportunities in collaboration with humans that they alone cannot even think of. As most profound technologies disappear and become an inseparable part of our daily lives, artificial intelligence is also believed to be working in our lives from the background, being invisible but also highly supportive all the time. A world of sensors and intelligence is to be the future of architecture, some experts suggest. Till present, artificial intelligence has been considered as a human companion, an equal partner in progress, but it is still not clear whether or when artificial intelligence will be able to surpass and replace the human intelligence. Whether it is artificial intelligence, cognitive intelligence, computational intelligence or whatever label we may assign it, artificial intelligence is going to be an inseparable part of our lives whether we believe or admit it or not. Highly complicated tasks that are beyond human imagination and power, too complex, too fast and too detailed, are being performed by artificial intelligence conveniently. But critiques also argue that once these tasks are done, artificial intelligence can take the role of humans, consequently forcing them out of their jobs and daily tasks. In Japan, from 1995 to 2010, 1.23 million construction and civil engineering jobs have been eliminated due to automation. A survey on the probability of computerisation of architecture and related disciplines shows that jobs that involve creative thinking, such as architectural and engineering managers, architects, interior designers, landscape architects, urban and regional planners, etc., are less likely to be automated as compared to jobs that require less critical thinking, such as cement masons and concrete finishers, paperhangers, plasterers and stucco masons, surveying and mapping technicians, etc.[7] Ethical issues relating to artificially intelligent architecture are also a significant concern, as surveillance, gender and racial biasedness issues are being discussed on all major international platforms. Only time will decide the fate of artificially intelligent architecture and whether it prevails or not, but what can be done today is to plan as flexibly as possible in order to accommodate the swiftly changing technologies and needs and to have scope for the future.

## Notes

1  Rem Koolhaas and Bruce Mau, "The Generic City," in *S,M,L,XL*, ed. Jennifer Sigler, 2nd ed. (New York: Monacelli Press, 1998), 1261.
2  So Kanno, Takahiro Yamaguchi and Hironori Sakamoto, "Semi-Senseless Drawing Modules #2 – Letters," *yang02.com* (website), accessed June 17, 2021, http://yang02.com/works/sdm2/.
3  teamLab, "teamLab Borderless: Mori Building Digital Art Museum," *teamLab Borderless* (website), accessed June 17, 2021, https://borderless.teamlab.art/.
4  Daito Manabe, Elevenplay, Kyle McDonald, Mikiko and Rhizomatiks Research, "Discrete Figures," *Discrete Figures* (website), accessed June 17, 2021, https://research.rhizomatiks.com/s/works/discrete_figures/en/.
5  For further details on the artificially intelligent architectural environments, author's papers can be consulted: Danyal Ahmed, "Senses, Experiences, Emotions, Memories: Artificial Intelligence *as a Design* Instead of *for a Design* in Contemporary Japan," *Intelligent Buildings International* 14, no. 2 (2022): 133–150, accessed June 19, 2023, https://doi.org/10.1080/17508975.2020.1764327.
   Danyal Ahmed and Junichiro Higaya, "Information, Communication, Feedback: The Festival Plaza (Japan World Exposition Osaka 1970), Center Pompidou and Sendai Mediatheque as Suggestive Examples of Artificially Intelligent Architecture," *Journal of Asian Architecture and Building Engineering* 21, no. 3 (2022): 701–716, accessed June 19, 2023, https://doi.org/10.1080/13467581.2021.1883621.
6  For further details on the topic of artificially intelligent smart homes, author's paper can be consulted: Danyal Ahmed, "Anthropomorphizing Artificial Intelligence: Towards a User-Centered Approach for Addressing the Challenges of Over-Automation and Design Understandability in Smart Homes," *Intelligent Buildings International* 13, no. 4 (2021): 227–240, accessed June 19, 2023, https://doi.org/10.1080/17508975.2020.1795612.
7  For further details author's paper can be consulted: Danyal Ahmed, "Artificial Intelligence and Contemporary Japanese Architecture – Any Relationship?" *Intelligent Buildings International* 12, no. 4 (2020): 295–308, accessed June 17, 2021, https://doi.org/10.1080/17508975.2019.1577212.

## Bibliography

Ahmed, Danyal. "Anthropomorphizing Artificial Intelligence: Towards a User-Centered Approach for Addressing the Challenges of Over-Automation and Design Understandability in Smart Homes." *Intelligent Buildings International* 13, no. 4 (2021): 227–240. https://doi.org/10.1080/17508975.2020.1795612.

Ahmed, Danyal. "Artificial Intelligence and Contemporary Japanese Architecture – Any Relationship?" *Intelligent Buildings International* 12, no. 4 (2020): 295–308. https://doi.org/10.1080/17508975.2019.1577212.

Ahmed, Danyal. "Senses, Experiences, Emotions, Memories: Artificial Intelligence *as a Design* Instead of *for a Design* in Contemporary Japan." *Intelligent Buildings International* 14, no. 2 (2022): 133–150. https://doi.org/10.1080/17508975.2020.1764327.

Kanno, So, Takahiro Yamaguchi and Hironori Sakamoto. "Semi-Senseless Drawing Modules #2 – Letters." *yang02.com* (website). Accessed June 17, 2021. http://yang02.com/works/sdm2/.

Koolhaas, Rem and Bruce Mau. "The Generic City." In *S,M,L,XL*. 2nd ed., edited by Jennifer Sigler, 1239–1264. New York: Monacelli Press, 1998.

Manabe, Daito, Elevenplay, Kyle McDonald, Mikiko and Rhizomatiks Research. "Discrete Figures." *Discrete Figures* (website). Accessed June 17, 2021. https://research.rhizomatiks.com/s/works/discrete_figures/en/.

teamLab. "teamLab Borderless: Mori Building Digital Art Museum." *teamLab Borderless* (website). Accessed June 17, 2021. https://borderless.teamlab.art/.

# Index

Note: Page numbers in *italics* indicate a figure and page numbers in **bold** indicate a table on the corresponding page.

747 Hangar at Heathrow Airport 132
*2001: A Space Odyssey*, artificial intelligence, theme of 97–98, 102

Abbott, Edwin 180
Abe, Kōbō 94
Abell, Thornton M. 109
AC Horn Company, rubber-based #5 coating 113
Aillaud, Émile 136
AI Winter 203
Alexander, Christopher 2, 165; *see also Notes on the Synthesis of Form*
Alpine Architecture 72
Altec Lansing, home music system by 116, 123
*Analyse Du Projet Lauréat* (Analysis of the Winning Project) 140
Apollo 13, origins of intelligent building 99, 102
Appleby, Sally 129–131
Apple's IIGS 182
Arai/Responsive House: mechanical systems of 77; primitive domestic robots of 74; responsive behavior of 74; simulation model, as 74; stabile/mobile house, as 77; structure of 74–77, *76*; technologically advanced residential module, as 74
ARAM Inc. 130
Archigram 90, 102, 132, 143, 145–146
Architectural Association School of Architecture 166, 177
*Architectural Design* magazine 162
Architectural Institute of Japan 88
architectural projects case studied **4**

*Architectural Relevance of Cybernetics, The* (Pask): architects, responsibilities of 162; architectural cybernetics, cybernetic theory of architecture 162; architectural designs, evolution built into 164; a*rchitectural holism* 163–166; a*rchitectural mutualism* 163–166; architecture and cybernetics 162; artificial intelligence computer programs, architecture and 166; Beer and 162; control, communication and system 165; cybernetics as formal science, developments toward 163; designing of systems, pre-1800s' architecture and 162–163; functionalism and mutualism 163–167; Gaudi's Parque Guell 164–165, 167, 196; "machine for living in" and 167; Program Evaluation and Review Technique (PERT) programming and 162; self-organising systems 166; smart homes, state of symbiosis 167; *Speculations*, cybernetic theory of architecture and 166; surrealism and 164; symbolic environments 164–165; traditional architects and system designers, cybernetics and 162; Victorian era, and 163
Architecture Machine Group (MIT): artificial intelligence computer programs and 166; artificially intelligent architecture, definition

of 44; cognitive psychology 44; Defense Advanced Research Projects Agency (DARPA), funds from 44; Groisser and 166; human-computer interaction 44; intelligent architecture machine, interaction with the real world of 44; intelligent architecture machine, personality like humans 44; intelligent behavior 44; introduction to 43–46; Massachusetts Institute of Technology (MIT) 2, 44–49; Media Lab 44; MIT's Artificial Intelligence Lab 44; multi-disciplinarity of 43–44; Office of Naval Research, funds from 44
Architecture of growth, concepts of 70–71
*Architecture of Quotation and Metaphor* (Isozaki) 81–82
Arnold, Christopher W. 125
art and technology 94
art, architecture and technology 94
artificial intelligence (AI): definitions of 1–2; evolution of 17n1; technological booms, first, second and third of 2–4, 203; transdisciplinarity of 1–2
artificial intelligence computer programs, architecture and 166
artificial intelligence programming language 181
artificially intelligent architecture: artificial intelligence (AI) and architecture, relationship of 1–2; Chartered Institution of Building Services Engineers UK, Talk 1; definitions of 1–3, 44; prospects of 203–205; TEDx Tohoku University Talk 1; transdisciplinarity of 1–2; twentieth century history, an overview of 2–3, 202–203
artificially intelligent environments, users, interaction between 204, 205n5
Art Nouveau 164
Asada, Takashi 156
Ascott, Roy 27–28, 52n13
Aspen, Colorado 181
Association for Rural Aid in Medicine (ARAM) Module: inspirations from 130–131; portable, flexible system of 130–131; standardised components of 131; structural system of 131; team of 130; *see also* Rogers, Richard

Astronomical Society of London 12
atomic bombing 74
*a-un* guardian warriors 96–97
autonomously operating machine, architecture as, characteristics of 81
avant-garde art movements 94

B&B Italia 133, *134*
Babbage, Charles: Difference Engine No. 1, mechanisms and functions of 12–16, *14*; *Laws of Mechanical Notation*, as a universal language 15–16; signs on Difference Engine No. 1, for expressing actions of 15–16
Barcelona Pavilion, Ludwig Mies van Der Rohe 121
Bauhaus 165
Beadle, Alfred Newman 108
Beatty, Chester 52n12
Beer, Stafford 52n12, 162
Belmont, Joseph 156
Bend Home Appliances, Automatic Washer and Automatic Dryer by 118
Bernardi, Theodore C. 109
Bibliotheca Alexandrina 203
Board of the East Side Union High School District, San Jose 124
Bobrow, Daniel G. 181
Boice, John R. 125
boomu 93
Bormioli, Rita 131
Botschi, Pierre 128, 130–131
Bowdler, Richard 52n12
Bowser Inc., Gas-Fired Automatic Incinor by 118
Boyd, Visscher 125
Brady, Jules 109
Brezorski, Slavko 67
Briggs, Asa 52n12
British Museum 140, 146
Brodey, Warren 174
Brunel, Isambard Kingdom 163
Brunelleschi 133
Brussels exposition 87
Bryant, Vernon C. 125
Buff, Conrad, III 108
Building Information Modelling (BIM) 203
Burckhardt, Michael 131
Bureau International des Expositions 82
Burton, Decimus 163

Calder, Lord Ritchie 23
Campbell, John Carden 109

Cape Kennedy, rocket launch 98, 102
Carnegie Mellon University 1
Case Study House # 17; appliances,
    short-listed for 118–121, 147n19;
    Ellwood and 118; handsome object,
    as 118; structural, spatial details
    of 118; *see also* Case Study House
    Program
Case Study House # 18; appliances of 123;
    Ellwood and 121; structural system
    of 121–123, *122*; *see also* Case
    Study House Program
Case Study House 1950; Soriano and
    116; structural system of 116;
    technologically advanced products
    used 116, *117*, 147n16; *see also*
    Case Study House Program
Case Study House Program: *Arts and
    Architecture* magazine and 108;
    houses, details of 110–123;
    inspiration for Richard Rogers, as
    110; new materials and techniques,
    used in 109–110; overview of
    108–110; participating architects
    108–109; selection of architects,
    criteria of 109–110; *see also* Eames
    House/Case Study House for 1949;
    Case Study House 1950; Case
    Study House # 17; Case Study
    House # 18; New Case Study
    House
*Cedric Price Works 1952–2003: A
    Forward-Minded Retrospective*
    (Hardingham) 178
Center Pompidou, Paris: brief of 138,
    145; *culture,* transdisciplinarities
    and 135–136; *curiosity*, design
    element of 135–136, 143;
    *flexibility,* transdisciplinarity and
    exchangeability of 139–142,
    *142*; *funny machine*, as 135, 143;
    giant space frame, inspiration
    from Osaka Expo '70 for 143;
    humanistic scale, granted to 143;
    impartiality of 138–139, *144*;
    information dissemination machine,
    as 138–141, 145–146; information
    network of 139; international
    competition for 136–138; kit-of-
    parts, structure as 142; *live centre
    of information*, as 140; living
    and complex organism, as 146;
    members of the jury for 136–138;
    Piano and 135–136, 143; piazza

of 135; Rogers and 135, 141,
    143; scaffolding-like exterior,
    inauguration of 136, *137*; spaceship
    landing, portrayed as 135; turning
    point in history of museum
    designing 136; urban machine, as
    143
Central Vacuum Corporation 123
Chernikhov, Iakov 72
Chesterman, G. 52n12
Chesterman, R. 52n12
Chiba, Makuhari 77
Ciborowski, Adolf 67
Città Nuova 72
City for the Dead 73
City in the Air 73
City on the Sea 73
Clarke, Arthur C. 97
Clark, John 28, **29**, 50, 52n12, 170
climate change 201
code-sprinkled schema, space as 72, 101
Colloquy of Mobiles: Brodey and 174–176;
    *Cybernetic Serendipity Exhibition
    of Cybernetic Art* 171–172, *173*;
    exhibition, objectives of 172;
    exhibition setup, team of 172–173,
    *175*; overview of 171–174,
    196–197; *socially oriented reactive
    and adaptive environment*, as
    173–174
*Comment, a case history and a plan, A*
    (Pask): reactive and adaptive
    environment, characteristics of
    177–178
Computer Aided City: artificially intelligent
    architecture on a city scale
    77–81, *78–80*; *brain of the city*,
    as 77, *79*; cable city, called as 77;
    centralised control center of 102;
    computer-aided environment of
    Festival Plaza, extension of 77;
    supercomputers, proposed for
    77–81; unbuilt, reasons behind 80
Computer-Aided Three-dimensional
    Interactive Application (CATIA)
    203
Concertone Tape Recorder 118
Confucius 201
Conrac Television Set 118
Constructivist City 72
*contemporary*, meaning of 109
Cook, Peter 132, 145, 188, 194
Cornberg, Sol 32
Crystal Palace, Exhibition 85, 163

Cultural Revolution 93
Curran, Susan 180
cybernetic environment, characteristics of (Isozaki) 73–74, 90
*Cybernetic Serendipity Exhibition of Cybernetic Art* 171–172, *173*
*Cybernetics: Or Control and Communication in the Animal and the Machine* 1–2

Dalmotron Talkmaster, electronic inter-communication system of 121
Data space, Negroponte 181
Davidson, J. R. 109
Davies, Mike 131
De Fantis' work 181
*deku-no-bō* (good for nothing) 97
Deme and Deku, *apparatuses* 88, 94, *95–96*, 97, 99, 102
Descartes, René: comprehension of the human mind and body, views on 9; human body vs. machine, views on 9–10; "I am, I exist", *thinking thing*, views on 9; *imaginari*, interpretations of 18n6
Design Research Unit company 130
de Vaucanson, Jacques: mechanical Duck, mechanism of 10, *11*
*Discrete Figures*, Manabe and team 203
Doggart, John 128–130
do-it-yourself (DIY) approach 130
Dordevic, Aleksandar 67
Dowson, Mark 172
Doxiadis Associates 67
Driberg, Tom, MP 52n12
Droege, Peter 157, 187–188, 190–191
Drucker, Peter 93

Eames, Charles 16, 108, 110, 112, 128
Eames House/Case Study House for 1949; artificially intelligent architecture, as 114; Eames and 110–116; generator of ideas, inherited ephemeralness of 110, *111–113*; overview of 110–116; self-decision-making artefacts of 114–116, 146n11; structural system, flexibility of 112–113; *see also* Case Study House Program
Eaton, Sally 131
Educational Facilities Laboratories, Inc. 123–124
E. F. Hauserman Company 126

Ehrenkrantz, Ezra D. 16, 125
*Eighth International Federation of Information Processing Societies Congress*, Tokyo 180
Ekuan, Kenji 157
Electric Labyrinth: 14th Triennale Di Milano: Festival Plaza's cybernetic environment, inspiration for 74; ideology behind 74; set-up of 74, *75*
Electro-Responsive Environment (Archigram) 90, 102
Ellwood, Craig 16, 108, 110, 116, 118, 121, 128
Emmons, Donn, FAIA 108
Emmons, Frederick E. 108–109
energy crisis 69
Engineers Collaborative 126
Entenza, John 108, 110, 143
*Environmental computing machine* 176
Environmental Ecology Laboratory 174–176
*Environmental Planning* (Isozaki's company) 94
environment as a system 73, 94
*Environment Society* 94
experimental art and environmental exhibitions 94
Extension to Design Research Unit: flexibility of 130; piano and 130; structural system of 130; team of 130; *see also* Rogers, Richard

*Face of Another, The* 94
FACOM 270–30 99
ferro-board decking 113, *113*
Festival Plaza: activities scheduled in 88–90; artificially controlled environment of 99; artificially intelligent environment, as 86–87; control system of 99–100; cybernetic environment of 90–91; Deme and Deku, *apparatuses* 88, 94, *95–96*, 97, 99, 102; *elastic*, space as in 91; floor equipment of 99; ideology behind 85–86; Isozaki and 88–100; levels as symbolic representations of past, present, future 86; man-machine symbiosis, achievement of 87; mobile equipment of 87, 91, *92*; non-physical aspects, exchange of under 86; performer-spectator-machine

symbiosis of 90–91; set-up/ installations of 86–88, *89*, 106n92; *software monuments*, software environment of 87–88; space-frame roof for 86; Tower of Maternity 86; Tower of the Sun, central communications organ, as 86; Tower of Youth 86; *see also* Japan World Exposition Osaka 1970

Flack, Peter 131

*Flatland: A Romance of Many Dimensions* (Abbott) 180

Fleetguard Factory 131

*Fluxus* 94

Foerster, Heinz Vow [sic] 182

Ford Foundation 123

Ford Motor's, assembly line of 72

Foster, Norman 127

Foster, Wendy 127

Franchini, Gianfranco 140

Francis, Frank 138

Frazer, John 37–41, 50–51, 176

Frazer, Julia 37–41, 50–51, 176

*From Manner to Rhetoric, and now* (Isozaki) 81

*From Space to Environment* 94

Fujie, Shuichi 88

Fukuda, Asao 83

Fuller, R. Buckminster 2, 23, 132

*Function, Structure and Symbol* (Tange): communication field, space as 66, 101; energetic, function and space as static, deterministic and decisive 63, 65–66, 72, 101; informational, function and space as pluralistic, elastic, selective and spontaneous 65–66, 72, 101; space in the age of information and communication, definition of 65

Fun Palace: 24/7 activities of 23; 70 Projects for (Clark) 28, **29**; artificially intelligent, on the basis of 50; boredom, overcame through a feedback loop in 26–27, 38, 40–41, 49–50; Civic Trust's Lea Valley Development Plan (East London) 23; cybernetic system, classification as a 23–30; *Fun Palace Cybernetics Committee*, responsibilities for 27–28, 50, 52n12; Fun Palace Foundation as a Charitable Trust 23; information dissemination machine, function as an 23–26; *Input of Unmodified* and *Output of Modified People* 23, 50; introduction to 22–26; Littlewood and 22–23, 49, 143, 146, 165; meta-information, definition of (Pask) 27; mobility and flexibility of 22–23; Pask and 26–30; Price and 22–26, 49–50, 52n12; *Proposals for a Cybernetic Theatre* (Pask), specifications, ergonomics and design of 26–27, 50; punch card questionnaires for 23; *Scientist's toy*, *magic doors*, representation of 28, 50; short-life toy, intended as 22–23, *24–25*; unconstructed, reasons behind 22–23; work and leisure: elimination of divisions, aim of 22

Gaki, famished demons 74

Galic, Risto 67

G and M Equipment Company, Intercom-Radio System 123

Garrone and Cusago, free-plan houses of 133

Gaudi, Antoni 164, 167

Gehry, Frank 203

General Water Heater Corporation, Water Heater by 118

generator: boredom, computer programs for 35–41, 50–51; classification of computer programs for 37–39, *39*; client's brief for 35–36; compatibility questionnaires, *blank* sheet for 36, 54n37; computer-aided design software 37; *computing package* for 37–41, *39*; developers of computer programs for (Frazer's) 37–39; elements of 35; generation of plans and improvements 37–41, 50–51; Gilman Paper Company 35; intelligence of its own, self-replicating information system of 36–41, *37–38*, 50–51; intelligent diary for 40; *intelligent modelling kit* for 40; intelligent program for 40–41; interactive interrogator for 40–41, 50–51; introduction to 35–36, 50–51; *Never look empty, never feel full*, design criteria for 36; perpetual architect of 40; re-definition of architecture 35–36;

responsive behavior of 35–36,
*37–38*; structure of 35; White
Oak Plantation, Yulee, Florida 35;
working model of *37–38*
*Generic City, The* (Koolhaas) 202
George, F. 52n12
Ghosts 74
Gill, Susan P. 188, 194
Gilman, Howard 35
Glass Reinforced Plastic 130, 142
Glymph, Jim 203
Goldacre, R. 28, 52n12
Goldschmied, Marco 129–131
Goodman, Richard 27–28
*Go-shintai* (divine body) 97
Gothic cathedrals as spaceships 135
grasshopper 203
Gray, Don 131
Great Exhibition of the Works of Industry
of All Nations/Great Exhibition
85
Gregory, Richard 52n12
Gregory, Steven 48
Groisser, Leon B. 44, 166
Guggenheim Bilbao 203

Hadid, Zaha 203
Haladay, Edward 58
Hall, Edward Twitchell 73
*Hanging robot* 99
Hardingham, Samantha 178, 182–183
hardware, physical appearances in a city as
70–71, 86–88, 94, 101
Harrison, Keith 33
Harvard University 128
Hayashi, Yujiro 156
Headquarters Building of the World Health
Organisation (W.H.O): core spaces
as visually communicating spaces
58; individuality and collectivism,
levels of 57–58; overview of
57–58; Tange and 57–58; unbuilt,
as 57
Hensman, Donald C. 108
Hercules 97
Herd, Charles M. 125
Hero of Alexandria: pneumatic
architectural automations, design
of 5–7, 17n3; temple doors, bird
movements at the top of a shrine,
automated mechanisms of 6
Hikotani, Kunikazu 83
Hines, Max H. 181

Hinton, Geoffrey 203
Hiroshima 74
Hisada, Toshihiko 67
Holmes, Andrew 130
Holt, Eric 131
Hotchkiss, Frank 188
human intelligence, replacement by
artificial intelligence, of 204–205
Hunt, Anthony 127–131
Hyams, Maurice 172

IBM 360/50, Iris 50 computer 139
Ibusuki, Machio 83
Incinor Disposal Unit 116, 145
*inflexible specification* 176
Inmos Microprocessor Factory 131
inter-architectural relations 69–70
interchangeability of space 71, 101–102,
127
intermedia and environmental art practices
94
International Concept Design Competition
for an Advanced Information
City/Campus City Competition,
Kawasaki: *2001 Kawasaki City
Plan* of 154–155; *Advanced
information and communication
society*, Japan as 153–154;
brief of 153, 157, 196; Campus
Area Network (CAN) and
160–161; *Campus City*, concept
of 155; Campus City Festival,
concept of, *International
Information Exposition* and
159–160; communication channels,
Community Antenna Television
(CATV) 154; Droege and 157,
187–188, 190–191; information-
intensive and humanistic city,
Kawasaki as 153; Intelligent
Network, concept of 159–160;
Intelligent Plazas, concept of
158; International Symposium on
Regional Information Systems
(IRIS) conference and 155; Isozaki
and 157; Japan Association of
Planning Administration and 155;
jurors and special advisors for
156–157, **156–157**; Kawasaki
Institute of Technology (KIT),
concept of, *science of information*
and 158–159; knowledge-
based economy, transition to

153–154; *linked city*, concept of 155; *Massachusetts Institute of Technology: Reports to the President 1988–89* and 157; MIT East Asian Architecture and Planning Program and 157; *New Media* infrastructure, *Teletopia Cities* of 154; participating organisations 152–153; *Technology For People: A Campus City Guide*, winning entry of 157, 188, 190; *Third Sector* of 154
international moment of youths 93
internet of things 204
invisible architecture 81, 90, 96
*Invisible City* (Isozaki), characteristics of cybernetic environment 71, 90
Ishihara, Shunsuke 156
Ishii, Takemochi 156
Isozaki, Arata 2–3, 16, 57–58, 67, 70–84, 88–102, 156, 196; cybernetic environments, transdisciplinarity of 1–2, 16, 57, 70–74, 94, 202; *see also* Plan for Skopje; A Plan for Tokyo
Italian Industry Pavilion, Japan World Exposition Osaka 1970 133, *134*
Ito, Kazutoshi 189, 195
Ito, Kunisuke 87
Ito, Saburo 156
Ito, Toyo 203
Iveson, Lalla 130
Iwasaki, Kei 189

Jakobson, Leo 188
James B. Lansing Speaker 118
Japan Association for Planning Administration 152, 186
Japanese, evolution of architecture 164
Japan Foundation 153
Japan International Cooperation Agency 153
Japan World Exposition Osaka 1970; centralised control room of 97–99, *98*; headquarters building of 83, 85; *Hello from the Countries of the World*, theme song 94; Isozaki and 93–100; landmark tower of 83, 85; master planners for 82; master plan of 83–85, *84*; overview of 82; plaza of human contacts, Expo as 82; political and festivity venue, as 93; *Progress and Harmony for Mankind*, theme for 82; Rice and 143; spatial harmony, achievement of 85; Symbol Zone, central civic communications axis 83; Theme Committee of 82; trunk facilities for 82, **83**, 84, *84*, 85–86, 88; Tsuboi and 143; *see also* Festival Plaza
Japnet, Kawasaki (Pask and Price): adaptable drawbridges 182; adaptable sensory partitions of 182; architectural mutualism, holism and 165; Architecture of Knowledge 180, 183, *184*, 185, 197; artificially intelligent post boxes, Techno Trees as 182–183; beyond the fifth generation 194; Book of Revelations 194; Campus Area Network (CAN) 193; City of Festivals 192–193; computeroid carapace 185–186; Discovery Museum 194–195; flexibility of 183; Fun Palace and 185; *Intelligent City Map*, *KIT Catalog* 192; Intelligent Network and 185; Intelligent Places, components of 192, **193**; *Intelligent Plaza* and 182; *Kawasaki Daichi* 194; *Kawasaki Suspension* 183–185; mythologies of water, wind, tree, light, fire, dream and, wood 195; overview of 177, 197; presentation panels of 178–183, 197; Price and 177–178; runner-up competition entries 194–196, 199n69; selection criteria for winning entry of 187; shortcomings of Pask's competition entry 195–196; team of winning entry 190, **191**; Technology for People: A Campus City Guide, winning entry for 190–192; *Techno Trees* or *People Poles*, concept of 179–180, 182–183, 197; torus, doughnut 180, 182–183, *184*; winning entries of 186–187, **188–189**
Jaquet-Droz, Pierre: Writer, Draughtsman and Musician, mechanisms of 12, *13*
Johnson, Philip 136
Jonckheere, A. R. 27–28
Jones, A. Quincy 108
Joroff, Michael 157

Kahn, Louis 132
Kamiya, Koji 58, 83, 86
Kaplicky, Jan 130
Kaprow, Allan 73
Kastl, Peter 125
Kato, Kan 156
Kato, Kunio 83
Kawasaki, Kiyoshi 83
Kawazoe, Noboru 86
Kaya, Seiji 82
Kelvinator Electric Range 116, 145
Kennedy, Roger 156
Kierulff Sound Corporation, HI-FI
    equipment by 118, *120*
Kiesler, Frederick 72
Kikutake, Kiyonori 83
Killingsworth, Edward A. 108
Knorr, Don R. 108
Knowledge Representation Language 181
Koenig, Pierre 109
Koh, Heiki 58
Koolhaas, Rem 202
Kraemer, Kenneth 157
KRL, Nelson's Hypertext, Winograd and
    Kaye's 181
Kubrick, Stanley 97
Kurashiki Town Hall 58
Kurokawa, Moriaki 58
Kurokawa, Noriaki 86

Laboratory of Architecture and Planning
    (MIT) 157
Labyrinth City 73
Laclotte, Michel 138
Lamlnar Fiberglas 118
Lascelles, 7ᵗʰ Earl of Harewood (George
    Henry Hubert) 23
Lefcoe, George 157
Lennox Industries 126
Lewis, Brian 52n12
Licklider, Joseph Carl Robnett: *Man-
    Computer Symbiosis* 44; *thinking
    center*, idea of 44–45
lightness, phenomenological concept of
    133–135
*Limits of Togetherness* (Pask) 180
Littlewood, Joan 22–23, 49, 143, 146, 165
Llull, Ramon: cipher wheel as a
    cryptographic device, inspired from
    7; Leibniz, Gottfried W., binary
    system and modern computer
    sciences 7; rotating discs and
    linguistic symbols, terms, and

alphabets, design of 7, *8*; theory of
    information 7
London, Hyde Park 85

MacDonald, A. G. 28
*Machine and Architecture, The* (Ellwood)
    121
Mc Intosh Amplifier 118
*Mainichi* Newspapers 152
Maki, Fumihiko 86
Makowski, Zygmunt Stanislaw 132
Manetti, Antonio 133
Marx, Leo 191
Massachusetts Institute of Technology
    (MIT) 44, 57, 157, **157**
Massachusetts Institute of Technology
    (M.I.T.) Boston Harbor: core spaces
    as visually communicating spaces
    58; individuality and collectivism,
    levels of 57–58; overview of 57–58;
    Tange and 57–58; team for 58;
    unbuilt, as 57
*matsuri-goto* 93
McAslan, John 131
McLuhan, Marshall 73
Menuhin, Yehudi 23
Mera, Koichi 189
Messervy, Julie Moir 191
metabolism 57, 71, 94, 194
*Micro Man: Computers and the Evolution
    of Consciousness* (Curran) 180
migrations 201
Mikado, Ian, MP 52n12
Minna No Mori Gifu Media Cosmos 203
Minsky, Marvin: intelligence, definition
    of 2–3; *Steps Toward Artificial
    Intelligence*, on inherent
    mysteriousness of intelligence 3
Mishevic, Radovan 67
Miura, Noriyuki 88
Mobile Structure for Sulphur Extraction
    133
Modern Architecture Movement, machine
    as metaphor 81
Montreal exposition 87
Moore, Nathalie 131
Mori, Hanae 156
Morioka, Yushi 88
Morris, Ingrid 128
Mozuna, Kikoh 188, 194
Musicolor System: *Color Music System*,
    Lerner and 167; defects of 171;
    inspirations from 167; intelligent

device, as 171; man-machine
symbiosis and 170–171, *172*;
mechanism of 167–170; overview
of 167, *168–169*, 196; synaesthesia,
inspiration for 170–171
Muto, Kiyoshi 67

Nagasu, Kazuji 156
Nakamori, Takahiro 88
Namiki, Yutaka 188
NASA, Houston 98, 102
Nash, John 162
National Radio Tuner 118
Navajo Pueblo 121
Negroponte, Nicholas 2–3, 16, 43–51,
165–166, 181; artificially intelligent
architecture: as responsive,
distinctive, exciting, automatic and
self-organizing 43–49; *see also*
Architecture Machine Group; *Soft
Architecture Machines*; Seek
Neoprene zip jointing system 128, 131
Nervi, Pier Luigi 132
Neutra, Richard J. 109
New Case Study House: Ellwood and
116–118; structural system, spatial
details of 116; technologically
advanced systems of 116–118, *117*;
*see also* Case Study House Program
Nezu, Koichiro 83
Niedermann, Ted 58
Niemeyer, Oscar 136
Nishiyama, Uzo 82, 93
Nomland, Kemper, Jr. 109
Nomland, Kemper, Sr. 109
*Notes on the Synthesis of Form* 2
NuTone, appliances by 123

Oberhofer, Alphons 131
*Observing Systems* (Foerster) 182
Okalux laminate 142
Okamoto, Taro 83, 86
Okano, Yoshio 188, 194
Okita, Saburo 156
Okuyama, Shinichi 188, 195
O'Neill, Brendan 131
*open plan* space 133
Osaka Prefecture, Senri Hills 82
Otaka, Masato 83
Ove Arup and Associates 140, 143
Oxford Corner House (OCH): B.E.A
[British European Airways] 52n22;
B.O.A.C [British Overseas Airways

Corporation] 52n22; British Rail
52n22; *Capacity of Building —
Activities* 32; Central Government
52n22; C.O.I.D 52n22; Eidophor
Projection System for, Peto
Scott Electrical Instruments *31*,
33, 50; Electronic Audio-Visual
Equipment and Techniques
(EAVET) 32–33, 50; *Extent of
ex-site Static Communications
possible: Internal Communication
& Exchange potential — Static
Communications* 32–33; *Factors
of obsolescence in relation to
constituent parts: Extent of inbuilt
flexibility required* 34–35; G.L.C.
[Greater London Council] 52n22;
Greater London Boroughs 52n22;
Housing: Local Government 52n22;
I.L.E.A [Inner London Education
Authority] 52n22; information
dissemination, internal and external
linkages of 32–33; introduction
to 30–32, *31*, 52n19; J. Lyons and
Company Limited 30, 50; life-
cycle, demolition of 34–35; L.T.E
[Long Term Evolution] 52n22;
Lyons Corner House, regeneration
to 30, *31*; memorandum to IBM,
400 carrels for information retrieval
for 34; Metropolitan Police 52n22;
Ministry of Education, Health,
Technology, Economic Affairs
52n22; OCH Feasibility Study
30; People's Nerve Centre, a
City Brain or a Self-Pace Public
Skill and Information Hive,
classification as (Price) 30, 50;
Price and 30–35; processing of
information, mediums for 32, 50;
*Static communications network in
the hive, providing audio, video
and print-out information facilities*
33–34; town hall, labor exchange or
an official letter, intended character
of 32

Pachinko parlors 195
Pangaro, Paul: cybernetics as derivation of
artificial intelligence, views on 1–2
PA organisation 132
Paracelsus: *Homunculus*: artificial
generation of men, recipe of 7, 9

*Parametricism* 203

Parker, Peter 127

Pask, Andrew Gordon Speedie 1, 3, 16–17, 23–28, 152, 161–186, 195–197; cybernetic environments 152, 161–166, 172, 177, 196–197, 202–203; *see also* Colloquy of Mobiles; Fun Palace; Japnet, Kawasaki; Musicolor System

PA Technology Laboratory: design team of 131; inspirations from 132; kit-of-parts approach of 132; structural system of 132; *see also* Rogers, Richard

Paxton, Joseph 163

Payne perimeter forced-air heating system 116

Peacock, Frank 127

Peattie, Lisa 191

Peters, Steven 48

Pevsner, Nikolaus Bernhard Leon 163

Piano, Renzo 3, 16, 108, 127, 129, 130–136, *137*, 140, 142–146

Piccinato, Luigi 67

Picon, Gaëtan 138

Piene, Otto 191

Pillorge, George 58

Pinker, R. 30, 52n12

Pittas, Michael 157

Plan for Skopje: City Gate and City Wall, focal points of 68; Isozaki and 67; open system, central civic communication axis of 68–69; overview of 67, 101; A Plan for Tokyo, as an extension of 67; Tange and 67–69; United Nations and 67; urban design and architectural competition for 67; vertical communication shafts 69, 101; visual communication, technique of 68; Yamanashi Communications Center, as an extension of 69

A Plan for Tokyo: architecture to an urban scale, expansion of 58–59; brain center, Tokyo as 62; City in the Air 58; city structure, transportation system and urban architecture, unity of 59–60; civic communications axis, of 59–62, *60*, *61*; communication or informational coupling, definition of 63, 65–66; ideas carried over from 57; individuality and collectivism, levels of 57–58; information in a metropolis, processing of 60–62, *61*; Isozaki and 58; linear and/or radial centripetal urban development/s, biological concepts of 59, *60*; metabolic and control functions 63; nervous system, organic composition of society as 63–64; open system, order of 58–62, *61*; Second Industrial Revolution, modern communication methods as 63; Tange and 57–62, 100; Tokyo as an organism, growth of 59; urban organisation, definition of 62; Wiener and communications, views of 63–64

Plateau Beaubourg 136

Pompidou, Georges Jean Raymond 135–136

pop art, new media 94

population explosion, Tokyo after the war 70

Porter, William 191

Pota, Ljube 67

Prestressed Steel and Reinforced-Polyester Structure 133

Price, Cedric 3, 16, 22–41, 49–51, 90, 132, 143, 145–146, 152, 165, 176–178, 197; artificially intelligent architecture: as interactive, self-generative and responsive 22–41; *see also* Fun Palace; Generator; Oxford Corner House (OCH)

Pritzker Architecture Prize 69, 133, 136

process alone is trustworthy, city wherein 72

Program Evaluation and Review Technique (PERT) programming 162

Prouvé, Jean 128, 132, 136

Raffles, Gerry 52n12

Rapson, Ralph 109

Ravnicar, Eduard 67

Ray, Bert E. 125

Reichardt, Jasia 172

Reliance Controls Electronics Factory: demolition of 128; flexible space, interchangeability of 127; inspirations from 127; kit-of-parts approach of 127; structural system of 127; *Team 4* and 127; *see also* Rogers, Richard

replacement of humans by artificial
   intelligence 205, 205n7
reproduction, division and feedback,
   constant state of a city 70–71
Rettberg, Randy 48
Revit 203
Rex, John 109
Rice, Peter 132, 143
Richmond, Winifred 191
Roche, Mark 131
Rogers House: flexibility of 128;
   inspirations from 128; participating
   architects of 128; precursor for
   Pompidou Center, Paris, as 128;
   standardised components of 128–
   129; *see also* Rogers, Richard
Rogers, Richard 3, 16, 108, 110, 127–133,
   135, *137*, 140–146; *see also*
   Association for Rural Aid in
   Medicine (ARAM) Module;
   Extension to Design Research
   Unit; PA Technology Laboratory;
   Reliance Controls Electronics
   Factory; Rogers House; Universal
   Oil Products Factory; Zip-Up
   Enclosures No 1 and No 2
Rogers, Susan 127–131
Rotival, Maurice 67
Rotor Company, Electric Barbecue Spit by
   118
Rotten, David 203
Russell, Richard 128

Saarinen, Eero 108
*Sagamiwan Urban Resort Festival, Surf 90*
   competition 178
*Saiji* (festivals) 93
Samuely, Felix J. 131
Sandberg, Willem 138
Sant'Elia, Antonia 72
Schöffer, Nicholas 167
School Construction Systems Development
   Project: change as the only
   constant, objectives of 123–124;
   Ehrenkrantz and 125; *erector sets,*
   structural details of 124, 126; goals
   of 124; industrialisation of building
   processes, aimed at 123–124; kit-
   of-parts, as 124; mock-up erected
   at 125; more variety, greater
   flexibility, higher quality, and
   lower costs 124–125; participating
   architects and architectural assistant

   of 125; *system*, classification as
   126–127
Schumacher, Patrick 203
Seagrams Building, New York 97
Seek: experimental set-up of 45–49, *46–49*;
   Ford Foundation, funds from
   47–48; *Life in a Computerized
   Environment* (Architecture Machine
   Group) 45; responsive behavior
   of 45–49, *46–49*; SOFTWARE
   exhibition, Jewish Museum 45–46;
   transdisciplinarity of 47–48; Urban
   Systems Laboratory (MIT) 47
*Seiji* (political affairs) 93
*Semi-Senseless Drawing Modules #2 –
   Letters*, Kanno, Yamaguchi and
   Sakamoto 203
Sendai Mediatheque 203
Servel Inc., Refrigerator by 118
Shell Structural System for the 14th Milan
   Triennale, Milan 133
Shimizu, Hiroshi 189
Shimokobe, Atsushi 156
Shioya, Koukichi 88
Shoji screens 74
simulation as city model, definition of
   (Isozaki) 73–74, 101
Slot, G. 52n12
smart buildings, districts and cities,
   elements of 69
smart homes 118–121, 123, 204, 205n6
Smith, Waugh 109
Smith, Whitney R., FAIA 109
Soane, John 162
Soedjatomoko [sic] 156
*Soft Architecture Machines* (Negroponte):
   applications of computers to
   architecture, characterization of 45;
   artificially intelligent architecture,
   brief historical narrative of 45, 48;
   *Epilogue: An Allegory* 45; string-
   and-ring machine 45
software, processes of a city as 70, 86–88,
   94, 101
Solomons, Gustave 58
Sone, Koichi 83
Sonnabend, Yolanda 172
Soriano, Raphael S. 16, 109–110, 116–117,
   128
Soundy, Richard 131
*Soviet Exhibition* 167
Space City 72
Spaulding, Sumner 109

Stanford University 181
Stanford University School Planning
    Laboratory, University of California
    124
Stans, Maurice 93
Straub, Calvin C. 108; structural system
    of 130
substantial, functional, structural, semiotic/
    symbolic, stages of urban design as
    72–73
Sulphur Extraction Plant 133
*Sunbeam:* artificially intelligent systems by
    114; *automatic*, products publicised
    as 114, *115*; Wafflemaster,
    Coffeemaster, Mixmaster,
    Ironmaster, Shavemaster, Toaster,
    etc. of 114, *115*
Sutcliffe, Mark 127
Sydney Opera House 132
System Research Ltd. 172

Tange, Kenzo 2–3, 16, 57–72, 82–88, 91,
    94, 100–102, 143; communications
    as the cement of society 57–70;
    cybernetic environments,
    transdisciplinarity of 1–2; *see
    also* Plan for Skopje; A Plan for
    Tokyo; Tsukiji Project in Tokyo;
    Yamanashi Communications Center
Taniguchi, Yoshio 67
Taut, Bruno 72
Taylor system 72
*teamLab Borderless: Mori Building Digital
    Art Museum* 203
technological disruptions 201
Temple Meads 163
Teshigahara, Hiroshi 94
theory of knowledge representation 181
*Theory of Process Planning, The* (Isozaki):
    continuous process of growth
    71–72, 103n30; elements in a
    spatial system, principles of 71–72,
    103n30; Library at Oita, Kyushu,
    as implementation of 71; Tange and
    70–72
Thermodulor furnace control 118
Thom, David 131
Thorens Record Changer 118
Thorne, David 108
threats of nuclear war 201
time axis of transformation, city as in 72
Time Magazine 91–93
Times Square 140, 146

Titelbaum, Mike 48
Tōhaku, Hasegawa 99
*Tokaido-Megalopolis: The Japanese
    Archipelago in the Future* (Tange)
    63
Tokyo Bay 77
Tokyo Institute of Technology 157
Transportation City 72
Tropical House 163
Truscon open webbed joists 113, *113*
Tsuboi, Yoshikatsu 65
Tsukiji Project in Tokyo: open system,
    central civic communication axis
    of 64; organic unity, among the
    city, transportation and urban
    architecture 65; A Plan for Tokyo,
    ideas carried over from 64;
    processing of information, within
    the city 64–65; Tange and 64–65;
    unbuilt, reasons behind 65; vertical
    cores, three dimensional lattice like
    system of 65
Tsukio, Yoshio 88

Ueda, Atsushi 83
Ukiyoe, from end of the shogunate 74
Ullathorne, Peter 130–131
United Nations Center for Regional
    Development 153
Universal Oil Products Factory: flexibility
    of 131; ideas carried over from 131;
    structural system of 131; team of
    131; *see also* Rogers, Richard
University of Toronto 203
unpredictable times 201–202
Urban Observatory: definition of 41, 43;
    *formation, situation, aspiration*:
    characteristics of 42–43; functions
    and displays of 41–42; *Museum
    of the Living City*, referred as 41;
    Philadelphia's City Hall, as an ideal
    space for 42; street: the measure
    of its quality is the measure of the
    city itself 41; *Urban Observatory:
    A Live Museum with a Data Pulse*
    43, *43*
*Using the Telephone in Family Therapy*
    (Hines) 181
Utzon, Jørn 138

Van den Broek and Bakema 67
van Doesburg, Theo 72
van Oosten, Niki 131

Vaughan, Robert 23
Vila, Enrique 188
Vincent, Ernest 48
visible to invisible architecture, transition
     from 81–82
Vitra Fire Station 203

Walker, Rodney 109
Ward, Robertson, Inland (company) from
     125–126
Watanabe, Sadao 58, 67
Watts, Tony 172
Wenzler, Fedor 67
Westcott, J. H. 52n12
Western-Holly Appliance Company,
     Automatic Built-in-Gas Cooking
     Units by 118, *119*
Westinghouse, appliances by 118
Westinghouse Electric Supply Company
     123
Wiener, Norbert 1–2, 63–65, 70–72,
     100–101; *see also Cybernetics: Or
     Control and Communication in the
     Animal and the Machine*
Wimbledon Common 128
Winder, Neil 131
Winograd, Terry 181
Wisconsin Prairie and Villa Savoye, Le
     Corbusier 121
Wong, Worley K. 109
Wood's, T. R. McKinnon 52n12, 170

World War I and II 3, 70, 91
Wren, Christopher 162
Wright, Frank Lloyd 164
Wurman, Richard Saul 3, 16, 41–43, 51;
     *see also* Urban Observatory
Wurster, William Wilson 109

Xerox PARC 181

Yamaguchi, Katsuhiro 94
Yamamoto, Yasuhiko 88
Yamanashi Communications Center:
     flexibility of 67; information and
     communication theories (Tange)
     and 66–67; open spatial structure
     of 66–67; A Plan for Tokyo, as an
     extension of 66–67; Tange and
     66–67; vertical or communication
     shafts of 67
Yamauchi, Daisuke 156
Yoshida, Hideo 64–65
Yoshikawa, Ken 83
Young, John 128–131, 140
Young, M. 52n12

Zip-Up Enclosures No 1 and No 2;
     do-it-yourself, approach of 130;
     monocoque construction technique,
     used for 129–130; participating
     architects of 129; structural system
     of, 130; *see also* Rogers, Richard

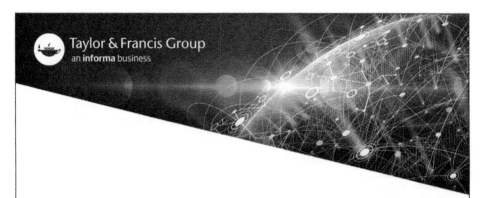

Printed and bound by CPI Group (UK) Ltd, Croydon, CR0 4YY

17/10/2024

01775704-0001